Equality

Other Titles from
HACKETT READINGS

Certainty
Free Will
God
The Good Life
The Idea of Race
Justice
Life and Death
Other Selves
Reality
Time

Equality

Edited, with Introductions, by
David Johnston
Columbia University

Hackett Publishing Company, Inc.
Indianapolis/Cambridge

06   05   04   03   02   01   00   1   2   3   4   5   6   7   8

For further information, please address:

Hackett Publishing Company, Inc.
P.O. Box 44937
Indianapolis, IN 46244-0937

www.hackettpublishing.com

Cover design by John Pershing

Library of Congress Cataloging-in-Publication Data

Equality / edited, with introductions by David Johnston
        p.   cm. — (Hackett readings in philosophy)
   ISBN 0-87220-481-2 (cloth) — ISBN 0-87220-480-4 (paper)
     1. Equality. I. Johnston, David, 1951–   I. Series
HM821.E68   2000
305—dc21   99-053665

The paper used in this publication meets the minimum standard requirements
of American National Standard for Information Sciences—Permanence of
Paper for Printed Materials, ANSI Z39.48-1984.
                                ∞

Contents

Introduction   vii

1. Plato, "Democracy and Equality," from *Republic*   1

2. Aristotle, "Proportional Equality," from *Politics*   9

3. Levellers, "An Agreement of the People"   18

4. Thomas Hobbes, "Equality in Nature and Society," from *Leviathan*   25

5. Jean-Jacques Rousseau, "The Genesis of Inequality," from *Discourse on the Origin and Foundations of Inequality Among Men*   32

6. Jean-Jacques Rousseau, "Sophy," from *Émile, or Education*   57

7. Edmund Burke, "Equality in Representation?" from *Reflections on the Revolution in France*   65

8. Alexis de Tocqueville, "Equality, Democracy, and Liberty," from *Democracy in America*   69

9. Karl Marx, "Human Equality," from *Critique of the Gotha Programme*   83

10. R. H. Tawney, "Equality in Historical Perspective," from *Equality*   90

11. F. A. von Hayek, "Equality, Value, and Merit," from *The Constitution of Liberty*   107

12. John Rawls, "Justice and Equality," from *A Theory of Justice*   124

13. Robert Nozick, "Equality versus Entitlement," from *Anarchy, State, and Utopia*   146

14. Amartya Sen, "Equality of What?"   160

15. Ronald Dworkin, "Equality of Resources"   178

16. Michael Walzer, "Complex Equality," from *Spheres of Justice*   208

17. Will Kymlicka, "Justice and Minority Rights," from *Multicultural Citizenship*   234

18. Iris Marion Young, "Displacing the Distributive Paradigm," from *Justice and the Politics of Difference*   243

Further Readings   266

For James L. Johnston, Jr.
who has thought about this subject
throughout his life

Introduction

> The difference of natural talents in different men is, in reality, much less than we are aware of . . .
> The difference between the most dissimilar characters, between a philosopher and a common street porter, for example, seems to arise not so much from nature, as from habit, custom, and education.[1]

Although the causes of human diversity have long been hotly disputed, few people deny that human beings differ markedly in talents and achievements as well as many other attributes. Despite these differences, it has often been claimed that people should be *regarded* or *treated* as equals, at least in some contexts. This claim is not a modern invention. The Greek historian Herodotus, writing nearly two and one-half thousand years ago, reports an imagined conversation about the attractions and weaknesses of several types of government in which the character Otanes, defending democracy, argues that popular rule "has the finest of all names to describe it—equality under law."[2] The idea of equality has been with us since the beginnings of moral and political philosophy.

If human beings are diverse, however, so is the idea of equality itself. Historically, most advocates of equality have defended one or more of four distinct conceptions of equality: moral, legal, political, and social equality.

Advocates of moral equality believe that people are—or should be regarded as being—equal to one another in value or worth, at least insofar as they are the subjects of moral reasoning. This view entails that when one deliberates about an action that can be expected to affect diverse people, one should give equal weight to the interests of all who would be affected. For example, if I were allocating places on lifeboats to passengers on a sinking ship, knowing that the lifeboats contain too few places to accommodate all passengers and that those who are not accommodated will die, a defender of the idea of moral equality would say that I would be morally wrong to give preference to some passengers solely because of their status, wealth, accomplishments, or abilities—or because of their ethnicity, class, or "race." If the passengers are equal in worth, then I should be equally concerned about all of them, even if it is impossible for me to save all from death.

Advocates of legal equality hold that all people—or at least all those to

---

1. Adam Smith, *An Inquiry into the Nature and Causes of the Wealth of Nations*, ed. by Edwin Cannan (New York: Random House/Modern Library, 1937), p. 15.

2. Herodotus, *Histories*, trans. by Aubrey de Selincourt (Harmondsworth, Middlesex: Penguin, 1954), Book III, para. 80.

whom the laws of a particular political association apply—should be subject to a single body of laws that is applied impartially to all. No one should be exempt from legal sanctions, nor should anyone enjoy legal privileges that are not extended to all. For much of the twentieth century, laws prohibited black Americans from using the same public facilities as whites in the American South. In addition, legal practices generally ensured that white defendants in criminal cases were tried before juries composed of other white citizens, whether the defendants' victims were white or black, while black defendants were often also tried before white juries. Conviction rates for black defendants were much higher than those for whites. These practices conferred de jure and de facto privileges on whites, violating the idea of equality before the law.

Proponents of the idea of political equality argue that all members of a political community should have an equal say with all others in the making of laws and the selection of political leaders. This idea is most obviously violated when some members are denied the right to vote. Until 1867, most members of the working class in England were denied the right to vote in parliamentary elections, and this right was extended to most agricultural laborers only in 1884. Women were denied the right to vote in both England and the United States until the early twentieth century, and black Americans, who were constitutionally guaranteed the right to vote after the American Civil War, were often faced with legal impediments that effectively denied many of them the opportunity to exercise that right until the 1960s. All these restrictions on the right to vote constituted violations of the idea of political equality.

Champions of social equality maintain that all people—or perhaps all members of a political association—should enjoy equal access to the things that enable people to lead good lives, such as income, wealth, medical care, education, and jobs. Social egalitarians often point to the highly unequal distribution of income and wealth in the United States, or to the considerable disparities in access to high quality medical care and educational resources, as evidence that the ideal of social equality is, for now at least, far from being attained.

In addition to being distinct from one another, moral, legal, political, and social equality are also internally complex ideas. Each of these labels actually represents a family of views, some of whose members are barely on speaking terms. One of the most common divisions is between those who believe that *opportunities* should be equal and those who believe that *outcomes* should be equal.

Some champions of social equality believe that that ideal would be attained if opportunities for high incomes were equalized, even if in the end incomes were highly unequal. According to this view, as long as everyone has an equal chance to compete for advantages, the idea of social equality does not require that everyone end up with equal or similar advantages. Yet other social egalitarians believe to the contrary that equality in opportunities is irrelevant or at best secondary to equality in results. From this point of view, equal opportunity has little value if some people end up rich while others become poor.

Similar divisions can be found among proponents of political equality. Does political equality entail only that all members of a political association be *eligible* to participate equally with all others in the making of laws and the selection of political leaders? Or does it entail that they *actually* participate equally? If the latter, then presumably some means to compel reluctant participants will have to be employed. Does political equality entail that all groups in society (or all major groups, or all groups of some particular kind) be represented equally in legislatures and other representative bodies? If so, then some form of proportional representation will have to be put into place. A particularly radical interpretation of the idea of political equality would require that legislative outcomes conform to some standard of equality. For example, it might be asserted that public expenditures should be spread equally among all the members of the political association. This assertion is drastically different from, and potentially in conflict with, the claim of an equal right of participation.

The ideas of legal and moral equality are also internally complex. Does legal equality require only that everyone be subject to the same laws, with no exemption or privilege for any? Or does it require that everyone have access to equally skilled legal advice (or that everyone actually receive equally skilled legal advice)? Similarly, does moral equality require that all people be regarded as equal in worth without further ado? Or is equal worth an opportunity-concept, something that must be earned or that can be lost or diminished because of one's conduct? If one of the passengers on my sinking ship had been a recidivist violent criminal, would I have been morally wrong to choose to save an innocent passenger instead of him? If Albert Einstein had been a passenger on the *Titanic*, would it have been morally wrong for those who directed passengers to lifeboats to give him priority over other passengers?

In addition to the tensions *within* each of the four families of views I have labelled moral, legal, political, and social equality, tensions exist *between* these four conceptions of equality (and many of their variants). For example, the idea of legal equality as it is usually understood requires that the law be blind to a great range of differences between those who are subject to it. To apply the law impartially means to apply it without regard to those differences. Yet to promote social equality, it may be necessary to apply the law in ways that are sensitive to differences of gender, or class, or "race," or of other kinds, as some proponents of affirmative action have argued. Legal equality and social equality are widely believed to stand in an uneasy relation to one another.

This sketch of various conceptions of equality and of some of the tensions within and between them offers only a taste of the many important questions about equality to which philosophers and social theorists have devoted their attention. No simple scheme is rich enough to do justice to their diverse conclusions, nor can any selection fairly represent the many thoughtful arguments that have been made about this subject. While I have tried to represent a wide range of views in this anthology, major omissions are inevitable. The selections from recent and contemporary writers are mainly theoretical rather than policy oriented. Consequently, there is little or no discussion in these selections about many specific issues that are of topical importance, such as affirmative action and gender equality. All, or nearly all, the authors represented discuss equality within the context of a political association, and none focuses on international equality, even though questions about equality and justice on an international scale have become increasingly salient in recent years.

Despite these limitations, I hope this anthology will open a small window through which its readers can eavesdrop on a cluster of conversations that have helped to shape their social world and will continue to do so for years. Although the authors represented here disagree with one another, often sharply, every one of their arguments is worth pondering. Most of all, I hope that readers will come away from this volume with an understanding that the arguments they encounter here are vital and consequential, and that the "equality" evoked by the title of this book is actually a range of "equalities," each of which stands on its own, to be endorsed, modified, or rejected—after all the relevant arguments and reasons have been weighed.

Acknowledgments

I wish to thank Naomi Choi and Frank Lovett for their superb assistance in the location and selection of items for inclusion in this anthology as well as for their thoughtful advice on editing.

Plato,
"Democracy and Equality,"
from *Republic*

Plato (c.428–348 B.C.E.) was a member of an aristocratic family in Athens and a student of the philosopher Socrates, who was put to death in 399 B.C.E., after being accused and tried for impiety and corrupting the youth. Socrates himself wrote nothing, but he appears as a character in nearly all of Plato's many dialogues. In 388 B.C.E, Plato founded the Academy of Athens, a school of philosophy and mathematics that became well known in antiquity. The Republic, *which is now the most famous of all of Plato's dialogues, was probably composed about 380 B.C.E. In this excerpt from Book 8 (of ten books), Socrates is in dialogue with Adeimantus, a much younger man who in real life was Plato's brother. After a lengthy discussion of the best possible form of government, which Plato believes would be an aristocracy—a regime in which the wisest citizens rule all others—Books 8 and 9 focus on a series of regimes that are in Plato's view inferior, including oligarchy and democracy. This passage describes how a democratic regime might arise out of an oligarchical one.*

It seems, then, that we must next consider democracy, how it comes into being, and what character it has when it does, so that, knowing in turn the character of a man who resembles it, we can present him for judgment.

That would be quite consistent with what we've been doing.

Well, isn't the city changed from an oligarchy to a democracy in some such way as this, because of its insatiable desire to attain what it has set before itself as the good, namely, the need to become as rich as possible?

In what way?

Since those who rule in the city do so because they own a lot, I suppose   c
they're unwilling to enact laws to prevent young people who've had no discipline from spending and wasting their wealth, so that by making loans to them, secured by the young people's property, and then calling those loans in, they themselves become even richer and more honored.

That's their favorite thing to do.

From Plato, *Republic*, trans. by G. M. A. Grube, revised by C. D. C. Reeve (Indianapolis: Hackett Publishing Company, 1992). Reprinted by permission of Hackett Publishing Company, Inc. All rights reserved.

So isn't it clear by now that it is impossible for a city to honor wealth and at the same time for its citizens to acquire moderation, but one or the
d   other is inevitably neglected?

That's pretty clear.

Because of this neglect and because they encourage bad discipline, oligarchies not infrequently reduce people of no common stamp to poverty.

That's right.

And these people sit idle in the city, I suppose, with their stings and weapons—some in debt, some disenfranchised, some both—hating those who've acquired their property, plotting against them and others, and
e   longing for a revolution.

They do.

The money-makers, on the other hand, with their eyes on the ground, pretend not to see these people,[1] and by lending money they disable any of the remainder who resist, exact as interest many times the principal sum,
556 and so create a considerable number of drones and beggars in the city.

A considerable number indeed.

In any case, they are unwilling to quench this kind of evil as it flares up in the city, either in the way we mentioned, by preventing people from doing whatever they like with their own property or by another law which would also solve the problem.

What law?

The second-best one, which compels the citizens to care about virtue by prescribing that the majority of voluntary contracts be entered into at
b   the lender's own risk, for lenders would be less shameless then in their pursuit of money in the city and fewer of those evils we are mentioning just now would develop.

Far fewer.

But as it is, for all these reasons, the rulers in the city treat their subjects in the way we described. But as for themselves and their children, don't they make their young fond of luxury, incapable of effort either mental or
c   physical, too soft to stand up to pleasures or pains, and idle besides?

Of course.

And don't they themselves neglect everything except making money, caring no more for virtue than the poor do?

Yes.

But when rulers and subjects in this condition meet on a journey or

---

1. Their eyes are on the ground because their appetite for money forces their souls to look downward.

some other common undertaking—it might be a festival, an embassy, or a campaign, or they might be shipmates or fellow soldiers—and see one another in danger, in these circumstances are the poor in any way despised by the rich? Or rather isn't it often the case that a poor man, lean and   *d* suntanned, stands in battle next to a rich man, reared in the shade and carrying a lot of excess flesh, and sees him panting and at a loss? And don't you think that he'd consider that it's through the cowardice of the poor that such people are rich and that one poor man would say to another when they met in private: "These people are at our mercy; they're good for nothing"?   *e*

I know very well that's what they would do.

Then, as a sick body needs only a slight shock from outside to become ill and is sometimes at civil war with itself even without this, so a city in the same condition needs only a small pretext—such as one side bringing in allies from an oligarchy or the other from a democracy—to fall ill and to fight with itself and is sometimes in a state of civil war even without any external influence.

Absolutely.   *557*

And I suppose that democracy comes about when the poor are victorious, killing some of their opponents and expelling others, and giving the rest an equal share in ruling under the constitution, and for the most part assigning people to positions of rule by lot.

Yes, that's how democracy is established, whether by force of arms or because those on the opposing side are frightened into exile.

Then how do these people live? What sort of constitution do they have? It's clear that a man who is like it will be democratic.   *b*

That is clear.

First of all, then, aren't they free? And isn't the city full of freedom and freedom of speech? And doesn't everyone in it have the license to do what he wants?

That's what they say, at any rate.

And where people have this license, it's clear that each of them will arrange his own life in whatever manner pleases him.

It is.

Then I suppose that it's most of all under this constitution that one finds people of all varieties.   *c*

Of course.

Then it looks as though this is the finest or most beautiful of the constitutions, for, like a coat embroidered with every kind of ornament, this city, embroidered with every kind of character type, would seem to be the most beautiful. And many people would probably judge it to be so, as women and children do when they see something multicolored.

They certainly would.

d   It's also a convenient place to look for a constitution.

Why's that?

Because it contains all kinds of constitutions on account of the license it gives its citizens. So it looks as though anyone who wants to put a city in order, as we were doing, should probably go to a democracy, as to a supermarket of constitutions, pick out whatever pleases him, and establish that.

e   He probably wouldn't be at a loss for models, at any rate.

In this city, there is no requirement to rule, even if you're capable of it, or again to be ruled if you don't want to be, or to be at war when the others are, or at peace unless you happen to want it. And there is no requirement in the least that you not serve in public office as a juror, if you happen to want to serve, even if there is a law forbidding you to do so. Isn't that a

558 divine and pleasant life, while it lasts?

It probably is—while it lasts.

And what about the calm of some of their condemned criminals? Isn't that a sign of sophistication? Or have you never seen people who've been condemned to death or exile under such a constitution stay on at the center of things, strolling around like the ghosts of dead heroes, without anyone staring at them or giving them a thought?

Yes, I've seen it a lot.

b   And what about the city's tolerance? Isn't it so completely lacking in small-mindedness that it utterly despises the things we took so seriously when we were founding our city,[2] namely, that unless someone had transcendent natural gifts, he'd never become good unless he played the right games and followed a fine way of life from early childhood? Isn't it magnificent the way it tramples all this underfoot, by giving no thought to what someone was doing before he entered public life and by honoring him if

c   only he tells them that he wishes the majority well?

Yes, it's altogether splendid!

Then these and others like them are the characteristics of democracy. And it would seem to be a pleasant constitution, which lacks rulers but not variety and which distributes a sort of equality to both equals and unequals alike.

We certainly know what you mean.

Consider, then, what private individual resembles it. Or should we first inquire, as we did with the city, how he comes to be?

---

2. [Earlier in the *Republic*, the participants in this dialogue, led by Socrates, developed an imagined city with the ostensible purpose of identifying the nature of justice.—D.J.]

Yes, we should.

Well, doesn't it happen like this? Wouldn't the son of that thrifty oligarch be brought up in his father's ways? d

Of course.

Then he too rules his spendthrift pleasures by force—the ones that aren't money-making and are called unnecessary.

Clearly.

But, so as not to discuss this in the dark, do you want us first to define which desires are necessary and which aren't?

I do.

Aren't those we can't desist from and those whose satisfaction benefits us rightly called necessary, for we are by nature compelled to satisfy them both? Isn't that so? e

Of course.

So we'd be right to apply the term "necessary" to them? *559*

We would.

What about those that someone could get rid of if he practiced from youth on, those whose presence leads to no good or even to the opposite? If we said that all of them were unnecessary, would we be right?

We would.

Let's pick an example of each, so that we can grasp the patterns they exhibit.

We should do that.

Aren't the following desires necessary: the desire to eat to the point of health and well-being and the desire for bread and delicacies? b

I suppose so.

The desire for bread is necessary on both counts; it's beneficial, and unless it's satisfied, we die.[3]

Yes.

The desire for delicacies is also necessary to the extent that it's beneficial to well-being.

Absolutely.

What about the desire that goes beyond these and seeks other sorts of foods, that most people can get rid of, if it's restrained and educated while they're young, and that's harmful both to the body and to the reason and moderation of the soul? Would it be rightly called unnecessary? c

It would indeed.

Then wouldn't we also say that such desires are spendthrift, while the earlier ones are money-making, because they profit our various projects?

Certainly.

---

3. Bread is here the "stuff of life." That's why one dies for want of it.

And won't we say the same about the desire for sex and about other desires?

Yes.

And didn't we say that the person we just now called a drone is full of such pleasures and desires, since he is ruled by the unnecessary ones, while
d a thrifty oligarch is ruled by his necessary desires?

We certainly did.

Let's go back, then, and explain how the democratic man develops out of the oligarchic one. It seems to me as though it mostly happens as follows.

How?

When a young man, who is reared in the miserly and uneducated manner we described, tastes the honey of the drones and associates with wild and dangerous creatures who can provide every variety of multi-colored pleasure in every sort of way, this, as you might suppose, is the
e beginning of his transformation from having an oligarchic constitution within him to having a democratic one.

It's inevitable that this is how it starts.

And just as the city changed when one party received help from like-minded people outside, doesn't the young man change when one party of his desires receives help from external desires that are akin to them and of the same form?

Absolutely.

And I suppose that, if any contrary help comes to the oligarchic party within him, whether from his father or from the rest of his household, who exhort and reproach him, then there's civil war and counterrevolution
560 within him, and he battles against himself.

That's right.

Sometimes the democratic party yields to the oligarchic, so that some of the young man's appetites are overcome, others are expelled, a kind of shame rises in his soul, and order is restored.

That does sometimes happen.

But I suppose that, as desires are expelled, others akin to them are being nurtured unawares, and because of his father's ignorance about how to
b bring him up, they grow numerous and strong.

That's what tends to happen.

These desires draw him back into the same bad company and in secret intercourse breed a multitude of others.

Certainly.

And, seeing the citadel of the young man's soul empty of knowledge, fine ways of living, and words of truth (which are the best watchmen and guardians of the thoughts of those men whom the gods love), they finally occupy that citadel themselves.

They certainly do.　　　　　　　　　　　　　　　　　　　　　　　*c*

And in the absence of these guardians, false and boastful words and beliefs rush up and occupy this part of him.

Indeed, they do.

Won't he then return to these lotus-eaters and live with them openly? And if some help comes to the thrifty part of his soul from his household, won't these boastful words close the gates of the royal wall within him to prevent these allies from entering and refuse even to receive the words of older private individuals as ambassadors? Doing battle and controlling things themselves, won't they call reverence foolishness and moderation　*d* cowardice, abusing them and casting them out beyond the frontiers like disenfranchised exiles? And won't they persuade the young man that measured and orderly expenditure is boorish and mean, and, joining with many useless desires, won't they expel it across the border?

They certainly will.

Having thus emptied and purged these from the soul of the one they've possessed and initiated in splendid rites, they proceed to return insolence, anarchy, extravagance, and shamelessness from exile in a blaze of torch-　*e* light, wreathing them in garlands and accompanying them with a vast chorus of followers. They praise the returning exiles and give them fine names, calling insolence good breeding, anarchy freedom, extravagance magnificence, and shamelessness courage. Isn't it in some such way as this that someone who is young changes, after being brought up with necessary desires, to the liberation and release of useless and unnecessary pleasures?　*561*

Yes, that's clearly the way it happens.

And I suppose that after that he spends as much money, effort, and time on unnecessary pleasures as on necessary ones. If he's lucky, and his frenzy doesn't go too far, when he grows older, and the great tumult within him has spent itself, he welcomes back some of the exiles, ceases to surrender himself completely to the newcomers, and puts his pleasures on an equal　*b* footing. And so he lives, always surrendering rule over himself to which-ever desire comes along, as if it were chosen by lot.[4] And when that is satisfied, he surrenders the rule to another, not disdaining any but satisfy-ing them all equally.

That's right.

And he doesn't admit any word of truth into the guardhouse, for if someone tells him that some pleasures belong to fine and good desires and others to evil ones and that he must pursue and value the former and　*c* restrain and enslave the latter, he denies all this and declares that all pleasures are equal and must be valued equally.

---

4. Many public officials were elected by lot in Athens. Socrates seems to have been opposed to this practice.

That's just what someone in that condition would do.

And so he lives on, yielding day by day to the desire at hand. Sometimes
d   he drinks heavily while listening to the flute; at other times, he drinks only
water and is on a diet; sometimes he goes in for physical training; at other
times, he's idle and neglects everything; and sometimes he even occupies
himself with what he takes to be philosophy. He often engages in politics,
leaping up from his seat and saying and doing whatever comes into his
mind. If he happens to admire soldiers, he's carried in that direction, if
money-makers, in that one. There's neither order nor necessity in his life,
but he calls it pleasant, free, and blessedly happy, and he follows it for as
long as he lives.

e   You've perfectly described the life of a man who believes in legal
equality.

I also suppose that he's a complex man, full of all sorts of characters,
fine and multicolored, just like the democratic city, and that many men and
women might envy his life, since it contains the most models of constitutions and ways of living.

That's right.

Then shall we set this man beside democracy as one who is rightly
562 called democratic?

Let's do so.

Aristotle,
"Proportional Equality,"
from *Politics*

*Aristotle (384–322 B.C.E.) was born in Macedonia, and at an early age
came to Athens to study at Plato's Academy. He then spent the middle part
of his life in travel, and may have tutored Alexander the Great. He returned to Athens and established his own school, the Lyceum, where he
taught until he was forced to flee the city a year before his death. Aristotle's
writings cover nearly the entire range of knowledge in his time, including
metaphysics and logic, physics and biology, ethics and politics. The following
selections are drawn from his* Politics *and focus on two contrasting conceptions of equality, which Aristotle calls numerical equality and proportional
equality.*

Book III

Chapter 9

The first thing one must grasp, however, is what people say the defining
marks of oligarchy and democracy are, and what oligarchic and democratic
justice are. For [1] they all grasp justice of a sort, but they go only to a
certain point and do not discuss the whole of what is just in the most
authoritative sense. For example, justice seems to be equality, and it is, but   *10*
not for everyone, only *for equals.* Justice also seems to be inequality, since
indeed it is, but not for everyone, only *for unequals.* They disregard the
"for whom," however, and judge badly. The reason is that the judgment
concerns themselves, and most people are pretty poor judges about what is
their own.   *15*

So since what is just is just *for certain people,* and consists in dividing
things and people in the same way, they agree about what constitutes
equality in the thing but disagree about it in the people. This is largely
because of what was just mentioned, that they judge badly about what
concerns themselves, but also because, since they are both speaking up to a   *20*

From Aristotle, *Politics,* trans. by C. D. C. Reeve (Indianapolis: Hackett Publishing
Company, 1998). Reprinted by permission of Hackett Publishing Company, Inc.
All rights reserved.

point about justice of a sort, they think they are speaking about what is unqualifiedly just. For one lot thinks that if they are unequal in one respect (wealth, say) they are wholly unequal, whereas the other lot thinks that if they are equal in one respect (freedom, say) they are wholly equal. But about the most authoritative considerations they do not speak.

25 For suppose people constituted a community and came together for the sake of property; then their participation in a city-state would be proportional to their property, and the oligarchic argument would as a result seem to be a powerful one. (For it is not just that someone who has contributed only one mina to a sum of one hundred minas should have equal shares in that sum, whether of the principal or of the interest, with 30 the one who has contributed all the rest.) But suppose [2] they do not do so only for the sake of life, but rather for the sake of living well, since otherwise there could be a city-state of slaves or animals, whereas in fact there is not, because these share neither in happiness nor in a life guided by deliberative choice.

And suppose [3] they do not do so for the sake of an alliance to safeguard themselves from being wronged by anyone, nor [4] to facilitate 35 exchange and mutual assistance, since otherwise the Etruscans and the Carthaginians, and all those who have treaties with one another would virtually be citizens of one city-state. To be sure, they have import agreements, treaties about refraining from injustice, and formal documents of 40 alliance, but no offices common to all of them have been established to deal with these matters; instead each city-state has different ones. Nor are 1280b those in one city-state concerned with what sort of people the others should be, or that none of those covered by the agreements should be unjust or vicious in any way, but only that neither city-state acts unjustly toward the other. But those who are concerned with good government give 5 careful attention to political virtue and vice. Hence it is quite evident that the city-state (at any rate, the one truly so called and not just for the sake of argument) must be concerned with virtue. For otherwise the community becomes an alliance that differs only in location from other alliances in 10 which the allies live far apart, and law becomes an agreement, "a guarantor of just behavior toward one another," as the sophist Lycophron[1] said, but not such as to make the citizens good and just.

It is evident that this is right. For even if [5] one were to bring their territories together into one, so that the city-state of the Megarians was attached to that of the Corinthians by walls, it still would not be a single 15 city-state. Nor would it be so if their citizens intermarried, even though this is one of the forms of community characteristic of city-states. Sim-

---

1. Lycophron is known only from the writings of Aristotle. He may have belonged to the school of Gorgias.

ilarly, if there were some who lived separately, yet not so separately as to share nothing in common, and had laws against wronging one another in their business transactions (for example, if one were a carpenter, another a farmer, another a cobbler, another something else of that sort, and their *20* number were ten thousand), yet they shared nothing else in common besides such things as exchange and alliance—not even in this case would there be a city-state.

What, then, is the reason for this? Surely, it is not because of the nonproximate nature of their community. For suppose they joined together while continuing to share in that way, but each nevertheless treated *25* his own household like a city-state, and the others like a defensive alliance formed to provide aid against wrongdoers only. Even then this still would not be thought a city-state by those who make a precise study of such things, if indeed they continued to associate with one another in the same manner when together as when separated.

Evidently, then, a city-state is not [5] a sharing of a common location, and does not exist for the purpose of [4] preventing mutual wrongdoing *30* and [3] exchanging goods. Rather, while these must be present if indeed there is to be a city-state, when all of them *are* present there is still not yet a city-state, but [2] only when households and families live well as a community whose end is a complete and self-sufficient life. But this will not be possible unless they do inhabit one and the same location and practice *35* intermarriage. That is why marriage connections arose in city-states, as well as brotherhoods, religious sacrifices, and the leisured pursuits of living together. For things of this sort are the result of friendship, since the deliberative choice of living together constitutes friendship. The end of the city-state is living well, then, but these other things are for the sake of the end. And a city-state is the community of families and villages in a *40* complete and self-sufficient life, which we say is living happily and nobly. *1281a*

So political communities must be taken to exist for the sake of noble actions, and not for the sake of living together. Hence those who contribute the most to *this* sort of community have a larger share in the city-state than those who are equal or superior in freedom or family but inferior in po- *5* litical virtue, and those who surpass in wealth but are surpassed in virtue.

It is evident from what has been said, then, that [1] those who dispute about constitutions all speak about a *part* of justice. *10*

. . .

Chapter 12

Since in every science and craft the end is a good, the greatest and best good is the end of the science or craft that has the most authority of all of *15* them, and this is the science of statesmanship. But the political good is

justice, and justice is the common benefit. Now everyone holds that what
is just is some sort of equality, and up to a point, at least, all agree with
what has been determined in those philosophical works of ours dealing
20   with ethical issues. For justice is something to someone, and they say it
should be something equal to those who are equal. But equality in what
and inequality in what, should not be overlooked. For this involves a
problem and political philosophy.

Someone might say, perhaps, that offices should be unequally distributed on the basis of superiority in any good whatsoever, provided the
people did not differ in their remaining qualities but were exactly simi-
25   lar, since where people differ, so does what is just and what accords
with merit. But if this is true, then those who are superior in complexion,
or height, or any other good whatsoever will get more of the things with
which political justice is concerned. And isn't that plainly false? The
30   matter is evident in the various sciences and capacities. For among flute
players equally proficient in the craft, those who are of better birth do not
get more or better flutes, since they will not play the flute any better if
they do. It is the superior performers who should also get the superior
35   instruments. If what has been said is somehow not clear, it will become so
if we take it still further. Suppose someone is superior in flute playing, but
is very inferior in birth or beauty; then, even if each of these (I mean birth
40   and beauty) is a greater good than flute playing, and is proportionately
more superior to flute playing than he is superior in flute playing, he
should still get the outstanding flutes. For the superiority in wealth and
1283a   birth would have to contribute to the performance, but in fact they contribute nothing to it.

Besides, according to this argument every good would have to be commensurable with every other. For if being a certain height counted more,
5   height in general would be in competition with both wealth and freedom.
So if one person is more outstanding in height than another is in virtue,
and if height in general is of more weight than virtue, then all goods would
be commensurable. For if a certain amount of size is better than a certain
amount of virtue, it is clear that some amount of the one is equal to some
amount of the other. Since this is impossible, it is clear that in political
10   matters, too, it is reasonable not to dispute over political office on the
basis of just any sort of inequality. For if some are slow runners and others
fast, this is no reason for the latter to have more and the former less: it is in
athletic competitions that such a difference wins honor. The dispute must
be based on the things from which a city-state is constituted. Hence the
15   well-born, the free, and the rich reasonably lay claim to office. For there
must be both free people and those with assessed property, since a city-
state cannot consist entirely of poor people, any more than of slaves. But if

these things are needed in a city-state, so too, it is clear, are justice and political virtue, since a city-state cannot be managed without these. Rather, without the former a city-state cannot exist, and without the latter *20* it cannot be well managed.

. . .

Book V

Chapter 1

Pretty well all the other topics we intended to treat have been discussed. *20* Next, after what has been said, we should investigate: [1] the sources of change in constitutions, how many they are and of what sort; [2] what things destroy each constitution; [3] from what sort into what sort they principally change; further, [4] the ways to preserve constitutions in general and each constitution in particular; and, finally, [5] the means by which each constitution is principally preserved.

We should take as our initial starting point that many constitutions have *25* come into existence because, though everyone agrees about justice (that is to say, proportional equality), they are mistaken about it, as we also mentioned earlier. For democracy arose from those who are equal in some respect thinking themselves to be unqualifiedly equal; for because they are equally free, they think they are unqualifiedly equal. Oligarchy, on the *30* other hand, arose from those who are unequal in some respect taking themselves to be wholly unequal; for being unequal in property, they take themselves to be unqualifiedly unequal. The result is that the former claim to merit an equal share of everything, on the grounds that they are all equal, whereas the latter, being unequal, seek to get more (for a bigger share is an unequal one). All these constitutions possess justice of a sort, *35* then, although unqualifiedly speaking they are mistaken. And this is why, when one or another of them does not participate in the constitution in accordance with their assumption,[2] they start faction. However, those who would be most justified in starting faction, namely, those who are outstandingly virtuous, are the least likely to do so. For they alone are the ones it *40* is most reasonable to regard as unqualifiedly unequal. There are also *1301b* certain people, those of good birth, who suppose that they do not merit a merely equal share because they are unequal in this way. For people are thought to be noble when they have ancestral wealth and virtue behind them.

These, practically speaking, are the origins and sources of factions, the *5* factors that lead people to start it. Hence the changes that are due to

2. About the nature of proportional equality.

faction are also of two kinds. [1] For sometimes people aim to change the established constitution to one of another kind—for example, from democracy to oligarchy, or from oligarchy to democracy, or from these to polity or aristocracy, or the latter into the former. [2] But sometimes
10 instead of trying to change the established constitution (for example, an oligarchy or a monarchy), they deliberately choose to keep it, but [2.1] want to have it in their own hands. Again, [2.2] it may be a question of degree: where there is an oligarchy, the aim may be to make the governing
15 class more oligarchic or less so; where there is a democracy, the aim may be to make it more democratic or less so; and similarly, in the case of the remaining constitutions, the aim may be to tighten or loosen them. Again, [2.3] the aim may be to change a certain part of the constitution, for example, to establish or abolish a certain office, as some say Lysander tried
20 to abolish the kingship in Sparta, and King Pausanias the overseership.[3] In Epidamnus too the constitution was partially altered, since a council replaced the tribal rulers, though it is still the case that only those members of the governing class who actually hold office are obliged to attend the public assembly when election to office is taking place. (Having a
25 single supreme official was also an oligarchic feature of this constitution.)

For faction is everywhere due to inequality, when unequals do not receive proportionately unequal things (for example, a permanent kingship is unequal if it exists among equals). For people generally engage in faction in pursuit of equality. But equality is of two sorts: numerical
30 equality and equality according to merit. By numerical equality I mean being the same and equal in number or magnitude. By equality according to merit I mean what is the same and equal in ratio. For example, three exceeds two and two exceeds one by a numerical amount. But four exceeds two and two exceeds one in ratio. For two and one are equal parts of four
35 and two, since both are halves. But, though people agree that what is unqualifiedly just is what is according to merit, they still disagree, as we said earlier. For some consider themselves wholly equal if they are equal in a certain respect, whereas others claim to merit an unequal share of everything if they are unequal in a certain respect.

That is also why two constitutions principally arise: democracy and
40 oligarchy. For good birth and virtue are found in a few people, whereas wealth and freedom are more widespread. For no city-state has a hundred
1302a good and well-born men, but there are rich ones in many places. But it is a

3. Lysander was a Spartan general and statesman who fought against Athens in the Peloponnesian war. He failed in his attempt to introduce elective monarchy in Sparta, and was killed in 395. Pausanias was largely responsible for the Greek victory over the Persians at the battle of Platea in 479.

bad thing for a constitution to be organized unqualifiedly and entirely in accord with either sort of equality. This is evident from what actually happens, since no constitution of this kind is stable. The reason is that when one begins from an erroneous beginning, something bad inevitably 5 results in the end. Hence numerical equality should be used in some cases, and equality according to merit in others. Nevertheless, democracy is more stable and freer from faction than oligarchy. For in oligarchies, *two* sorts of faction arise, one among the oligarchs themselves and another against the people. In democracies, on the other hand, the only faction is 10 against the oligarchs, since there is none worth mentioning among the people themselves. Besides, a constitution based on the middle classes is closer to a democracy than to an oligarchy, and it is the most secure constitution of this kind. 15

. . .

Book VI

Chapter 2

The fundamental principle of the democratic constitution is freedom. 40 For it is commonly asserted that freedom is shared only in this sort of constitution, since it is said that all democracies have it as their aim. One *1317b* component of freedom is ruling and being ruled in turn. For democratic justice is based on numerical equality, not on merit.[4] But if this is what justice is, then of necessity the multitude must be in authority, and what- 5 ever seems right to the majority, this is what is final and this is what is just, since they say that each of the citizens should have an equal share. The result is that the poor have more authority than the rich in democracies. For they are the majority, and majority opinion is in authority. This, then, is one mark of freedom which all democrats take as a goal of their constitu- 10 tion. Another is to live as one likes. This, they say, is the result of freedom, since that of slavery is not to live as one likes. This, then, is the second goal of democracy. From it arises the demand not to be ruled by anyone, or failing that, to rule and be ruled in turn. In this way the second goal 15 contributes to freedom based on equality.

From these presuppositions and this sort of principle arise the following democratic features: [1] Having all choose officials from all. [2] Having all rule each and each in turn rule all. [3] Having all offices, or all that do 20

---

4. Numerical equality (*to ison kata arithmon*) involves equal participation in politi- cal office by each citizen, and so an interchange of ruling and being ruled, it does not seem necessarily to involve equality of property, since none of the ways of establishing it discussed in VI.3 involves a redistribution of property.

not require experience or skill, filled by lot. [4] Having no property assessment for office, or one as low as possible. [5] Having no office, or few besides military ones, held twice or more than a few times by the same person. [6] Having all offices or as many as possible be short-term. [7]
25   Having all, or bodies selected from all, decide all cases, or most of them, and the ones that are most important and involve the most authority, such as those having to do with the inspection of officials, the constitution, or private contracts. [8] Having the assembly have authority over everything or over all the important things, but having no office with authority over
30   anything or over as little as possible. The council is the most democratic office in city-states that lack adequate resources to pay everyone, but where such resources exist even this office is stripped of its power. For when the people are well paid, they take all decisions into their own hands (as we said in the inquiry preceding this one). [9] Having pay provided,
35   preferably for everyone, for the assembly, courts, and public offices, or failing that, for service in the offices, courts, council, and assemblies that are in authority, or for those offices that require their holders to share a mess. Besides, since oligarchy is defined by family, wealth, and education,
40   their opposition (low birth, poverty, and vulgarity) are held to be characteristically democratic. [10] Furthermore, it is democratic to have no office be permanent; and if such an office happens to survive an ancient change,
1318a   to strip it of its power, at least, and have it filled by lot rather than by election.

    Theses, then, are the features commonly found in democracies. And from the type of justice that is agreed to be democratic, which consists in
5   everyone having numerical equality, comes what is held to be most of all a democracy and a rule by the people, since equality consists in the poor neither ruling more than the rich nor being alone in authority, but in all ruling equally on the basis of numerical equality, since in that way they
10   would consider equality and freedom to be present in the constitution.

Chapter 3

    The next problem that arises is how they will achieve this equality. Should they divide assessed property so that the property of five hundred citizens equals that of a thousand others, and then give equal power to the thousand as to the five hundred?[5] Or is this not the way to produce numerical equality? Should they instead divide as before, then take an

---

5. We have two groups, one of five hundred (the rich), another of one thousand (the poor), each of which has the same amount of property. If we so distribute political power that each group has the same amount, have we treated both the rich and the poor as numerical equality demands?

equal number of citizens from the five hundred as from the thousand and *15*
give them authority over the elections and the courts? Is this the constitution that is most just from the point of view of democratic justice? Or is it
the one based on quantity? For democrats say that whatever seems just to
the greater number constitutes justice, whereas oligarchs say that it is
whatever seems just to those with the most property. For they say that
quantity of property should be the deciding factor. But both views are *20*
unequal and unjust. For if justice is whatever the few decide, we have
tyranny, since if one person has more than the others who are rich, then,
from the point of view of oligarchic justice, it is just for him alone to rule.
On the other hand, if justice is what the numerical majority decide, they
will commit injustice by confiscating the property of the wealth few. . . . *25*

What sort of equality there might be, then, that both would agree on is
something we must investigate in light of the definitions of justice they
both give. For they both say that the opinion of the majority of the citizens
should be in authority. So let this stand, though not fully. Instead, since
there are in fact two classes in a city-state, the rich and the poor, whatever *30*
is the opinion of both or of a majority of each should have authority. But if
they are opposed, the opinion of the majority (that is to say, the group
whose assessed property is greater) should prevail. Suppose, for example,
that there are ten rich citizens and twenty poor ones, and that six of the
rich have voted against fifteen of the poorer ones, whereas four of the rich
have sided with the poor, and five of the poor with the rich. When the *35*
assessed properties of both the rich and the poor on each side are added
together, the side whose assessed property is greater should have authority. If the amounts happen to be equal, this should be considered a failure
for both sides, as it is at present when the assembly or the court is split, and *40*
the question must be decided by lot or something else of that sort. *1318b*

Even if it is very difficult to discover the truth about what equality and
justice demand, however, it is still easier than to persuade people of it
when they have the power to be acquisitive. For equality and justice are
always sought by the weaker party; the strong pay no heed to them.

Levellers,
"An Agreement of the People"

The Levellers were Puritan radicals during the English Civil War of the 1640s. Led by John Lilburne (c.1614–1657) and Richard Overton (fl.1631–1664), they represented small property owners, farmers, tradesmen, and artisans. Their influence reached its peak in the period between the military defeat of King Charles I in 1647 and his execution in early 1649. The document reprinted here is dated December 10, 1648 and was presented to Parliament on January 20, 1649. In it, the Levellers defend the principles of political equality—with restrictions—and religious toleration, as well as a number of additional liberties.

An Agreement of the People of England, and the Places Therewith Incorporated, for a Firm and Present Peace Upon Grounds of Common Right and Freedom.

Having by our late labours and hazards made it appear to the world at how high a rate we value our just freedom, and God having so far owned our cause as to deliver the enemies thereof into our hands, we do now hold ourselves bound, in mutual duty to each other, to take the best care we can for the future, to avoid both the danger of returning into a slavish condition and the chargeable remedy of another war. For as it cannot be imagined that so many of our countrymen would have opposed us in this quarrel if they had understood their own good, so may we safely promise to ourselves, that when our common rights and liberties shall be cleared, their endeavours will be disappointed, that seek to make themselves our masters. Since therefore our former oppressions, and not-yet-ended troubles, have been occasioned either by want of frequent national meetings in council, or by the undue or unequal constitution thereof, or by rendering those meetings ineffectual, we are fully agreed and resolved to provide that hereafter our Representatives be neither left for uncertainty for time, nor be unequally constituted, nor made useless to the ends for which they are intended. In order whereunto we declare and agree:

I. That to prevent the many inconveniences apparently arising from

From John Lilburne, *Foundations of Freedom or an Agreement of the People* (London: R. Smithurst, 1648).

the long continuance of the same persons in authority, this present Parliament be dissolved upon or before the last day of April, in the year of our Lord 1649.

II. That the people of England being at this day very unequally distributed by counties, cities, or boroughs, for the election of their representatives, be more indifferently proportioned, and to this end, that the Representative of the whole nation shall consist of 300 persons; and in each county and the places thereto subjoined there shall be chosen to make up the said Representative at all times, the several numbers hereunder mentioned. * * *

III. The Manner of Elections: 1. That the electors in every division shall be natives or denizens of England, such as have subscribed this Agreement, not persons receiving alms, but such as are assessed ordinarily towards the relief of the poor; not servants to, or receiving wages from, any particular person. And in all elections (except for the Universities) they shall be men of one-and-twenty years old or upwards, and housekeepers, dwelling within the division for which the election is. Provided that until the end of seven years next ensuing the time herein limited for the end of this present Parliament, no person shall be admitted to, or have any hand or voice in, such elections, who have adhered to, or assisted the King against the Parliament in any of these wars or insurrections; or who shall make or join in, or abet any forcible opposition against this Agreement; and that such as shall not subscribe it before the time limited for the end of this Parliament, shall not have vote in the next election; neither if they subscribe afterwards, shall they have any voice in the election next succeeding their subscription, unless their subscription were six months before the same.

2. That until the end of fourteen years such persons, and such only, may be elected for any division, who by the rule aforesaid are to have voice in elections in one place or other; provided that of those, none shall be eligible for the first or second Representatives who have not voluntarily assisted the Parliament against the King, either in person before the fourteenth of June, 1645, or else in money, plate, horse, or arms, lent upon the propositions, before the end of May, 1643, or who have joined in, or abetted the treasonable engagement in London in the year 1647, or who declared or engaged themselves for a cessation of arms with the Scots who invaded the nation the last summer, or for compliance with the actors in any the insurrections of the same summer, or with the Prince of Wales or his accomplices in the revolted fleet.

3. That whoever, being by the rules in the two next preceding articles incapable of election, or to be elected, shall assume to vote in, or be present

at, such elections for the first or second Representative, or being elected, shall presume to sit or vote in either of the said Representatives, shall incur the pain of confiscation of the moiety of his estate to the use of the public, in case he have any estate visible, to the value of fifty pounds. And if he have not such an estate, then he shall incur the pain of imprisonment for three months. And if any person shall forcibly oppose, molest, or hinder the people (capable of electing as aforesaid) in their quiet and free election of their representatives; then each person so offending shall incur the pain of confiscation of his whole state, both real and personal; and if he have not an estate to the value of fifty pounds, shall suffer imprisonment during one whole year without bail or mainprize; provided that the offender in each such case be convicted within three months next after the committing of his offence.

4. That for the more convenient election of representatives, each county, with the several places thereto conjoined, wherein more than three representatives are to be chosen, shall be divided by a due proportion into so many parts, as each part may elect two, and no part above three, representatives. And for the making of these divisions, two persons be chosen in every hundred, lathe, or wapentake, by the people therein (capable of electing as aforesaid), which people shall on the last Tuesday in February next between eleven and three of the clock, be assembled together for that end at the chief town or usual meeting place in the same hundred, lathe, or wapentake. And that the persons in every hundred, lathe, or wapentake, so chosen, or the major part of them, shall on the fourteenth day after their election meet at the common hall of the county-town, and divide the county into parts as aforesaid, and also appoint a certain place in each respective part of the division, wherein the people shall always meet for the choice of their representatives, and shall make returns of the said divisions, and certain places of meeting therein, into the Parliament records in writing under the hands and seals of the major part of them present; and also cause the same to be published in every parish in the county before the end of March now next ensuing. And for the more equal division of the City of London for the choice of its representatives, there shall one person be chosen by the people in every parish in the said City (capable of election as aforesaid) upon the last Tuesday in February aforesaid; on which day they shall assemble in each parish for the same purpose between two and four of the clock. And that the persons so chosen, or the major part of them, shall upon the fourteenth day after their election meet in the Guild Hall of the said City, and divide the same City into eight equal parts or divisions, and appoint a certain place in every division respectively, wherein the people of that division shall always meet for the choice of their repre-

sentatives, and shall make return thereof, and cause the same to be published in the manner prescribed to the several counties, as in this article.

5. That for the better provision for true and certain returns of persons elected, the chief public officer in every division aforesaid, who shall be present at the beginning of the election, and in the absence of every such officer, then any person eligible as aforesaid, whom the people at that time assembled shall choose for that end, shall regulate the elections, and by poll or otherwise clearly distinguish the judge thereof, and make true return thereof in writing indented under the hands and seals of himself, and of six or more of the electors, into the Parliament's records, within one-and-twenty days after the election, and for default thereof, or for making any false return, shall forfeit £100 to the public use.

IV. That one hundred and fifty members at least be always present in each sitting of the Representatives at the passing of any law, or doing of any act whereby the people are to be bound.

V. That every Representative shall within twenty days after their first meeting, appoint a Council of State for the managing of public affairs until the first day of the next Representative, and the same council to act and proceed therein, according to such instructions and limitations as the Representatives shall give, and not otherwise.

VI. That to the end all officers of state may be certainly accomptable, and no factions made to maintain corrupt interests, no member of a Council of State, nor any officer of any salary forces in army or garrison, nor any treasurer or receiver of public moneys, shall (which such) be elected to be a representative; and in case any such election shall be, the same to be void; and in case any lawyer shall be chosen of any Representative or Council of State, then he shall be incapable of practice as lawyer during that trust.

VII. That the power of the People's Representatives extend (without the consent or concurrence of any other person or persons) to the enacting, altering, repealing, and declaring of laws; to the erecting and abolishing officers of courts of justice, and to whatsoever is not in this Agreement excepted or reserved from them.

As particularly:

1. We do not empower our Representatives to continue in force, or make, any laws, oaths, covenants, whereby to compel by penalties or otherwise any person to anything in or about matters of faith, religion, or God's worship, or to restrain any person from the professing his faith, or exercise of religion according to his conscience in any house or place (except such as are, or shall be, set apart for the public worship); nevertheless the instruction or directing of the nation in a public way for the matters of

faith, worship, or discipline (so it be not compulsive or express popery) is referred to their discretion.

2. We do not empower them to impress or constrain any person to serve in war either by sea or land, every man's conscience being to be satisfied in the justness of that cause wherein he hazards his life.

3. That after the dissolution of this present Parliament, none of the people be at any time questioned for anything said or done in reference to the late wars or public differences, otherwise than in execution or pursuance of the determination of the present House of Commons against such as have adhered to the King or his interest against the people; and saving that accomptants for public moneys received, shall remain accomptable for the same.

4. That in any laws hereafter to be made, no person by virtue of any tenure, grant, charter, patent, degree or birth, shall be privileged from subjection thereto, or [from] being bound thereby as well as others.

5. That all privileges or exemptions of any persons from the laws, or from the ordinary course of legal proceedings, by virtue of any tenure, grant, charter, patent, degree or birth, or of any place of residence or refuge, shall be henceforth void and null, and the like not to be made nor revived again.

6. That the Representatives intermeddle not with the execution of laws, or give judgment upon any man's person or estate, where no law hath been before provided, save only in calling to an accompt, and punishing public officers for abusing or failing their trust.

7. That no member of any future Representative be made either receiver, treasurer or other officer during that employment, saving to be a member of the Council of State.

8. That no Representative shall in any wise render up, or give, or take away any the foundations of common right, liberty or safety contained in this Agreement, nor shall level men's estates, destroy propriety, or make all things common.

VIII. That the Council of State, in case of imminent danger or extreme necessity, may in each interval summon a Representative to be forthwith chosen and to meet, so as the sessions thereof continue not above forty days, and so it dissolve two months before the appointed time for the meeting of the next Representative.

IX. That all securities given by the public faith of the nation shall be made good by the next and all future Representatives save that the next Representative may continue or make null, in part or in whole, all gifts of moneys made by the present House of Commons to their own members, or to any of the Lords, or to any of the attendants of either of them.

X. That every officer or leader of any forces in any present or future army or garrison, that shall resist the orders of the next or any future Representative (except such Representative shall expressly violate this Agreement), shall forthwith after his or their resistance, by virtue of this Agreement, lose the benefit and protection of all the laws of the land, and die without mercy.

These things we declare to be essential to our just freedoms, and to a thorough composure of our long and woeful distractions. And therefore we are agreed and resolved to maintain these certain rules of government and all that join therein, with our utmost possibilities, against all opposition whatsoever.

These following particulars were offered to be inserted in the Agreement, but adjudged fit, as the most eminent grievances to be redressed by the next Representative:

1. It shall not be in their power to punish or cause to be punished any person or persons for refusing to answer to questions against themselves in criminal cases.

2. That it shall not be in their power to continue or constitute any proceedings in law, that shall be longer than three or four months in finally determining of any cause past all appeal, or to continue the laws (or proceedings therein) in any other language than in the English tongue.

3. It shall not be in their power to continue or make any laws to abridge any person from trading unto any parts beyond the seas, unto which any are allowed to trade, or to restrain trade at home.

4. It shall not be in their power to continue excise longer than twenty days after the beginning of the next Representative, nor to raise moneys by any other way except by an equal rate, proportionably to men's real or personal estates; wherein all persons not worth above thirty pound shall be exempted from bearing any part of public charge, except to the poor and other accustomary charge of the place where they dwell.

5. It shall not be in their power to make or continue any law whereby men's estates, or any part thereof, shall be exempted from payment of their debts; or to continue or make any law to imprison any man's person for debts of that nature.

6. It shall not be in their power to make or continue any law for taking away any man's life except for murder, or for endeavouring by force to destroy this Agreement; but [they] shall use their uttermost endeavour to propound punishments equal to offences, that so men's lives, limbs, liberties and estates may not as hitherto be liable to be taken away upon trivial or slight occasion; and shall have special care to keep all sorts of people from misery and beggary.

7. They shall not continue or make a law to deprive any person in case or trial from the benefit of witnesses, as well for as against him.

8. They shall not continue the grievance and oppression of tithes longer than to the end of the first Representative; in which time they shall provide for and satisfy all impropriators. Neither shall they force any person to pay toward the maintenance of the public ministers, who out of conscience cannot submit thereunto, but shall provide for them in some other unoppressive way.

9. They shall not continue or make a law for any other ways of judgment or conviction of life, liberty, or estate, but only by twelve sworn men of the neighbourhood.

10. They shall not continue or make a law to allow any person to take above six pound per cent. for loan of money for a year.

11. They shall not disable any person from bearing any office in the commonwealth for any opinion or practice in religion, thought contrary to the public way.

Unto these I shall add:

1. That the next Representative be most earnestly pressed for the ridding of this kingdom of those vermin and caterpillars, the lawyers, the chief bane of this poor nation; to erect a court of justice in every hundred in the nation, for the ending of all differences arising in that hundred, by twelve men of the same hundred annually chosen by freemen of that hundred, with express and plain rules in English made by the Representative, or supreme authority of the nation, for them to guide their judgments by.

2. That for the preventing of fraud, thefts, and deceits, there be forthwith in every county or shire in England, and the Dominion of Wales, erected a county record for the perfect registering of all conveyances, bills, and bonds, &c., upon a severe and strict penalty.

3. That in case there be any need, after the erection of hundred courts, of mayors, sheriffs, justices of the peace, deputy lieutenants, &c.; that the people capable of election of Parliamentmen in the foregoing Agreement, be restored by the Representative unto their native, just, and undoubted right by common consent, from amongst themselves annually to choose all the foresaid officers in such manner as shall be plainly and clearly described and laid down by the supreme authority of the nation; and that when any subsidies or public taxes be laid upon the nation, the freemen of every division or hundred capable of election as aforesaid, choose out persons by common consent from amongst themselves, for the equal division of their assessments.

4. That the next Representative be earnestly desired to abolish all base tenures.

Thomas Hobbes,
"Equality in Nature and Society,"
from *Leviathan*

Thomas Hobbes (1588–1679) was educated at Oxford and spent most of his adult life as a tutor and private secretary in the household of one of the wealthiest families in England. From 1640 to 1650 he lived in France, and for a time tutored the future King Charles II. He returned to England in 1651, where he lived the rest of his life in peace despite his controversial writings. In addition to Leviathan, *his greatest political work, he published widely used translations of Thucydides and Homer as well as works on mathematics and science. The main argument of* Leviathan, *which Hobbes wrote near the end of the English Civil War, is that the only way to ensure lasting peace is to accept an absolute sovereign with final authority to resolve all disputes. In this excerpt, Hobbes explains his views on moral equality and legal equality, as well as the responsibilities of the state (or "commonwealth") for the welfare of its members.*

CHAP. XIII

Nature has made men so equal in the faculties of body and mind; as that though there be found one man sometimes manifestly stronger in body, or of quicker mind than another; yet when all is reckoned together, the difference between man, and man, is not so considerable, as that one man can thereupon claim to himself any benefit to which another may not pretend as well as he. For as to the strength of body, the weakest has strength enough to kill the strongest, either by secret machination, or by confederacy with others, that are in the same danger with himself.

And as to the faculties of the mind (setting aside the arts grounded upon words, and especially that skill of proceeding upon general, and infallible rules, called Science; which very few have, and but in few things; as being not a native faculty, born with us; nor attained, (as Prudence,) while we look after something else), I find yet a greater equality amongst

From Thomas Hobbes, *Leviathan, or the Matter, Forme, and Power of a Commonwealth, Ecclesiastical and Civill* (London: Andrew Crooke, 1651).

men, than that of strength. For Prudence is but Experience, which equal
time equally bestows on all men, in those things they equally apply themselves unto. That which may perhaps make such equality incredible is but
a vain conceit of one's own wisdom, which almost all men think they have
in a greater degree than the Vulgar; that is, than all men but themselves,
and a few others, whom by Fame, or for concurring with themselves, they
approve. For such is the nature of men, that howsoever they may acknowledge many others to be more witty, or more eloquent, or more learned; Yet
they will hardly believe there be many so wise as themselves: For they see
their own wit at hand, and other men's at a distance. But this proves rather
that men are in that point equal, than unequal. For there is not ordinarily a
greater sign of the equal distribution of any thing, than that every man is
contented with his share.

From this equality of ability arises equality of hope in the attaining of
our Ends. And therefore if any two men desire the same thing, which
nevertheless they cannot both enjoy, they become enemies; and in the way
to their End (which is principally their own conservation, and sometimes
their delectation only), endeavor to destroy or subdue one another. And
from hence it comes to pass that where an Invader has no more to fear than
another man's single power; if one plant, sow, build, or possess a convenient Seat, others may probably be expected to come prepared with forces
united, to dispossess and deprive him, not only of the fruit of his labor, but
also of his life or liberty. And the Invader again is in the like danger of
another.

And from this diffidence of one another, there is no way for any man to
secure himself so reasonable as Anticipation; that is, by force or wiles, to
master the persons of all men he can, so long, till he see no other power
great enough to endanger him: And this is no more than his own conservation requires, and is generally allowed. Also because there be some, that
taking pleasure in contemplating their own power in the acts of conquest,
which they pursue farther than their security requires; if others, that
otherwise would be glad to be at ease within modest bounds, should not by
invasion increase their power, they would not be able, long time, by standing only on their defence, to subsist. And by consequence, such augmen-
tation of dominion over men, being necessary to a man's conservation, it
ought to be allowed him.

Again, men have no pleasure (but on the contrary a great deal of grief)
in keeping company, where there is no power able to over-awe them all. For
every man looks that his companion should value him, at the same rate he
sets upon himself: And upon all signs of contempt or undervaluing, naturally endeavors, as far as he dares (which among them that have no
common power to keep them in quiet, is far enough to make them destroy

each other), to extort a greater value from his contemners, by damage; and from others, by the example.

So that in the nature of man, we find three principal causes of quarrel. First, Competition; Secondly, Diffidence; Thirdly, Glory.

The first makes men invade for Gain; the second, for Safety; and the third, for Reputation. The first use Violence, to make themselves Masters of other men's persons, wives, children, and cattle; the second, to defend them; the third, for trifles, as a word, a smile, a different opinion, and any other sign of undervalue, either direct in their Persons, or by reflection in their Kindred, their Friends, their Nation, their Profession, or their Name.

Hereby it is manifest, that during the time men live without a common Power to keep them all in awe, they are in that condition which is called War; and such a war, as is of every man against every man. For War, consists not in Battle only, or the act of fighting; but in a tract of time wherein the Will to contend by Battle is sufficiently known: and therefore the notion of *Time*, is to be considered in the nature of War; as it is in the nature of Weather. For as the nature of Foul weather lies not in a shower or two of rain; but in an inclination thereto of many days together: So the nature of War consists not in actual fighting; but in the known disposition thereto, during all the time there is no assurance to the contrary. All other time is Peace.

Whatever therefore is consequent to a time of War, where every man is Enemy to every man; the same is consequent to the time wherein men live without other security, than what their own strength and their own invention shall furnish them withall. In such condition there is no place for Industry; because the fruit thereof is uncertain: and consequently no Culture of the Earth; no Navigation, nor use of the commodities that may be imported by Sea; no commodious Building; no Instruments of moving and removing such things as require much force; no Knowledge of the face of the Earth; no account of Time; no Arts; no Letters; no Society; and which is worst of all, continual fear, and danger of violent death; And the life of man, solitary, poor, nasty, brutish, and short.

It may seem strange to some man that has not well weighed these things that Nature should thus dissociate, and render men apt to invade and destroy one another: and he may therefore, not trusting to this Inference made from the Passions, desire perhaps to have the same confirmed by Experience. Let him therefore consider with himself, when taking a journey, he arms himself, and seeks to go well accompanied; when going to sleep, he locks his doors; when even in his house he locks his chests; and this when he knows there be Laws and public Officers, armed, to revenge all injuries shall be done him; what opinion he has of his fellow subjects, when he rides armed; of his fellow Citizens, when he locks his doors; and of his children and servants, when he locks his chests. Does he not there as much accuse mankind by his actions, as I do by my words? But neither of us accuse man's nature in it. The Desires and other Passions of man are in themselves no Sin. No more are the Actions that proceed from those Passions, till they know a Law that forbids them: which till Laws be made they cannot know: nor can any Law be made, till they have agreed upon the Person that shall make it.

It may peradventure be thought, there was never such a time, nor condition of war as this; and I believe it was never generally so over all the world: but there are many places where they live so now. For the savage people in many places of *America*, except the government of small Families, the concord whereof depends on natural lust, have no government at all; and live at this day in that brutish manner, as I said before. However, it may be perceived what manner of life there would be where there were no common Power to fear; by the manner of life which men that have formerly lived under a peaceful government use to degenerate into, in a civil War.

But though there had never been any time wherein particular men were in a condition of war one against another; yet in all times, Kings and Persons of Sovereign authority, because of their Independency, are in continual jealousies, and in the state and posture of Gladiators; having their weapons pointing, and their eyes fixed on one another; that is, their Forts, Garrisons, and Guns upon the Frontiers of their Kingdoms; and continual Spies upon their neighbors; which is a posture of War. But because they uphold thereby the Industry of their Subjects; there does not follow from it, that misery, which accompanies the Liberty of particular men.

To this war of every man against every man, this also is consequent; that nothing can be Unjust. The notions of Right and Wrong, Justice and Injustice have there no place. Where there is no common Power, there is no Law: where no Law, no Injustice. Force, and Fraud, are in war the two Cardinal virtues. Justice and Injustice are none of the Faculties neither of the Body, nor Mind. If they were, they might be in a man that were alone in the world, as well as his Senses, and Passions. They are Qualities that relate to men in Society, not in Solitude. It is consequent also to the same condition that there be no Property, no Dominion, no *Mine* and *Thine* distinct; but only that to be every man's that he can get; and for so long, as he can keep it. And thus much for the ill condition which man by mere Nature is actually placed in; though with a possibility to come out of it, consisting partly in the Passions, partly in his Reason.

The Passions that incline men to Peace are Fear of Death; Desire of such things as are necessary to commodious living; and a Hope by their Industry to obtain them. And Reason suggest convenient Articles of

Peace, upon which men may be drawn to agreement. These Articles are they, which otherwise are called the Laws of Nature. . . .

CHAP. XV

The question who is the better man has no place in the condition of mere Nature; where (as has been shown before) all men are equal. The inequality that now is, has been introduced by the Laws civil. I know that *Aristotle* in the first book of his *Politics*, for a foundation of his doctrine, makes men by Nature, some more worthy to Command, meaning the wiser sort (such as he thought himself to be for his Philosophy); others to Serve (meaning those that had strong bodies, but were not Philosophers as he), as if Master and Servant were not introduced by consent of men, but by difference of Wit: which is not only against reason; but also against experience. For there are very few so foolish, that had not rather govern themselves, than be governed by others: Nor when the wise in their own conceit contend by force with them who distrust their own wisdom, do they always, or often, or almost at any time, get the Victory. If Nature therefore have made men equal, that equality is to be acknowledged: or if Nature have made men unequal; yet because men that think themselves equal will not enter into conditions of Peace, but upon Equal terms, such equality must be admitted. And therefore for the ninth law of Nature, I put this, *That every man acknowledge other for his Equal by Nature.* The breach of this Precept is *Pride.*

On this law depends another, *That at the entrance into conditions of Peace, no man require to reserve to himself any Right, which he is not content should be reserved to every one of the rest.* As it is necessary for all men that seek peace, to lay down certain Rights of Nature; that is to say, not to have liberty to do all they list: so is it necessary for man's life, to retain some; as right to govern their own bodies; enjoy air, water, motion, ways to go from place to place; and all things else without which a man cannot live, or not live well. If in this case, at the making of Peace, men require for themselves that which they would not have to be granted to others, they do contrary to the precedent law, that commands the acknowledgment of natural equality, and therefore also against the law of Nature. The observers of this law, are those we call *Modest*, and the breakers *Arrogant* men. The Greeks call the violation of this law πλεονεξία; that is, a desire of more than their share.

Also if *a man be trusted to judge between man and man*, it is a precept of the Law of Nature *that he deal Equally between them.* For without that, the Controversies of men cannot be determined but by War. He therefore that is partial in judgment does what in him lies, to deter men from the use of Judges, and Arbitrators; and consequently (against the fundamental Law of Nature) is the cause of War.

The observance of this law, from the equal distribution to each man of that which in reason belongs to him, is called Equity, and (as I have said before) distributive Justice: the violation, *Acception of persons,* προσωποληψιά.

And from this follows another law, *That such things as cannot be divided, be enjoyed in Common, if it can be; and if the quantity of the thing permit, without Stint; otherwise Proportionately to the number of them that have Right.* For otherwise the distribution is Unequal, and contrary to Equity.

But some things there be that can neither be divided nor enjoyed in common. Then, The Law of Nature, which prescribes Equity, requires, *That the Entire Right; or else (making the use alternate) the First Possession be determined by Lot.* For equal distribution is of the Law of Nature; and other means of equal distribution cannot be imagined.

CHAP. XXX

The safety of the People requires further, from him, or them that have the Sovereign Power, that Justice be equally administered to all degrees of People; that is, that as well as the rich and mighty, as poor and obscure persons, may be righted of the injuries done them; so as the great may have no greater hope of impunity when they do violence, dishonor, or any Injury to the meaner sort, than when one of these does the like to one of them: For in this consists Equity; to which, as being a Precept of the Law of Nature, a Sovereign is as much subject as any of the meanest of his People. All breaches of the Law are offences against the Commonwealth: but there be some that are also against private Persons. Those that concern the Commonwealth only may without breach of Equity be pardoned; for every man may pardon what is done against himself, according to his own discretion. But an offence against a private man, cannot in Equity be pardoned, without the consent of him that is injured; or reasonable satisfaction.

The Inequality of Subjects proceeds from the Acts of Sovereign Power; and therefore has no more place in the presence of the Sovereign; that is to say, in a Court of Justice, than the Inequality between Kings and their Subjects, in the presence of the King of Kings. The honor of great Persons is to be valued for their beneficence and the aids they give to men of inferior rank, or not at all. And the violences, oppressions, and injuries they do are not extenuated, but aggravated by the greatness of their persons; because they have least need to commit them. The consequences of this partiality towards the great proceed in this manner. Impunity makes Insolence; Insolence Hatred; and Hatred, an Endeavour to pull down all oppressing and contumelious greatness, though with the ruin of the Commonwealth.

To Equal Justice appertains also the Equal imposition of Taxes; the Equality whereof depends not on the Equality of riches, but on the Equality of the debt that every man owes to the Commonwealth for his defence. It is not enough for a man to labor for the maintenance of his life; but also to fight (if need be), for the securing of his labor. They must either do as the Jews did after their return from captivity in re-edifying the Temple, build with one hand, and hold the Sword in the other; or else they must hire others to fight for them. For the Impositions that are laid on the People by the Sovereign Power are nothing else but the Wages due to them that hold the public Sword, to defend private men in the exercise of several Trades and Callings. Seeing then the benefit that every one receives thereby is the enjoyment of life, which is equally dear to poor, and rich; the debt which a poor man owes them that defend his life is the same which a rich man owes for the defence of his; saving that the rich, who have the service of the poor, may be debtors not only for their own persons, but for many more. Which considered, the Equality of Imposition, consists rather in the Equality of that which is consumed, than of the riches of the persons that consume the same. For what reason is there that he which labors much, and sparing the fruits of his labor, consumes little, should be more charged than he that living idly, gets little, and spends all he gets; seeing the one has no more protection from the Commonwealth than the other? But when the Impositions are laid upon those things which men consume, every man pays Equally for what he uses; Nor is the Commonwealth defrauded by the luxurious waste of private men.

And whereas many men, by accident unevitable, become unable to maintain themselves by their labor; they ought not to be left to the Charity of private persons; but to be provided for (as far-forth as the necessities of Nature require) by the Laws of the Commonwealth. For as it is Uncharitablenesse in any man to neglect the impotent; so it is in the Sovereign of a Commonwealth, to expose them to the hazard of such uncertain Charity.

But for such as have strong bodies, the case is otherwise: they are to be forced to work; and to avoid the excuse of not finding employment, there ought to be such Laws as may encourage all manner of Arts; as Navigation, Agriculture, Fishing, and all manner of Manufacture that requires labor. The multitude of poor and yet strong people still increasing, they are to be transplanted into Countries not sufficiently inhabited: where nevertheless, they are not to exterminate those they find there; but constrain them to inhabit closer together, and not range a great deal of ground, to snatch what they find; but to court each little Plot with art and labor, to give them their sustenance in due season. And when all the world is overcharged with Inhabitants, then the last remedy of all is War; which provides for every man by Victory, or Death.

5

Jean-Jacques Rousseau, "The Genesis of Inequality," from *Discourse on the Origin and Foundations of Inequality Among Men*

Born in Geneva, Jean-Jacques Rousseau (1712–1778) had a turbulent youth and unstable life. Unsuccessful as a tutor, he lived mainly in or around Paris from 1742 until 1762, when he was forced to flee because of the hostile reactions provoked by his most influential works, On the Social Contract *and* Émile, *both of which were published in that year. Eventually he returned to spend his last years in Paris and its environs. Rousseau first achieved widespread notice after the publication of his provocative* Discourse on the Sciences and the Arts *in the early 1750s. He followed this work with the similarly provocative* Discourse on the Origin and Foundations of Inequality Among Men. *The bulk of the excerpt below is drawn from the second half of this* Discourse, *in which Rousseau, having sketched an idyllic portrait of the prehistoric natural state of human beings, proposes an account of the gradual development of artificial inequalities in human society.*

What is the Origin of Inequality Among Men, and is it Authorized by the Natural Law?

It is of man that I have to speak, and the question I am examining indicates to me that I am going to be speaking to men, for such questions are not proposed by those who are afraid to honor the truth. I will therefore confidently defend the cause of humanity before the wise men who invite me to do so, and I will not be displeased with myself if I make myself worthy of my subject and my judges.

I conceive of two kinds of inequality in the human species: one which I call natural or physical, because it is established by nature and consists in the difference of age, health, bodily strength, and qualities of mind or soul.

From Jean-Jacques Rousseau, *The Basic Political Writings*, trans. by Donald A. Cress (Indianapolis: Hackett Publishing Company, 1988). Reprinted by permission of Hackett Publishing Company, Inc. All rights reserved.

The other may be called moral or political inequality, because it depends on a kind of convention and is established, or at least authorized, by the consent of men. This latter type of inequality consists in the different privileges enjoyed by some at the expense of others, such as being richer, more honored, more powerful than they, or even causing themselves to be obeyed by them.

There is no point in asking what the source of natural inequality is, because the answer would be found enunciated in the simple definition of the word. There is still less of a point in asking whether there would not be some essential connection between the two inequalities, for that would amount to asking whether those who command are necessarily better than those who obey, and whether strength of body or mind, wisdom or virtue are always found in the same individuals in proportion to power or wealth. Perhaps this is a good question for slaves to discuss within earshot of their masters, but it is not suitable for reasonable and free men who seek the truth.

Precisely what, then, is the subject of this discourse? To mark, in the progress of things, the moment when, right taking the place of violence, nature was subjected to the law. To explain the sequence of wonders by which the strong could resolve to serve the weak, and the people to buy imaginary repose at the price of real felicity.

. . .

It is easy to see that, among the differences that distinguish men, several of them pass for natural ones which are exclusively the work of habit and of the various sorts of life that men adopt in society. Thus a robust or delicate temperament, and the strength or weakness that depend on it, frequently derive more from the harsh or effeminate way in which one has been raised than from the primitive constitution of bodies. The same holds for mental powers; and not only does education make a difference between cultivated minds and those that are not, it also augments the difference among the former in proportion to their culture; for were a giant and a dwarf walking on the same road, each step they both take would give a fresh advantage to the giant. Now if one compares the prodigious diversity of educations and lifestyles in the different orders of the civil state with the simplicity and uniformity of animal and savage life, where all nourish themselves from the same foods, live in the same manner, and do exactly the same things, it will be understood how much less the difference between one man and another must be in the state of nature than in that of society, and how much natural inequality must increase in the human species through inequality occasioned by social institutions.

But even if nature were to affect, in the distribution of her gifts, as many preferences as is claimed, what advantage would the most favored men derive from them, to the detriment of others, in a state of things that allowed practically no sort of relationships among them? Where there is no love, what use is beauty? What use is wit for people who do not speak, and ruse to those who have no dealing with others? I always hear it repeated that the stronger will oppress the weaker. But let me have an explanation of the meaning of the word "oppression." Some will dominate with violence; others will groan, enslaved to all their caprices. That is precisely what I observe among us; but I do not see how this could be said of savage men, to whom it would be difficult even to explain what servitude and domination are. A man could well lay hold of the fruit another has gathered, the game he has killed, the cave that served as his shelter. But how will he ever succeed in making himself be obeyed? And what can be the chains of dependence among men who possess nothing? If someone chases me from one tree, I am free to go to another; if someone torments me in one place, who will prevent me from going elsewhere? Is there a man with strength sufficiently superior to mine and who is, moreover, sufficiently depraved, sufficiently lazy and sufficiently ferocious to force me to provide for his subsistence while he remains idle? He must resolve not to take his eyes off me for a single instant, to keep me carefully tied down while he sleeps, for fear that I may escape or that I would kill him. In other words, he is obliged to expose himself voluntarily to a much greater hardship than the one he wants to avoid and gives me. After all that, were his vigilance to relax for an instant, were an unforeseen noise to make him turn his head, I take twenty steps into the forest; my chains are broken, and he never sees me again for the rest of his life.

Without needlessly prolonging these details, anyone should see that, since the bonds of servitude are formed merely from the mutual dependence of men and the reciprocal needs that unite them, it is impossible to enslave a man without having first put him in the position of being incapable of doing without another. This being a situation that did not exist in the state of nature, it leaves each person free of the yoke, and renders pointless the law of the strongest.

After having proved that inequality is hardly observable in the state of nature, and that its influence there is almost nonexistent, it remains for me to show its origin and progress in the successive developments of the human mind. After having shown that *perfectibility*, social virtues, and the other faculties that natural man had received in a state of potentiality could never develop by themselves, that to achieve this development they required the chance coming together of several unconnected causes that might never have come into being and without which he would have remained eternally in his primitive constitution, it remains for me to consider and to bring together the various chance happenings that were able to perfect human reason while deteriorating the species, make a being evil while rendering it habituated to the ways of society, and, from so distant a beginning, finally bring man and the world to the point where we see them now.

. . .

[After an account of the origins of the family and the differentiation of gender roles, Rousseau continues:]

In this new state, with a simple and solitary life, very limited needs, and the tools they had invented to provide for them, since men enjoyed a great deal of leisure time, they used it to procure for themselves many types of conveniences unknown to their fathers; and that was the first yoke they imposed on themselves without realizing it, and the first source of evils they prepared for their descendants. For in addition to their continuing thus to soften body and mind (those conveniences having through habit lost almost all their pleasure, and being at the same time degenerated into true needs), being deprived of them became much more cruel than possessing them was sweet; and they were unhappy about losing them without being happy about possessing them.

At this point we can see a little better how the use of speech was established or imperceptibly perfected itself in the bosom of each family; and one can further conjecture how various particular causes could have extended the language and accelerated its progress by making it more necessary. Great floods or earthquakes surrounded the inhabited areas with water or precipices. Upheavals of the globe detached parts of the mainland and broke them up into islands. Clearly among men thus brought together and forced to live together, a common idiom must have been formed sooner than among those who wandered freely about the forests of the mainland. Thus it is quite possible that after their first attempts at navigation, the islanders brought the use of speech to us; and it is at least quite probable that society and languages came into being on islands and were perfected there before they were known on the mainland.

Everything begins to take on a new appearance. Having previously wandered about the forests and having assumed a more fixed situation, men slowly came together and united into different bands, eventually forming in each country a particular nation, united by mores and characteristic features, not by regulations and laws, but by the same kind of life and foods and by the common influence of the climate. Eventually a permanent proximity cannot fail to engender some intercourse among different families. Young people of different sexes live in neighboring huts; the passing intercourse demanded by nature soon leads to another, through frequent contact with one another, no less sweet and more permanent. People become accustomed to consider different objects and to make comparisons. Imperceptibly they acquire the ideas of merit and beauty which produce feelings of preference. By dint of seeing one another, they can no longer get along without seeing one another again. A sweet and tender feeling insinuates itself into the soul and at the least opposition becomes an impetuous fury. Jealousy awakens with love; discord triumphs, and the sweetest passion receives sacrifices of human blood.

In proportion as ideas and sentiments succeed one another and as the mind and heart are trained, the human race continues to be tamed, relationships spread and bonds are tightened. People grew accustomed to gather in front of their huts or around a large tree; song and dance, true children of love and leisure, became the amusement or rather the occupation of idle men and women who had flocked together. Each one began to look at the others and to want to be looked at himself, and public esteem had a value. The one who sang or danced the best, the handsomest, the strongest, the most adroit or the most eloquent became the most highly regarded. And this was the first step toward inequality and, at the same time, toward vice. From these first preferences were born vanity and contempt on the one hand, and shame and envy on the other. And the fermentation caused by these new leavens eventually produced compounds fatal to happiness and innocence.

As soon as men had begun mutually to value one another, and the idea of esteem was formed in their minds, each one claimed to have a right to it, and it was no longer possible for anyone to be lacking it with impunity. From this came the first duties of civility, even among savages; and from this every voluntary wrong became an outrage, because along with the harm that resulted from the injury, the offended party saw in it contempt for his person, which often was more insufferable than the harm itself. Hence each man punished the contempt shown him in a manner proportionate to the esteem in which he held himself; acts of revenge became terrible, and men became bloodthirsty and cruel. This is precisely the stage reached by most of the savage people known to us; and it is for want of having made adequate distinctions among their ideas or of having noticed how far these peoples already were from the original state of nature that many have hastened to conclude that man is naturally cruel, and that he needs civilization in order to soften him. On the contrary, nothing is so gentle as man in his primitive state, when, placed by nature at an equal distance from the stupidity of brutes and the fatal enlightenment of civil man, and limited equally by instinct and reason to protecting himself from the harm that threatens him, he is restrained by natural pity from needlessly harming anyone himself, even if he has been harmed. For according to the axiom of the wise Locke, *where there is no property, there is no injury.*

But it must be noted that society in its beginning stages and the relations already established among men required in them qualities different from those they derived from their primitive constitution; that, with morality beginning to be introduced into human actions, and everyone, prior to the existence of laws, being sole judge and avenger of the offenses he had received, the goodness appropriate to the pure state of nature was no longer what was appropriate to an emerging society; that it was necessary for punishments to become more severe in proportion as the occasions for giving offense became more frequent; and that it was for the fear of vengeance to take the place of the deterrent character of laws. Hence although men had become less forebearing, and although natural pity had already undergone some alteration, this period of the development of human faculties, maintaining a middle position between the indolence of our primitive state and the petulant activity of our egocentrism, must have been the happiest and most durable epoch. The more one reflects on it, the more one finds that this state was the least subject to upheavals and the best for man, and that he must have left it only by virtue of some fatal chance happening that, for the common good, ought never have happened. The example of savages, almost all of whom have been found in this state, seems to confirm that the human race had been made to remain in it always; that this state is the veritable youth of the world; and that all the subsequent progress has been in appearance so many steps toward the perfection of the individual, and in fact toward the decay of the species.

As long as men were content with the rustic huts, as long as they were limited to making their clothing out of skins sewn together with thorns or fish bones, adorning themselves with feathers and shells, painting their bodies with various colors, perfecting or embellishing their bows and arrows, using sharp-edged stones to make some fishing canoes or some crude musical instruments; in a word, as long as they applied themselves exclusively to tasks that a single individual could do and to the arts that did not require the cooperation of several hands, they lived as free, healthy, good and happy as they could in accordance with their nature; and they continued to enjoy among themselves the sweet rewards of independent intercourse. But as soon as one man needed the help of another, as soon as one man realized that it was useful for a single individual to have provisions for two, equality disappeared, property came into existence, labor became necessary. Vast forests were transformed into smiling fields which had to be watered with men's sweat, and in which slavery and misery were soon seen to germinate and grow with the crops.

Metallurgy and agriculture were the two arts whose invention produced this great revolution. For the poet, it is gold and silver; but for the philosopher, it is iron and wheat that have civilized men and ruined the human race. Thus they were both unknown to the savages of America, who for that reason have always remained savages. Other peoples even appear to have remained barbarous, as long as they practiced one of those arts without the other. And perhaps one of the best reasons why Europe has been, if not sooner, at least more constantly and better governed than the other parts of the world, is that it is at the same time the most abundant in iron and the most fertile in wheat.

It is very difficult to guess how men came to know and use iron, for it is incredible that by themselves they thought of drawing the ore from the mine and performing the necessary preparations on it for smelting it before they knew what would result. From another point of view, it is even less plausible to attribute this discovery to some accidental fire, because mines are set up exclusively in arid places devoid of trees and plants, so that one would say that nature had taken precautions to conceal this deadly secret from us. Thus there remains only the extraordinary circumstance of some volcano that, in casting forth molten metal, would have given observers the idea of imitating this operation of nature. Even still we must suppose them to have had a great deal of courage and foresight to undertake such a difficult task and to have envisaged so far in advance the advantages they could derive from it. This is hardly suitable for minds already better trained than theirs must have been.

As for agriculture, its principle was known long before its practice was established, and it is hardly possible that men, constantly preoccupied with deriving their subsistence from trees and plants, did not rather quickly get the idea of the methods used by nature to grow plant life. But their industry probably did not turn in that direction until very late either because trees, which, along with hunting and fishing, provided their nourishment, had no need of their care; or for want of knowing how to use wheat; or for want of tools with which to cultivate it; or for want of foresight regarding future needs; or, finally, for want of the means of preventing others from appropriating the fruits of their labors. Having become more industrious, it is believable that, with sharp stones and pointed sticks, they began by cultivating some vegetables or roots around their huts long before they knew how to prepare wheat and had the tools necessary for large-scale cultivation. Moreover, to devote oneself to that occupation and to sow the lands, one must be resolved to lose something at first in order to gain a great deal later: a precaution quite far removed from the mind of the savage man, who, as I have said, finds it quite difficult to give thought in the morning to what he will need at night.

The invention of the other arts was therefore necessary to force the human race to apply itself to that of agriculture. Once men were needed in order to smelt and forge the iron, other men were needed in order to feed them. The more the number of workers increased, the fewer hands there were to obtain food for the common subsistence, without there being fewer mouths to consume it; and since some needed foodstuffs in exchange for their iron, the others finally found the secret of using iron to multiply foodstuffs. From this there arose farming and agriculture, on the one hand, and the art of working metals and multiplying their uses, on the other.

From the cultivation of land, there necessarily followed the division of land; and from property once recognized, the first rules of justice. For in order to render everyone what is his, it is necessary that everyone can have something. Moreover, as men began to look toward the future and as they saw that they all had goods to lose, there was not one of them who did not have to fear reprisals against himself for wrongs he might do to another. This origin is all the more natural as it is impossible to conceive of the idea of property arising from anything but manual labor, for it is not clear what man can add, beyond his own labor, in order to appropriate things he has not made. It is labor alone that, in giving the cultivator a right to the product of the soil he has tilled, consequently gives him a right, at least until the harvest, and thus from year to year. With this possession continuing uninterrupted, it is easily transformed into property. When the ancients, says Grotius, gave Ceres the epithet of legislatrix, gave the name Thesmophories to a festival celebrated in her honor, they thereby made it apparent that the division of lands has produced a new kind of right: namely, the right of property, different from that which results from the natural law.

Things in this state could have remained equal, if talents had been equal, and if the use of iron and the consumption of foodstuffs had always been in precise balance. But this proportion, which was not maintained by anything, was soon broken. The strongest did the most work; the most adroit turned theirs to better advantage: the most ingenious found ways to shorten their labor. The farmer had a greater need for iron, or the blacksmith had a greater need for wheat; and in laboring equally, the one earned a great deal while the other barely had enough to live. Thus it is that natural inequality imperceptibly manifests itself together with inequality occasioned by the socialization process. Thus it is that the differences among men, developed by those of circumstances, make themselves more noticeable, more permanent in their effects, and begin to influence the fate of private individuals in the same proportion.

With things having reached this point, it is easy to imagine the rest. I will not stop to describe the successive invention of the arts, the progress of languages, the testing and use of talents, the inequality of fortunes, the use or abuse of wealth, nor all the details that follow these and that everyone can easily supply. I will limit myself exclusively to taking a look at the human race placed in this new order of things.

Thus we find here all our faculties developed, memory and imagination in play, egocentrism looking out for its interests, reason rendered active, and the mind having nearly reached the limit of the perfection of which it is capable. We find here all the natural qualities put into action, the rank and fate of each man established not only on the basis of the quantity of goods and the power to serve or harm, but also on the basis of mind, beauty, strength or skill, on the basis of merit or talents. And since these qualities were the only ones that could attract consideration, he was soon forced to have them or affect them. It was necessary, for his advantage, to show himself to be something other than what he in fact was. Being something and appearing to be something became two completely different things; and from this distinction there arose grand ostentation, deceptive cunning, and all the vices that follow in their wake. On the other hand, although man had previously been free and independent, we find him, so to speak, subject, by virtue of a multitude of fresh needs, to all of nature and particularly to his fellowmen, whose slave in a sense he becomes even in becoming their master; rich, he needs their services; poor, he needs their help; and being midway between wealth and poverty does not put him in a position to get along without them. It is therefore necessary for him to seek incessantly to interest them in his fate and to make them find their own profit, in fact or in appearance, in working for his. This makes him two-faced and crooked with some, imperious and harsh with others, and puts him in the position of having to abuse everyone he needs when he cannot make them fear them and does not find it in his interests to be of useful service to them. Finally, consuming ambition, the zeal for raising the relative level of his fortune, less out of real need than in order to put himself above others, inspires in all men a wicked tendency to harm one another, a secret jealousy all the more dangerous because, in order to strike its blow in greater safety, it often wears the mask of benevolence; in short, competition and rivalry on the one hand, opposition of interest[s] on the other, and always the hidden desire to profit at the expense of someone else. All these ills are the first effect of property and the inseparable offshoot of incipient inequality.

Before representative signs of wealth had been invented, it could hardly have consisted of anything but lands and livestock, the only real goods men can possess. Now when inheritances had grown in number and size to the point of covering the entire landscape and of all bordering on one another, some could no longer be enlarged except at the expense of others; and the supernumeraries, whom weakness or indolence had prevented from acquiring an inheritance in their turn, became poor without having lost anything, because while everything changed around them, they alone had not changed at all. Thus they were forced to receive or steal their subsistence from the hands of the rich. And from that there began to arise, according to the diverse characters of the rich and the poor, domination and servitude, or violence and thefts. For their part, the wealthy had no sooner known the pleasure of domination, than before long they disdained all others, and using their old slaves to subdue new ones, they thought of nothing but the subjugation and enslavement of their neighbors, like those ravenous wolves which, on having once tasted human flesh, reject all other food and desire to devour only men.

Thus, when both the most powerful or the most miserable made of their strength or their needs a sort of right to another's goods, equivalent, according to them, to the right of property, the destruction of equality was followed by the most frightful disorder. Thus the usurpations of the rich, the acts of brigandage by the poor, the unbridled passions of all, stifling natural pity and the still weak voice of justice, made men greedy, ambitious and wicked. There arose between the right of the strongest and the right of the first occupant a perpetual conflict that ended only in fights and murders. Emerging society gave way to the most horrible state of war; since the human race, vilified and desolated, was no longer able to retrace its steps or give up the unfortunate acquisitions it had made, and since it labored only toward its shame by abusing the faculties that honor it, it brought itself to the brink of its ruin. *Horrified by the newness of the ill, both the poor man and the rich man hope to flee from wealth, hating what they once had prayed for.*

It is not possible that men should not have eventually reflected upon so miserable a situation and upon the calamities that overwhelm them. The rich in particular must have soon felt how disadvantageous to them it was to have a perpetual war in which they alone paid all the costs, and in which the risk of losing one's life was common to all and the risk of losing one's goods was personal. Moreover, regardless of the light in which they tried to place their usurpations, they knew full well that they were established on nothing but a precarious and abusive right, and that having been acquired merely by force, force might take them away from them without their having any reason to complain. Even those enriched exclusively by industry could hardly base their property on better claims. They could very well say: "I am the one who built that wall; I have earned this land with my labor." In response to them it could be said: "Who gave you the boundary lines? By what right do you claim to exact payment at our expense for labor we did not impose upon you? Are you unaware that a multitude of your brothers perish or suffer from need of what you have in excess, and that you needed explicit and unanimous consent from the human race for you to help yourself to anything from the common subsistence that went beyond your own?" Bereft of valid reasons to justify himself and sufficient forces to defend himself; easily crushing a private individual, but himself crushed by troops of bandits; alone against all and unable on account of mutual jealousies to unite with his equals against enemies united by the common hope of plunder, the rich, pressed by necessity, finally conceived the most thought-out project that ever entered the human mind. It was to use in his favor the very strength of those who attacked him, to turn his adversaries into his defenders, to instill in them other maxims, and to give them other institutions which were as favorable to him as natural right was unfavorable to him.

With this end in mind, after having shown his neighbors the horror of a situation which armed them all against each other and made their possessions as burdensome as their needs, and in which no one could find safety in either poverty or wealth, he easily invented specious reasons to lead them to his goal. "Let us unite," he says to them, "in order to protect the weak from oppression, restrain the ambitious, and assure everyone of possessing what belongs to him. Let us institute rules of justice and peace to which all will be obliged to conform, which will make special exceptions for no one, and which will in some way compensate for the caprices of fortune by subjecting the strong and the weak to mutual obligations. In short, instead of turning our forces against ourselves, let us gather them into one supreme power that governs us according to wise laws, that protects and defends all the members of the association, repulses common enemies, and maintains us in an eternal concord."

Considerably less than the equivalent of this discourse was needed to convince crude, easily seduced men who also had too many disputes to settle among themselves to be able to get along without arbiters, and too much greed and ambition to be able to get along without masters for long. They all ran to chain themselves, in the belief that they secured their liberty, for although they had enough sense to realize the advantages of a political establishment, they did not have enough experience to foresee its dangers. Those most capable of anticipating the abuses were precisely those who counted on profiting from them; and even the wise saw the need to be resolved to sacrifice one part of their liberty to preserve the other, just as a wounded man has his arm amputated to save the rest of his body.

Such was, or should have been, the origin of society and laws, which gave new fetters to the weak and new forces to the rich, irretrievably destroyed natural liberty, established forever the law of property and of inequality, changed adroit usurpation into an irrevocable right, and for the profit of a few ambitious men henceforth subjected the entire human race to labor, servitude and misery. It is readily apparent how the establishment of a single society rendered indispensable that of all the others, and how, to stand head to head against the united forces, it was necessary to unite in turn. Societies, multiplying or spreading rapidly, soon covered the entire surface of the earth; and it was no longer possible to find a single corner in the universe where someone could free himself from the yoke and withdraw his head from the often ill-guided sword which everyone saw perpetually hanging over his own head. With civil right thus having become the common rule of citizens, the law of nature no longer was operative except between the various societies, when, under the name of the law of nations, it was tempered by some tacit conventions in order to make intercourse possible and to serve as a substitute for natural compassion which, losing between one society and another nearly all the force it had between one man and another, no longer resides anywhere but in a few great cosmopolitan souls, who overcome the imaginary barriers that separate peoples, and who, following the example of the sovereign being who has created them, embrace the entire human race in their benevolence.

Remaining thus among themselves in the state of nature, the bodies politic soon experienced the inconveniences that had forced private individuals to leave it; and that state became even more deadly among these great bodies than that state had among the private individuals of whom they were composed. Whence came the national wars, battles, murders, and reprisals that make nature tremble and offend reason, and all those horrible prejudices that rank the honor of shedding human blood among the virtues. The most decent people learned to consider it one of their duties to kill their fellow men. Finally, men were seen massacring one another by the thousands without knowing why. More murders were committed in a single day of combat and more horrors in the capture of a single city than were committed in the state of nature during entire centuries over the entire face of the earth. Such are the first effects one glimpses of the division of mankind into different societies. Let us return to the founding of these societies.

I know that many have ascribed other origins to political societies, such as conquests by the most powerful, or the union of the weak; and the choice among these causes is indifferent to what I want to establish. Nevertheless, the one I have just described seems to me the most natural, for the following reasons. 1. In the first case, the right of conquest, since it is not a right, could not have founded any other, because the conqueror and conquered peoples always remain in a state of war with one another, unless the nation, returned to full liberty, were to choose voluntarily its conqueror as its leader. Until then, whatever the capitulations that may have been made, since they have been founded on violence alone and are consequently null by this very fact, on this hypothesis there can be neither true society nor body politic, nor any other law than that of the strongest. 2. These words *strong* and *weak* are equivocal in the second case, because in the interval between the establishment of the right of property or of the first occupant and that of political governments, the meaning of these terms is better rendered by the words *poor* and *rich*, because, before the laws, man did not in fact have any other means of placing his equals in subjection except by attacking their goods or by giving them part of his. 3. Since the poor had nothing to lose but their liberty, it would have been utter folly for them to have voluntarily surrendered the only good remaining to them, gaining nothing in return. On the contrary, since the rich men were, so to speak, sensitive in all parts of their goods, it was much easier to do them harm, and consequently they had to take greater precautions to protect themselves. And finally it is reasonable to believe that a thing was invented by those to whom it is useful rather than by those to whom it is harmful.

Incipient government did not have a constant and regular form. The lack of philosophy and experience permitted only present inconveniences to be perceived, and there was thought of remedying the others only as they presented themselves. Despite all the labors of the wisest legislators, the political state always remained imperfect, because it was practically the work of chance and, because it had been badly begun, time, in discovering faults and suggesting remedies, could never repair the vices of the constitution. People were continually patching it up, whereas they should have begun by clearing the air and putting aside all the old materials, as Lycurgus did in Sparta, in order to raise a good edifice later on. At first, society consisted merely of some general conventions that all private individuals promised to observe, and concerning which the community became the guarantor for each of them. Experience had to demonstrate how weak such a constitution was, and how easy it was for lawbreakers to escape conviction or punishment for faults of which the public alone was to be witness and judge. The law had to be evaded in a thousand ways; inconveniences and disorders had to multiply continually in order to make them finally give some thought to confiding to private individuals the dangerous trust of public authority, and to make them entrust to magistrates the care of enforcing the observance of the deliberations of the people. For to say that the leaders were chosen before the confederation was brought about and that the ministers of the laws existed before the laws themselves is a supposition that does not allow of serious debate.

It would be no more reasonable to believe that initially the peoples threw themselves unconditionally and for all time into the arms of an absolute master, and that the first means of providing for the common security dreamed up by proud and unruly men was to rush headlong into slavery. In fact, why did they give themselves over to superiors, if not to defend themselves against oppression and to protect their goods, their liberties and their lives, which are, as it were, the constitutive elements of their being? Now, since, in relations between men, the worst that can happen to someone is for him to see himself at the discretion of someone else, would it not have been contrary to good sense to begin by surrendering into the hands of a leader the only things for whose preservation they needed his help? What equivalent could he have offered them for the concession of so fine a right? And if he had dared to demand it on the pretext of defending them, would he not have immediately received the reply given in the fable: "what more will the enemy do to us?" It is therefore incontestable, and it is a fundamental maxim of all political right, that peoples have given themselves leaders in order to defend their liberty and not to enslave themselves. *If we have a prince,* Pliny said to Trajan, *it is so that he may preserve us from having a master.*

[Our] political theorists produce the same sophisms about the love of liberty that [our] philosophers have made about the state of nature. By the things they see they render judgments about very different things they have not seen; and they attribute to men a natural inclination to servitude owing to the patience with which those who are before their eyes endure their servitude, without giving a thought to the fact that it is the same for liberty as it is for innocence and virtue: their value is felt only as long as one has them oneself, and the taste for them is lost as soon as one has lost them. "I know the delights of your country," said Brasidas to a satrap who compared the life of Sparta to that of Persepolis, "but you cannot know the pleasures of mine."

As an unbroken steed bristles his mane, paws the ground with his hoof, and struggles violently at the mere approach of the bit, while a trained horse patiently endures the whip and the spur, barbarous man does not bow his head for the yoke that civilized man wears without a murmur, and he prefers the most stormy liberty to tranquil subjection. Thus it is not by the degradation of enslaved peoples that man's natural dispositions for or against servitude are to be judged, but by the wonders that all free peoples have accomplished to safeguard themselves from oppression. I know that enslaved peoples do nothing but boast of the peace and tranquillity they enjoy in their chains and that *they give the name 'peace' to the most miserable slavery.* But when I see free peoples sacrificing pleasures, tranquillity, wealth, power, and life itself for the preservation of this sole good which is regarded so disdainfully by those who have lost it; when I see animals born free and abhorring captivity break their heads against the bars of their prison; when I see multitudes of utterly naked savages scorn European pleasures and brave hunger, fire, sword and death, simply to preserve their independence, I sense that it is inappropriate for slaves to reason about liberty.

As for paternal authority, from which several have derived absolute government and all society, it is enough, without having recourse to the contrary proofs of Locke and Sidney, to note that nothing in the world is farther from the ferocious spirit of despotism than the gentleness of that authority which looks more to the advantage of the one who obeys than to the utility of the one who commands; that by the law of nature, the father is master of the child as long as his help is necessary for him; that beyond this point they become equals, and the son, completely independent of the father, then owes him merely respect and not obedience; for gratitude is clearly a duty that must be rendered, but not a right that can be demanded. Instead of saying that civil society derives from paternal power, on the contrary it must be said that it is from civil society that this power draws its principal force. An individual was not recognized as the father of several children until the children remained gathered about him. The goods of the father, of which he is truly the master, are the goods that keep his children in a state of dependence toward him, and he can cause their receiving a share in his estate to be consequent upon the extent to which they will have well merited it from him by continuous deference to his wishes. Now, far from having some similar favor to expect from their despot (since they belong to him as personal possessions—they and all they possess—or at least he claims this to be the case), subjects are reduced to receiving as a favor what he leaves them of their goods. He does what is just when he despoils them; he does them a favor when he allows them to live.

In continuing thus to examine facts from the viewpoint of right, no more solidity than truth would be found in the belief that the establishment of tyranny was voluntary; and it would be difficult to show the validity of a contract that would obligate only one of the parties, where all the commitments would be placed on one side with none on the other, and that it would turn exclusively to the disadvantage of the one making the commitments. This odious system is quite far removed from being, even today, that of wise and good monarchs, and especially of the kings of France, as may be seen in various places in their edicts, and particularly in the following passage of a famous writing published in 1667 in the name of and by order of Louis XIV: *Let it not be said therefore that the sovereign is not subject to the laws of his state, for the contrary statement is a truth of the law of nations, which flattery has on occasion attacked, but which good princes have always defended as a tutelary divinity of their states. How much more legitimate is it to say, with the wise Plato, that the perfect felicity of a kingdom is that a prince be obeyed by his subjects, that the prince obey the law, and that the law be right and always directed to the public good.* I will not stop to investigate whether, with liberty being the most noble of man's faculties, he degrades his nature, places himself on the level of animals enslaved by instinct, offends even his maker, when he unreservedly renounces the most precious of all his gifts, and allows himself to commit all the crimes he forbids us to commit, in order to please a ferocious or crazed master; nor whether this sublime workman should be more irritated at seeing his finest work destroyed rather than at seeing it dishonored. [I will disregard, if you will, the authority of Barbeyrac, who flatly declares, following Locke, that no one can sell his liberty to the point of submitting himself to an arbitrary power that treats him according to its fancy. *For,* he adds, *this would be selling his own life, of which he is not the master.*] I will merely ask by what right those who have not been afraid of debasing themselves to this degree have been able to subject their posterity to the same ignominy and to renounce for it goods that do not depend on their liberality, and without which life itself is burdensome to all who are worthy of it.

Pufendorf says that just as one transfers his goods to another by conventions and contracts, one can also divest himself of his liberty in favor of someone. That, it seems to me, is very bad reasoning; for, in the first place, the goods I give away become something utterly foreign to me, and it is a matter of indifference to me whether or not these goods are abused; but it is important to me that my liberty is not abused, and I cannot expose myself to becoming the instrument of crime without making myself guilty of the evil I will be forced to commit. Moreover, since the right of property is merely the result of convention and human institution, every man can dispose of what he possesses as he sees fit. But it is not the same for the essential gifts of nature such as life and liberty, which everyone is allowed to enjoy, and of which it is at least doubtful that one has the right to divest himself. In giving up the one he degrades his being; in giving up the other he annihilates that being insofar as he can. And because no temporal goods can compensate for the one or the other, it would offend at the same time both nature and reason to renounce them, regardless of the price. But even if one could give away his liberty as he does his goods, the difference

would be very great for the children who enjoy the father's goods only by
virtue of a transmission of his right; whereas, since liberty is a gift they
receive from nature in virtue of being men, their parents had no right to
divest them of it. Thus, just as violence had to be done to nature in order
to establish slavery, nature had to be changed in order to perpetuate this
right. And the jurists, who have gravely pronounced that the child of a
slave woman is born a slave, have decided, in other words, that a man is not
born a man.

Thus it appears certain to me not only that governments did not begin
with arbitrary power, which is but their corruption and extreme limit, and
which finally brings them back simply to the law of the strongest, for
which they were initially to have been the remedy; but also that even if
they had begun thus, this power, being illegitimate by its nature, could not
have served as a foundation for the rights of society, nor, as a consequence,
for the inequality occasioned by social institutions.

Without entering at present into the investigations that are yet to be
made into the nature of the fundamental compact of all government, I
restrict myself, in following common opinion, to considering here the
establishment of the body politic as a true contract between the populace
and the leaders it chooses itself: a contract by which the two parties
obligate themselves to observe the laws that are stipulated in it and that
form the bonds of their union. Since, with respect to social relations, the
populace has united all its wills into a single one, all the articles on which
this will is explicated become so many fundamental laws obligating all the
members of the state without exception, and one of these regulates the
choice and power of the magistrates charged with watching over the
execution of the others. This power extends to everything that can maintain the constitution, without going so far as to change it. To it are joined
honors that make the laws and their ministers worthy of respect, and, for
the ministers personally, prerogatives that compensate them for the troublesome labors that a good administration requires. The magistrate, for his
part, obligates himself to use the power entrusted to him only in accordance with the intention of the constituents, to maintain each one in the
peaceful enjoyment of what belongs to him, and to prefer on every occasion the public utility to his own interest.

Before experience had shown or knowledge of the human heart had
made men foresee the inevitable abuses of such a constitution, it must have
seemed all the better because those who were charged with watching over
its preservation were themselves the ones who had the greatest interest in
it. For since the magistracy and its rights were established exclusively on
fundamental laws, were they to be destroyed, the magistracy would immediately cease to be legitimate; the people would no longer be bound to

obey them. And since it was not the magistrate but the law that had constituted the essence of the state, everyone would rightfully return to his natural liberty.

The slightest attentive reflection on this point would confirm this by new reasons, and by the nature of the contract it would be seen that it could not be irrevocable. For were there no superior power that could guarantee the fidelity of the contracting parties or force them to fulfill their reciprocal commitments, the parties would remain sole judges in their own case, and each of them would always have the right to renounce the contract as soon as he should find that the other party violated the conditions of the contract, or as soon as the conditions should cease to suit him. It is on this principle that it appears the right to abdicate can be founded. Now to consider, as we are doing, only what is of human institution, if the magistrate, who has all the power in his hands and who appropriates to himself all the advantages of the contract, nevertheless had the right to renounce the authority, a fortiori the populace, which pays for all the faults of the leaders, should have the right to renounce their dependence. But the horrible dissensions, the infinite disorders that this dangerous power would necessarily bring in its wake, demonstrate more than anything else how much need human governments had for a basis more solid than reason alone, and how necessary it was for public tranquillity that the divine will intervened to give to sovereign authority a sacred and inviolable character which took from the subjects the fatal right to dispose of it. If religion had brought about this good for men, it would be enough to oblige them to cherish and adopt it, even with its abuses, since it spares even more blood than fanaticism causes to be shed. But let us follow the thread of our hypothesis.

The various forms of government take their origin from the greater or lesser differences that were found among private individuals at the moment of institution. If a man were eminent in power, virtue, wealth or prestige, he alone was elected magistrate, and the state became monarchical. If several men, more or less equal among themselves, stood out over all the others, they were elected jointly, and there was an aristocracy. Those whose fortune or talents were less disproportionate, and who least departed from the state of nature, kept the supreme administration and formed a democracy. Time made evident which of these forms was the most advantageous to men. Some remained in subjection only to the laws; the others soon obeyed masters. Citizens wanted to keep their liberty; the subjects thought only of taking it away from their neighbors, since they could not endure others enjoying a good they themselves no longer enjoyed. In a word, on the one hand were riches and conquests, and on the other were happiness and virtue.

In these various forms of government all the magistratures were at first elective; and when wealth did not prevail, preference was given to merit, which gives a natural ascendancy, and to age, which gives experience in conducting business and cool-headedness in deliberation. The elders of the Hebrews, the gerontes of Sparta, the senate of Rome, and even the etymology of our word *seigneur* show how much age was respected in former times. The more elections fell upon men of advanced age, the more frequent elections became, and the more their difficulties were made to be felt. Intrigues were introduced; factions were formed; parties became embittered; civil wars flared up. Finally, the blood of citizens was sacrificed to the alleged happiness of the state, and people were on the verge of falling back into the anarchy of earlier times. The ambition of the leaders profited from these circumstances to perpetuate their offices within their families. The people, already accustomed to dependence, tranquillity and the conveniences of life, and already incapable of breaking their chains, consented to let their servitude increase in order to secure their tranquillity. Thus it was that the leaders, having become hereditary, grew accustomed to regard their magistratures as family property, to regard themselves as the proprietors of the state (of which at first they were but the officers), to call their fellow citizens their slaves, to count them like cattle in the number of things that belonged to them, and to call themselves equals of the gods and kings of kings.

If we follow the progress of inequality in these various revolutions, we will find that the first stage was the establishment of the law and of the right of property, the second stage was the institution of the magistracy, and the third and final stage was the transformation of legitimate power into arbitrary power. Thus the class of rich and poor was authorized by the first epoch, that of the strong and the weak by the second, and that of master and slave by the third: the ultimate degree of inequality and the limit to which all the others finally lead, until new revolutions completely dissolve the government or bring it nearer to its legitimate institution.

To grasp the necessity of this progress, we must consider less the motives for the establishment of the body politic than the form it takes in its execution and the disadvantages that follow in its wake. For the vices that make social institutions necessary are the same ones that make their abuses inevitable. And with the sole exception of Sparta, where the law kept watch chiefly over the education of children, and where Lycurgus established mores that nearly dispensed with having to add laws to them, since laws are generally less strong than passions and restrain men without changing them, it would be easy to prove that any government that always moved forward in conformity with the purpose for which it was founded without being corrupted or altered, would have been needlessly instituted, and that a country where no one eluded the laws and abused the magistrature would need neither magistracy nor laws.

Political distinctions necessarily lend themselves to civil distinctions. The growing inequality between the people and its leaders soon makes itself felt among private individuals, and is modified by them in a thousand ways according to passions, talents and events. The magistrate cannot usurp illegitimate power without producing protégés for himself to whom he is forced to yield some part of it. Moreover, citizens allow themselves to be oppressed only insofar as they are driven by blind ambition; and looking more below than above them, domination becomes more dear to them than independence, and they consent to wear chains in order to be able to give them in turn to others. It is very difficult to reduce to obedience someone who does not seek to command; and the most adroit politician would never succeed in subjecting men who wanted merely to be free. But inequality spreads easily among ambitious and cowardly souls always ready to run the risks of fortune and, almost indifferently, to dominate or serve, according to whether it becomes favorable or unfavorable to them. Thus it is that there must have come a time when the eyes of people were beguiled to such an extent that its leaders merely had to say to the humblest men, "Be great, you and all your progeny," and he immediately appeared great to everyone as well as in his own eyes, and his descendants were elevated even more in proportion as they were at some remove from him. The more remote and uncertain the cause, the more the effect increased; the more loafers one could count in a family, the more illustrious it became.

If this were the place to go into detail, I would easily explain how [even without government involvement] the inequality of prestige and authority becomes inevitable among private individuals,[1] as soon as they are united

---

1. Distributive justice would still be opposed to this rigorous equality of the state of nature, if it were workable in civil society. And since all the members of the state owe it services proportionate to their talents and forces, the citizens for their part should be distinguished and favored in proportion to their services. It is in this sense that one must understand a passage of Isocrates, in which he praises the first Athenians for having known well how to distinguish which of the two sorts of equality was the more advantageous, one of which consists in portioning out indifferently to all citizens the same advantages, and the other in distributing them according to each one's merit. These able politicians, adds the orator, in banishing that unjust equality that makes no differentiation between wicked and good men, adhered inviolably to that equality which rewards and punishes each according to one's merit. But first, no society has ever existed, regardless of the degree of corruption they could have achieved, in which no differentiation between wicked and good men was made. And in the matter of mores, where the law cannot set a

in one single society and are forced to make comparisons among themselves and to take into account the differences they discover in the continual use they have to make of one another. These differences are of several sorts, but in general, since wealth, nobility or rank, power and personal merit are the principal distinctions by which someone is measured in society, I would prove that the agreement or conflict of these various forces is the surest indication of a well- or ill-constituted state. I would make it apparent that among these four types of inequality, since personal qualities are the origin of all the others, wealth is the last to which they are ultimately reduced, because it readily serves to buy all the rest, since it is the most immediately useful to well-being and the easiest to communicate. This observation enables one to judge rather precisely the extent to which each people is removed from its primitive institution, and of the progress it has made toward the final stage of corruption. I would note how much that universal desire for reputation, honors, and preferences, which devours us all, trains and compares our talents and strengths; how much it excites and multiplies the passions; and, by making all men competitors, rivals, or rather enemies, how many setbacks, successes and catastrophes of every sort it causes every day, by making so many contenders run the same course. I would show that it is to this ardor for making oneself the topic of conversation, to this furor to distinguish oneself which nearly always keeps us outside ourselves, that we owe what is best and worst among men, our virtues and vices, our sciences and our errors, our conquerors and our philosophers, that is to say, a multitude of bad things against a small number of good ones. Finally, I would prove that if one sees a handful of powerful and rich men at the height of greatness and fortune while the mob grovels in obscurity and misery, it is because the former prize the things they enjoy only to the extent that the others are deprived of them; and because, without changing their position, they would cease to be happy, if the people ceased to be miserable.

---

sufficiently precise measurement to serve as a rule for the magistrate, the law very wisely prohibits him from the judgment of persons, leaving him merely the judgment of actions, in order not to leave the fate or the rank of citizens to his discretion. Only mores as pure as those of the ancient Romans could withstand censors; such tribunals would soon have overturned everything among us. It is for public esteem to differentiate between wicked and good men. The magistrate is judge only of strict law [*droit*]; but the populace is the true judge of mores—an upright and even enlightened judge on this point, occasionally deceived but never corrupted. The ranks of citizens ought therefore to be regulated not on the basis of their personal merit, which would be to leave to the magistrate the means of making an almost arbitrary application of the law, but upon the real services which they render to the state and which lend themselves to a more precise reckoning.

But these details alone would be the subject of a large work in which one would weigh the advantages and the disadvantages of every government relative to the rights of the state of nature, and where one would examine all the different faces under which inequality has appeared until now and may appear in [future] ages, according to the nature of these governments and the upheavals that time will necessarily bring in its wake. We would see the multitude oppressed from within as a consequence of the very precautions it had taken against what menaced it from without. We would see oppression continually increase, without the oppressed ever being able to know where it would end or what legitimate means would be left for them to stop it. We would see the rights of citizens and national liberties gradually die out, and the protests of the weak treated like seditious murmurs. We would see politics restrict the honor of defending the common cause to a mercenary portion of the people. We would see arising from this the necessity for taxes, the discouraged farmer leaving his field, even during peacetime, and leaving his plow in order to gird himself with a sword. We would see the rise of fatal and bizarre rules in the code of honor. We would see the defenders of the homeland sooner or later become its enemies, constantly holding a dagger over their fellow citizens, and there would come a time when we would hear them say to the oppressor of their country:*"If you order me to plunge my sword into my brother's breast or my father's throat, and into my pregnant wife's entrails, I will do so, even though my right hand is unwilling."*

From the extreme inequality of conditions and fortunes, from the diversity of passions and talents, from useless arts, from pernicious arts, from frivolous sciences there would come a pack of prejudices equally contrary to reason, happiness and virtue. One would see the leaders fomenting whatever can weaken men united together by disuniting them; whatever can give society an air of apparent concord while sowing the seeds of real division; whatever can inspire defiance and hatred in the various classes through the opposition of their rights and interests, and can as a consequence strengthen the power that contains them all.

It is from the bosom of this disorder and these upheavals that despotism, by gradually raising its hideous head and devouring everything it had seen to be good and healthy in every part of the state, would eventually succeed in trampling underfoot the laws and the people, and in establishing itself on the ruins of the republic. The times that would precede this last transformation would be times of troubles and calamities; but in the end everything would be swallowed up by the monster, and the peoples would no longer have leader or laws, but only tyrants. Also, from that moment on, there would no longer be any question of mores and virtue, for wherever despotism, *in which decency affords no hope*, reigns, it tolerates no other master. As soon as it speaks, there is neither probity nor duty to consult, and the blindest obedience is the only virtue remaining for slaves.

Here is the final stage of inequality, and the extreme point that closes the circle and touches the point from which we started. Here all private individuals become equals again, because they are nothing. And since subjects no longer have any law other than the master's will, nor the master any rule other than his passions, the notions of good and the principles of justice again vanish. Here everything is returned solely to the law of the strongest, and consequently to a new state of nature different from the one with which we began, in that the one was the state of nature in its purity, and this last one is the fruit of an excess of corruption. Moreover, there is so little difference between these two states, and the governmental contract is so utterly dissolved by despotism, that the despot is master only as long as he is the strongest; and as soon as he can be ousted, he has no cause to protest against violence. The uprising that ends in the strangulation or the dethronement of a sultan is as lawful an act as those by which he disposed of the lives and goods of his subjects the day before. Force alone maintained him; force alone brings him down. Thus everything happens in accordance with the natural order, and whatever the outcome of these brief and frequent upheavals may be, no one can complain about someone else's injustice, but only of his own imprudence or his misfortune.

In discovering and following thus the forgotten and lost routes that must have led man from the natural state to the civil state; in reestablishing, with the intermediate positions I have just taken note of, those that time constraints on me have made me suppress or that the imagination has not suggested to me, no attentive reader can fail to be struck by the immense space that separates these two states. It is in this slow succession of things that he will see the solution to an infinity of moral and political problems which the philosophers are unable to resolve. He will realize that, since the human race of one age is not the human race of another age, the reason why Diogenes did not find his man is because he searched among his contemporaries for a man who no longer existed. Cato, he will say, perished with Rome and liberty because he was out of place in his age; and this greatest of men merely astonished the world, which five hundred years earlier he would have governed. In short, he will explain how the soul and human passions are imperceptibly altered and, as it were, change their nature; why, in the long run, our needs and our pleasures change their objects; why, with original man gradually disappearing, society no longer offers to the eyes of the wise man anything but an assemblage of artificial men and factitious passions which are the work of all these new relations and have no true foundation in nature. What reflection teaches us on this subject is perfectly confirmed by observation: savage man and civilized man differ so greatly in the depths of their hearts and in their inclinations, that what constitutes the supreme happiness of the one would reduce the other to despair. Savage man breathes only tranquillity and liberty; he wants simply to live and rest easy; and not even the unperturbed tranquillity of the Stoic approaches his profound indifference for any other objects. On the other hand, the citizen is always active and in a sweat, always agitated, and unceasingly tormenting himself in order to seek still more laborious occupations. He works until he dies; he even runs to his death in order to be in a position to live, or renounces life in order to acquire immortality. He pays court to the great whom he hates and to the rich whom he scorns. He stops at nothing to obtain the honor of serving them. He proudly crows about his own baseness and their protection; and proud of his slavery, he speaks with disdain about those who do not have the honor of taking part in it. What a spectacle for the Carib are the difficult and envied labors of the European minister! How many cruel deaths would that indolent savage not prefer to the horror of such a life, which often is not mollified even by the pleasure of doing good. But in order to see the purpose of so many cares, the words *power* and *reputation* would have to have a meaning in his mind; he would have to learn that there is a type of men who place some value on the regard the rest of the world has for them, and who know how to be happy and content with themselves on the testimony of others rather than on their own. Such, in fact, is the true cause of all these differences; the savage lives in himself; the man accustomed to the ways of society is always outside himself and knows how to live only in the opinion of others. And it is, as it were, from their judgment alone that he draws the sentiment of his own existence. It is not pertinent to my subject to show how, from such a disposition, so much indifference for good and evil arises, along with such fine discourse on morality; how, with everything reduced to appearances, everything becomes factitious and bogus: honor, friendship, virtue, and often even our vices, about which we eventually find the secret of boasting; how, in a word, always asking others what we are and never daring to question ourselves on this matter, in the midst of so much philosophy, humanity, politeness, and sublime maxims, we have merely a deceitful and frivolous exterior: honor without virtue, reason without wisdom, and pleasure without happiness. It is enough for me to have proved that this is not the original state of man, and that this is only the spirit of society, and the inequality that society engenders, which thus change and alter all our natural inclinations.

I have tried to set forth the origin and progress of inequality, the establishment and abuse of political societies, to the extent that these things can be deduced from the nature of man by the light of reason alone, and independently of the sacred dogmas that give to sovereign authority the sanction of divine right. It follows from this presentation that, since inequality is practically non-existent in the state of nature, it derives its force and growth from the development of our faculties and the progress of the human mind, and eventually becomes stable and legitimate through the establishment of property and laws. Moreover, it follows that moral inequality, authorized by positive right alone, is contrary to natural right whenever it is not combined in the same proportion with physical inequality: a distinction that is sufficient to determine what one should think in this regard about the sort of inequality that reigns among all civilized people, for it is obviously contrary to the law of nature, however it may be defined, for a child to command an old man, for an imbecile to lead a wise man, and for a handful of people to gorge themselves on superfluities while the starving multitude lacks necessities.

6

Jean-Jacques Rousseau, "Sophy," from *Émile, or Education*

Émile, published in 1762, is a treatise on education in the form of a discussion of the proper course of instruction from birth to adulthood of a single fictional character, Émile. During Rousseau's lifetime it was the most influential of all his works. In this excerpt, Rousseau discusses the qualities of an ideal fictional companion to Émile, Sophy. Rousseau's argument raises important questions about equality and inequalities based on gender.

Sophy, or Woman

Sophy should be as truly a woman as Émile is a man, *i.e.*, she must possess all those characters of her sex which are required to enable her to play her part in the physical and moral order. Let us inquire to begin with in what respects her sex differs from our own.

But for her sex, a woman is a man; she has the same organs, the same needs, the same faculties. The machine is the same in its construction; its parts, its working, and its appearance are similar. Regard it as you will, the difference is only in degree.

Yet where sex is concerned man and woman are unlike; each is the complement of the other; the difficulty in comparing them lies in our inability to decide, in either case, what is a matter of sex, and what is not. General differences present themselves to the comparative anatomist and even to the superficial observer; they seem not to be a matter of sex; yet they are really sex differences, though the connection eludes our observation. How far such differences may extend we cannot tell; all we know for certain is that where man and woman are alike we have to do with the characteristics of the species; where they are unlike, we have to do with the characteristics of sex. Considered from these two standpoints, we find so many instances of likeness and unlikeness that it is perhaps one of the greatest of marvels how nature has contrived to make two being so like and yet so different.

From Jean-Jacques Rousseau, *Émile, or Education*, trans. by Barbara Foxley (London: Dent, 1911).

These resemblances and differences must have an influence on the moral nature; this inference is obvious, and it is confirmed by experience; it shows the vanity of the disputes as to the superiority or the equality of the sexes; as if each sex, pursuing the path marked out for it by nature, were not more perfect in that very divergence than if it more closely resembled the other. A perfect man and a perfect woman should no more be alike in mind than in face, and perfection admits of neither less nor more.

In the union of the sexes each alike contributes to the common end, but in different ways. From this diversity springs the first difference which may be observed between man and woman in their moral relations. The man should be strong and active; the woman should be weak and passive; the one must have both the power and the will; it is enough that the other should offer little resistance.

When this principle is admitted, it follows that woman is specially made for man's delight. If man in his turn ought to be pleasing in her eyes, the necessity is less urgent, his virtue is in his strength, he pleases because he is strong. I grant you this is not the law of love, but it is the law of nature, which is older than love itself.

If woman is made to please and to be in subjection to man, she ought to make herself pleasing in his eyes and not provoke him to anger; her strength is in her charms, by their means she should compel him to discover and use his strength. The surest way of arousing his strength is to make it necessary by resistance. Thus pride comes to the help of desire and each exults in the other's victory. This is the origin of attack and defence, of the boldness of one sex and the timidity of the other, and even of the shame and modesty with which nature has armed the weak for the conquest of the strong.

Who can possibly suppose that nature has prescribed the same advances to the one sex as to the other, or that the first to feel desire should be the first to show it? What strange depravity of judgment! The consequences of the act being so different for the two sexes, is it natural that they should enter upon it with equal boldness? How can any one fail to see that when the share of each is so unequal, if the one were not controlled by modesty as the other is controlled by nature, the result would be the destruction of both, and the human race would perish through the very means ordained for its continuance?

Women so easily stir a man's senses and fan the ashes of a dying passion, that if philosophy ever succeeded in introducing this custom into any unlucky country, especially if it were a warm country where more women are born than men, the men, tyrannised over by the women, would at last become their victims, and would be dragged to their death without the least chance of escape.

Female animals are without this sense of shame, but what of that? Are their desires as boundless as those of women, which are curbed by this shame? The desires of the animals are the result of necessity, and when the need is satisfied, the desire ceases; they no longer make a feint of repulsing the male, they do it in earnest. Their seasons of complaisance are short and soon over. Impulse and restraint are alike the work of nature. But what would take the place of this negative instinct in women if you rob them of their modesty?

The Most High has deigned to do honour to mankind; he has endowed man with boundless passions, together with a law to guide them, so that man may be alike free and self-controlled; though swayed by these passions man is endowed with reason by which to control them. Woman is also endowed with boundless passions; God has given her modesty to restrain them. Moreover, he has given to both a present reward for the right use of their powers, in the delight which springs from that right use of them, *i.e.*, the taste for right conduct established as the law of our behaviour. To my mind this is far higher than the instinct of the beasts.

Whether the woman shares the man's passion or not, whether she is willing or unwilling to satisfy it, she always repulses him and defends herself, though not always with the same vigour, and therefore not always with the same success. If the siege is to be successful, the besieged must permit or direct the attack. How skilfully can she stimulate the efforts of the aggressor. The freest and most delightful of activities does not permit of any real violence; reason and nature are alike against it; nature, in that she has given the weaker party strength enough to resist if she chooses; reason, in that actual violence is not only most brutal in itself, but it defeats its own ends, not only because the man thus declares war against his companion and thus gives her a right to defend her person and her liberty even at the cost of the enemy's life, but also because the woman alone is the judge of her condition, and a child would have no father if any man might usurp a father's rights.

Thus the different constitution of the two sexes leads us to a third conclusion, that the stronger party seems to be master, but is as a matter of fact dependent on the weaker, and that, not by any foolish custom of gallantry, nor yet by the magnanimity of the protector, but by an inexorable law of nature. For nature has endowed woman with a power of stimulating man's passions in excess of man's power of satisfying those passions, and has thus made him dependent on her goodwill, and compelled him in his turn to endeavour to please her, so that she may be willing to yield to his superior strength. Is it weakness which yields to force, or is it voluntary self-surrender? This uncertainty constitutes the chief charm of the man's victory, and the woman is usually cunning enough to leave him in doubt. In this respect the woman's mind exactly resembles her body; far from being ashamed of her weakness, she is proud of it; her soft muscles offer no resistance, she professes that she cannot lift the lightest weight; she would be ashamed to be strong. And why? Not only to gain an appearance of refinement; she is too clever for that; she is providing herself beforehand with excuses, with the right to be weak if she chooses.

The experience we have gained through our vices has considerably modified the views held in older times; we rarely hear of violence for which there is so little occasion that it would hardly be credited. Yet such stories are common enough among the Jews and ancient Greeks; for such views belong to the simplicity of nature, and have only been uprooted by our profligacy. If fewer deeds of violence are quoted in our days, it is not that men are more temperate, but because they are less credulous, and a complaint which would have been believed among a simple people would only excite laughter among ourselves; therefore silence is the better course. There is a law in Deuteronomy, under which the outraged maiden was punished, along with her assailant, if the crime were committed in a town; but if in the country or in a lonely place, the latter alone was punished. "For," says the law, "the maiden cried for help, and there was none to hear." From this merciful interpretation of the law, girls learnt not to let themselves be surprised in lonely places.

This change in public opinion has had a perceptible effect on our morals. It has produced our modern gallantry. Men have found that their pleasures depend, more than they expected, on the goodwill of the fair sex, and have secured this goodwill by attentions which have had their reward.

See how we find ourselves led unconsciously from the physical to the moral constitution, how from the grosser union of the sexes spring the sweet laws of love. Woman reigns, not by the will of man, but by the decrees of nature herself; she had the power long before she showed it. That same Hercules who proposed to violate all the fifty daughters of Thespis was compelled to spin at the feet of Omphale, and Samson, the strong man, was less strong than Delilah. This power cannot be taken from woman; it is hers by right; she would have lost it long ago, were it possible.

The consequences of sex are wholly unlike for man and woman. The male is only a male now and again, the female is always a female, or at least all her youth; everything reminds her of her sex; the performance of her functions requires a special constitution. She needs care during pregnancy and freedom from work when her child is born; she must have a quiet, easy life while she nurses her children; their education calls for patience and gentleness, for a zeal and love which nothing can dismay; she forms a bond between father and child, she alone can win the father's love for his children and convince him that they are indeed his own. What loving care is required to preserve a united family! And there should be no question of virtue in all this, it must be a labour of love, without which the human race would be doomed to extinction.

The mutual duties of the two sexes are not, and cannot be, equally binding on both. Women do wrong to complain of the inequality of man-made laws; this inequality is not of man's making, or at any rate it is not the result of mere prejudice, but of reason. She to whom nature has entrusted the care of the children must hold herself responsible for them to their father. No doubt every breach of faith is wrong, and every faithless husband, who robs his wife of the sole reward of the stern duties of her sex, is cruel and unjust; but the faithless wife is worse; she destroys the family and breaks the bonds of nature; when she gives her husband children who are not his own, she is false both to him and them, her crime is not infidelity but treason. To my mind, it is the source of dissension and of crime of every kind. Can any position be more wretched than that of the unhappy father who, when he clasps his child to his breast, is haunted by the suspicion that this is the child of another, the badge of his own dishonour, a thief who is robbing his own children of their inheritance. Under such circumstances the family is little more than a group of secret enemies, armed against each other by a guilty woman, who compels them to pretend to love one another.

Thus it is not enough that a wife should be faithful; her husband, along with his friends and neighbours, must believe in her fidelity; she must be modest, devoted, retiring; she should have the witness not only of a good conscience, but of a good reputation. In a word, if a father must love his children, he must be able to respect their mother. For these reasons it is not enough that the woman should be chaste, she must preserve her reputation and her good name. From these principles there arises not only a moral difference between the sexes, but also a fresh motive for duty and propriety, which prescribes to women in particular the most scrupulous attention to their conduct, their manners, their behavior. Vague assertions as to the equality of the sexes and the similarity of their duties are only empty words; they are no answer to my argument.

It is a poor sort of logic to quote isolated exceptions against laws so firmly established. Women, you say, are not always bearing children. Granted; yet that is their proper business. Because there are a hundred or so of large towns in the world where women live licentiously and have few children, will you maintain that it is their business to have few children? And what would become of your towns if the remote country districts, with their simpler and purer women, did not make up for the barrenness of your fine ladies? There are plenty of country places where women with only four or five children are reckoned unfruitful. In conclusion, although here and there a woman may have few children,[1] what difference does it make? Is it any the less a woman's business to be a mother? And do not the general laws of nature and morality make provision for this state of things?

Even if there were these long intervals, which you assume, between the periods of pregnancy, can a woman suddenly change her way of life without danger? Can she be a nursing mother to-day and a soldier to-morrow? Will she change her tastes and her feelings as a chameleon changes his colour? Will she pass at once from the privacy of household duties and indoor occupations to the buffeting of the winds, the toils, the labours, the perils of war? Will she be now timid,[2] now brave, now fragile, now robust? If the young men of Paris find a soldier's life too hard for them, how would a woman put up with it, a woman who has hardly ventured out of doors without a parasol and who has scarcely put a foot to the ground? Will she make a good soldier at an age when even men are retiring from this arduous business?

There are countries, I grant you, where women bear and rear children with little or no difficulty, but in those lands the men go half-naked in all weathers, they strike down the wild beasts, they carry a canoe as easily as a knapsack, they pursue the chase for 700 or 800 leagues, they sleep in the open on the bare ground, they bear incredible fatigues and go many days without food. When women become strong, men become still stronger; when men become soft, women become softer; change both the terms and the ratio remains unaltered.

I am quite aware that Plato, in the *Republic*, assigns the same gymnastics to women and men. Having got rid of the family there is no place for women in his system of government, so he is forced to turn them into men. That great genius has worked out his plans in detail and has provided for every contingency; he has even provided against a difficulty which in all likelihood no one would ever have raised; but he has not succeeded in meeting the real difficulty. I am not speaking of the alleged community of

1. Without this the race would necessarily diminish; all things considered, for its preservation each woman ought to have about four children, for about half the children born die before they can become parents, and two must survive to replace the father and mother. See whether the towns will supply them?

2. Women's timidity is yet another instinct of nature against the double risk she runs during pregnancy.

wives which has often been laid to his charge; this assertion only shows that his detractors have never read his works. I refer to that political promiscuity under which the same occupations are assigned to both sexes alike, a scheme which could only lead to intolerable evils; I refer to that subversion of all the tenderest of our natural feelings, which he sacrificed to an artificial sentiment which can only exist by their aid. Will the bonds of convention hold firm without some foundation in nature? Can devotion to the state exist apart from the love of those near and dear to us? Can patriotism thrive except in the soil of that miniature fatherland, the home? Is it not the good son, the good husband, the good father, who makes the good citizen?

When once it is proved that men and women are and ought to be unlike in constitution and in temperament, it follows that their education must be different. Nature teaches us that they should work together, but that each has its own share of the work; the end is the same, but the means are different, as are also the feelings which direct them. We have attempted to paint a natural man, let us try to paint a helpmeet for him.

You must follow nature's guidance if you would walk aright. The native characters of sex should be respected as nature's handiwork. You are always saying, "Women have such and such faults, from which we are free." You are misled by your vanity; what would be faults in you are virtues in them; and things would go worse, if they were without these so-called faults. Take care that they do not degenerate into evil, but beware of destroying them.

On the other hand, women are always exclaiming that we educate them for nothing but vanity and coquetry, that we keep them amused with trifles that we may be their masters; we are responsible, so they say, for the faults we attribute to them. How silly! What have men to do with the education of girls? What is there to hinder their mothers educating them as they please? There are no colleges for girls; so much the better for them! Would God there were none for the boys, their education would be more sensible and more wholesome. Who is it that compels a girl to waste her time on foolish trifles? Are they forced, against their will, to spend half their time over their toilet, following the examples set them by you? Who prevents you teaching them, or having them taught, whatever seems good in your eyes? Is it our fault that we are charmed by their beauty and delighted by their airs and graces, if we are attracted and flattered by the arts they learn from you, if we love to see them prettily dressed, if we let them display at leisure the weapons by which we are subjugated? Well then, educate them like men. The more women are like men, the less influence they will have over men, and then men will be masters indeed.

All the faculties common to both sexes are not equally shared between them, but taken as a whole they are fairly divided. Woman is worth more as a woman and less as a man; when she makes a good use of her own rights, she has the best of it; when she tries to usurp our rights, she is our inferior. It is impossible to controvert this, except by quoting exceptions after the usual fashion of the partisans of the fair sex.

To cultivate the masculine virtues in women and to neglect their own is evidently to do them an injury. Women are too clear-sighted to be thus deceived; when they try to usurp our privileges they do not abandon their own; with this result: they are unable to make use of two incompatible things, so they fall below their own level as women, instead of rising to the level of men. If you are a sensible mother you will take my advice. Do not try to make your daughter a good man in defiance of nature. Make her a good woman, and be sure it will be better both for her and us.

Does this mean that she must be brought up in ignorance and kept to housework only? Is she to be man's handmaid or his helpmeet? Will he dispense with her greatest charm, her companionship? To keep her a slave will he prevent her knowing and feeling? Will he make an automaton of her? No, indeed, that is not the teaching of nature, who has given women such a pleasant easy wit. On the contrary, nature means them to think, to will, to love, to cultivate their minds as well as their persons; she puts these weapons in their hands to make up for their lack of strength and to enable them to direct the strength of men. They should learn many things, but only such things as are suitable.

When I consider the special purpose of women, when I observe her inclinations or reckon up her duties, everything combines to indicate the mode of education she requires. Men and women are made for each other, but their mutual dependence differs in degree; man is dependent on woman through his desires; woman is dependent on man through her desires and also through her needs; he could do without her better than she can do without him. She cannot fulfill her purpose in life without his aid, without his goodwill, without his respect; she is dependent on our feelings, on the price we put upon her virtue, and the opinion we have of her charms and her deserts. Nature herself has decreed that woman, both for herself and her children, should be at the mercy of man's judgment.

7

Edmund Burke,
"Equality in Representation?"
from *Reflections on the Revolution in France*

*Edmund Burke (1729–1797) was a member of the British Parliament from
1765 to 1794. He was also a philosopher and the author of an influential
work on aesthetics. He supported the American Revolution of 1776, but was
highly critical of the French Revolution, which began in 1789. In this excerpt from his* Reflections on the Revolution in France, *published in
1790, Burke considers the revolutionaries' demand for equality in political
representation.*

Believe me, Sir, those who attempt to level, never equalize. In all societies, consisting of various descriptions of citizens, some description
must be uppermost. The levellers therefore only change and pervert the
natural order of things; they load the edifice of society, by setting up in the
air what the solidity of the structure requires to be on the ground. The
associations of tailors and carpenters, of which the republic (of Paris, for
instance) is composed, cannot be equal to the situation, into which, by the
worst of usurpations, an usurpation on the prerogatives of nature, you
attempt to force them.

The chancellor of France at the opening of the states, said, in a tone of
oratorial flourish, that all occupations were honourable. If he meant only,
that no honest employment was disgraceful, he would not have gone
beyond the truth. But in asserting, that any thing is honourable, we imply
some distinction in its favour. The occupation of a hair-dresser, or of a
working tallow-chandler, cannot be a matter of honour to any person—to
say nothing of a number of other more servile employments. Such descriptions of men ought not to suffer oppression from the state; but the state
suffers oppression, if such as they, either individually or collectively, are
permitted to rule. In this you think you are combating prejudice, but you
are at war with nature.

I do not, my dear Sir, conceive you to be of that sophistical captious
spirit, or of that uncandid dulness as to require, for every general observation or sentiment, an explicit detail of the correctives and exceptions,

From Edmund Burke, *Reflections on the Revolution in France* (London: J. Dodsley,
1790).

which reason will presume to be included in all the general propositions which come from reasonable men. You do not imagine that I wish to confine power, authority, and distinction to blood, and names, and titles. No, Sir. There is no qualification for government, but virtue and wisdom, actual or presumptive. Wherever they are actually found, they have in whatever state, condition, profession or trade, the passport of Heaven to human place and honour. Woe to the country which would madly and impiously reject the service of the talents and virtues, civil, military, or religious, that are given to grace and to serve it; and would condemn to obscurity every thing formed to diffuse lustre and glory around a state. Woe to that country too, that passing into the opposite extreme, considers a low education, a mean contracted view of things, a sordid mercenary occupation, as a preferable title to command. Every thing ought to be open; but not indifferently to every man. No rotation; no appointment by lot; no mode of election operating in the spirit of sortition or rotation, can be generally good in a government conversant in extensive objects. Because they have no tendency, direct or indirect, to select the man with a view to the duty, or to accommodate the one to the other, I do not hesitate to say, that the road to eminence and power, from obscure condition, ought not to be made too easy, nor a thing too much of course. If rare merit be the rarest of all rare things, it ought to pass through some sort of probation. The temple of honour ought to be seated on an eminence. If it be open through virtue, let it be remembered too, that virtue is never tried but by some difficulty, and some struggle.

Nothing is a due and adequate representation of a state, that does not represent its ability, as well as its property. But as ability is a vigorous and active principle, and as property is sluggish, inert, and timid, it never can be safe from the invasions of ability, unless it be, out of all proportion, predominant in the representation. It must be represented too in great masses of accumulation, or it is not rightly protected. The characteristic essence of property, formed out of the combined principles of its acquisition and conservation, is to be *unequal*. The great masses therefore which excite envy, and tempt rapacity, must be put out of the possibility of danger. Then they form a natural rampart about the lesser properties in all their gradations. The same quantity of property, which is by the natural course of things divided among many, has not the same operation. Its defensive power is weakened as it is diffused. In this diffusion each man's portion is less than what, in the eagerness of his desires, he may flatter himself to obtain by dissipating the accumulations of others. The plunder of the few would indeed give but a share inconceivably small in the distribution to the many. But the many are not capable of making this calculation; and those who lead them to rapine, never intend this distribution.

The power of perpetuating our property in our families is one of the most valuable and interesting circumstances belonging to it, and that which tends the most to the perpetuation of society itself. It makes our weakness subservient to our virtue; it grafts benevolence even upon avarice. The possessors of family wealth, and of the distinction which attends hereditary possession (as most concerned in it) are the natural securities for this transmission. With us, the house of peers is formed upon this principle. It is wholly composed of hereditary property and hereditary distinction; and made therefore the third of the legislature; and in the last event, the sole judge of all property in all its subdivisions. The house of commons too, though not necessarily, yet in fact, is always so composed in the far greater part. Let those large proprietors be what they will, and they have their chance of being amongst the best, they are at the very worst, the ballast in the vessel of the commonwealth. For though hereditary wealth, and the rank which goes with it, are too much idolized by creeping sycophants, and the blind abject admirers of power, they are too rashly slighted in shallow speculations of the petulant, assuming, short-sighted coxcombs of philosophy. Some decent regulated pre-eminence, some preference (not exclusive appropriation) given to birth, is neither unnatural, nor unjust, nor impolitic.

It is said, that twenty-four millions ought to prevail over two hundred thousand. True; if the constitution of a kingdom be a problem of arithmetic. This sort of discourse does well enough with the lamp-post for its second: to men who *may* reason calmly, it is ridiculous. The will of the many, and their interest, must very often differ; and great will be the difference when they make an evil choice. A government of five hundred country attornies and obscure curates is not good for twenty-four millions of men, though it were chosen by eight and forty millions; nor is it the better for being guided by a dozen of persons of quality, who have betrayed their trust in order to obtain that power. At present, you seem in every thing to have strayed out of the high road of nature. The property of France does not govern it. Of course property is destroyed, and rational liberty has no existence. All you have got for the present is a paper circulation, and a stock-jobbing constitution: and as to the future, do you seriously think that the territory of France, upon the republican system of eighty-three independent municipalities (to say nothing of the parts that compose them) can ever be governed as one body, or can ever be set in motion by the impulse of one mind? When the National Assembly has completed its work, it will have accomplished its ruin. These commonwealths will not long bear a state of subjection to the republic of Paris. They will not bear that this one body should monopolize the captivity of the king, and the dominion over the assembly calling itself National. Each will keep its own portion of the spoil of the church to itself; and it will not suffer either that spoil, or the more just fruits of their industry, or the natural produce of their soil, to be sent to swell the insolence, or pamper the luxury of the mechanics of Paris. In this they will see none of the equality, under the pretence of which they have been tempted to throw off their allegiance to their sovereign, as well as the ancient constitution of their country. There can be no capital city in such a constitution as they have lately made. They have forgot, that when they framed democratic governments, they had virtually dismembered their country. The person whom they persevere in calling king, has not power left to him by the hundredth part sufficient to hold together this collection of republics. The republic of Paris will endeavour indeed to complete the debauchery of the army, and illegally to perpetuate the assembly, without resort to its constituents, as the means of continuing its depotism. It will make efforts, by becoming the heart of a boundless paper circulation, to draw every thing to itself; but in vain. All this policy in the end will appear as feeble as it is now violent.

8

Alexis de Tocqueville, "Equality, Democracy, and Liberty," from *Democracy in America*

Alexis de Tocqueville (1805–1859) was an active politician in France during the first half of the nineteenth century, serving for a decade as a member of the Chamber of Deputies and briefly as Foreign Minister. As a young man he travelled to America and on his return to France, he composed Democracy in America, *his most famous work, while still in his twenties. Later in his life he produced another classic of historical and political analysis,* The Old Regime and the French Revolution. *The selections below describe Tocqueville's concern with what he saw as the irresistible rising tide of social equality. Tocqueville believed that by observing the effects of this tide in America, Europeans would be able to prepare themselves for its revolutionary impact.*

Amongst the novel objects that attracted my attention during my stay in the United States, nothing struck me more forcibly than the general equality of conditions. I readily discovered the prodigious influence which this primary fact exercises on the whole course of society, by giving a certain direction to public opinion, and a certain tenor to the laws; by imparting new maxims to the governing powers, and peculiar habits to the governed.

I speedily perceived that the influence of this fact extends far beyond the political character and the laws of the country, and that it has no less empire over civil society than over the Government; it creates opinions, engenders sentiments, suggests the ordinary practices of life, and modifies whatever it does not produce.

The more I advanced in the study of American society, the more I perceived that the equality of conditions is the fundamental fact from which all others seem to be derived, and the central point at which all my observations constantly terminated.

I then turned my thoughts to our own hemisphere, where I imagined that I discerned something analogous to the spectacle which the New World presented to me. I observed that the equality of conditions is daily

From Alexis de Tocqueville, *Democracy in America*, 2 vols., trans. by Henry Reeve (London: Saunders and Otley, 1835).

progressing towards those extreme limits which it seems to have reached in the United States; and that the democracy which governs the American communities appears to be rapidly rising into power in Europe.

I hence conceived the idea of the book which is now before the reader.

It is evident to all alike that a great democratic revolution is going on amongst us; but there are two opinions as to its nature and consequences. To some it appears to be a novel accident, which as such may still be checked; to others, it seems irresistible, because it is the most uniform, the most ancient, and the most permanent tendency which is to be found in history.

Let us recollect the situation of France seven hundred years ago, when the territory was divided amongst a small number of families, who were the owners of the soil and the rulers of the inhabitants; the right of governing descended with the family inheritance from generation to generation; force was the only means by which man could act on man; and landed property was the sole source of power.

Soon, however, the political power of the clergy was founded, and began to exert itself: the clergy opened its ranks to all classes, to the poor and the rich, the villain and the lord; equality penetrated into the Government through the Church, and the being who as a serf must have vegetated in perpetual bondage, took his place as a priest in the midst of nobles, and not unfrequently above the heads of kings.

The different relations of men became more complicated and more numerous as society gradually became more stable and more civilized. Thence the want of civil laws was felt; and the order of legal functionaries soon rose from the obscurity of the tribunals and their dusty chambers, to appear at the court of the monarch, by the side of the feudal barons in their ermine and their mail.

Whilst the kings were running themselves by their great enterprises, and the nobles exhausting their resources by private wars, the lower orders were enriching themselves by commerce. The influence of money began to be perceptible in State affairs. The transactions of business opened a new road to power, and the financier rose to a station of political influence in which he was at once flattered and despised.

Gradually the spread of mental acquirements, and the increasing taste for literature and art, opened chances of success to talent; science became a means of government, intelligence led to social power, and the man of letters took a part in affairs of the State.

The value attached to the privileges of birth decreased in the exact proportion in which new paths were struck out to advancement. In the eleventh century, nobility was beyond all price; in the thirteenth it might be purchased; it was conferred for the first time in 1270; and equality was thus introduced into the Government by the aristocracy itself.

In the course of these seven hundred years, it sometimes happened that in order to resist the authority of the Crown, or to diminish the power of their rivals, the nobles granted a certain share of political rights to the people. Or, more frequently, the king permitted the lower orders to enjoy a degree of power, with the intention of repressing the aristocracy.

In France the kings have always been the most active and the most constant of levellers. When they were strong and ambitious, they spared no pains to raise the people to the level of the nobles; when they were temperate or weak, they allowed the people to rise above themselves. Some assisted the democracy by their talents, others by their vices. Louis XI and Louis XIV reduced every rank beneath the throne to the same subjection; Louis XV descended, himself and all his Court, into the dust.

As soon as land was held on any other than a feudal tenure, and personal property began in its turn to confer influence and power, every improvement which was introduced in commerce or manufacture was a fresh element of the equality of conditions. Henceforward every new discovery, every new want which it engendered, and every new desire which craved satisfaction, was a step towards the universal level. The taste for luxury, the love of war, the sway of fashion, and the most superficial as well as the deepest passions of the human heart, co-operated to enrich the poor and to impoverish the rich.

From the time when the exercise of the intellect became the source of strength and of wealth, it is impossible not to consider every addition to science, every fresh truth, and every new idea as a germ of power placed within the reach of the people. Poetry, eloquence, and memory, the grace of wit, the glow of imagination, the depth of thought, and all the gifts which are bestowed by Providence with an equal hand, turned to the advantage of the democracy; and even when they were in the possession of its adversaries, they still served its cause by throwing into relief the natural greatness of man; its conquests spread, therefore, with those of civilization and knowledge; and literature became an arsenal, where the poorest and the weakest could always find weapons to their hand.

In perusing the pages of our history, we shall scarcely meet with a single great event, in the lapse of seven hundred years, which has not turned to the advantage of equality.

The Crusades and the wars of the English decimated the nobles and divided their possessions: the erection of communities introduced an element of democratic liberty into the bosom of feudal monarchy; the invention of fire-arms equalized the villain and the noble on the field of battle;

printing opened the same resources to the minds of all classes; the post was organized so as to bring the same information to the door of the poor man's cottage, and to the gate of the palace, and Protestantism proclaimed that all men are alike able to find the road to heaven. The discovery of America offered a thousand new paths to fortune and placed riches and power within the reach of the adventurous and the obscure.

If we examine what has happened in France at intervals of fifty years, beginning with the eleventh century, we shall invariably perceive that a twofold revolution has taken place in the state of society. The noble has gone down on the social ladder, and the *roturier* has gone up; the one descends and the other rises. Every half-century brings them nearer to each other, and they will very shortly meet.

Nor is this phenomenon at all peculiar to France. Withersoever we turn our eyes we shall witness the came continual revolution throughout the whole of Christendom.

The various occurrences of national existence have everywhere turned to the advantage of democracy; all men have aided it by their exertions: those who have intentionally laboured in its cause, and those who have served it unwillingly; those who have fought for it and those who have declared themselves its opponents,—have all been driven along in the same track, have all laboured to one end, some ignorantly and some unwillingly; all have been blind instruments in the hands of God.

The gradual development of the equality of conditions is therefore a providential fact, and it possesses all the characteristics of a Divine decree: it is universal, it is durable, it constantly eludes all human interference, and all events as well as men contribute to its progress.

Would it, then, be wise to imagine that a social impulse which dates from so far back, can be checked by the efforts of a generation? Is it credible that the democracy which has annihilated the feudal system, and vanquished kings, will respect the citizen and the capitalist? Will it stop now that it is grown so strong, and its adversaries so weak?

None can say which way we are going, for all terms of comparison are wanting: the equality of conditions is more complete in the Christian countries of the present day, than it has been at any time, or in any part of the world; so that the extent of what already exists prevents us from foreseeing what may be yet to come.

The whole book which is here offered to the public has been written under the impression of a kind of religious dread produced in the author's mind by the contemplation of so irresistible a revolution, which has advanced for centuries in spite of such amazing obstacles, and which is still proceeding in the midst of the ruins it has made.

It is not necessary that God himself should speak in order to disclose to us the unquestionable signs of his will; we can discern them in the habitual course of nature, and in the invariable tendency of events: I know, without a special revelation, that the planets move in the orbits traced by the Creator's finger.

If the men of our time were led by attentive observation, and by sincere reflection, to acknowledge that the gradual and progressive development of social equality is at once the past and future of their history, this solitary truth would confer the sacred character of a Divine decree upon the change. To attempt to check democracy would be in that case to resist the will of God; and the nations would then be constrained to make the best of the social lot awarded to them by Providence.

The Christian nations of our age seem to me to present a most alarming spectacle; the impulse which is bearing them along is so strong that it cannot be stopped, but it is not yet so rapid that it cannot be guided: their fate is in their hands; yet a little while and it may be so no longer.

The first duty which is at this time imposed upon those who direct our affairs is to educate the democracy; to warm its faith, if that be possible; to purify its morals; to direct its energies, to substitute a knowledge of business for its inexperience, and an acquaintance with its true interests for its blind propensities; to adapt its government to time and place, and to modify it in compliance with the occurrences and the actors of the age. A new science of politics is indispensable to a new world.

This, however, is what we think of least; launched in the middle of a rapid stream, we obstinately fix our eyes on the ruins which may still be desired upon the shore we have left, whilst the current sweeps us along, and drives us backwards toward the gulf.

In no country in Europe has the great social revolution which I have been describing made such rapid progress as in France; but it has always been borne on by chance. The heads of the State have never had any forethought for its exigencies, and its victories have been obtained without their consent or without their knowledge. The most powerful, the most intelligent, and the most moral classes of the nation have never attempted to connect themselves with it in order to guide it. The people has consequently been abandoned to its wild propensities, and it has grown up like those outcasts who receive their education in the public streets, and who are unacquainted with aught but the vices and wretchedness of society. The existence of a democracy was seemingly unknown, when on a sudden it took possession of the supreme power. Everything was then submitted to its caprices; it was worshipped as the idol of strength; until, when it was enfeebled by its own excesses, the legislator conceived the rash project of annihilating its power, instead of instructing it and correcting its vices; no attempt was made to fit it to govern, but all were bent on excluding it from the government.

The consequence of this has been that the democratic revolution has been effected only in the material parts of society, without that concomitant change in laws, ideas, customs and manners which was necessary to render such a revolution beneficial. We have gotten a democracy, but without the conditions which lessen its vices and render its natural advantages more prominent; and although we already perceive the evils it brings, we are ignorant of the benefits it may confer.

While the power of the Crown, supported by the aristocracy, peaceably governed the nations of Europe, society possessed, in the midst of its wretchedness, several different advantages which can now scarcely be appreciated or conceived.

The power of a part of his subjects was an insurmountable barrier to the tyranny of the prince; and the monarch, who felt the almost divine character which he enjoyed in the eyes of the multitude, derived a motive for the just use of his power from the respect which he inspired.

High as they were placed above the people, the nobles could not but take that calm and benevolent interest in its fate which the shepherd feels towards his flock; and without acknowledging the poor as their equals, they watched over the destiny of those whose welfare Providence had entrusted to their care.

The people never having conceived the idea of a social condition different from its own, and entertaining no expectation of ever ranking with its chiefs, received benefits from them without discussing their rights. It grew attached to them when they were clement and just, and it submitted without resistance or servility to their exactions, as to the inevitable visitations of the arm of God. Custom, and the manners of the time, had moreover created a species of law in the midst of violence, and established certain limits to oppression.

As the noble never suspected that any one would attempt to deprive him of the privileges which he believed to be legitimate, and as the serf looked upon his own inferiority as a consequence of the immutable order of nature, it is easy to imagine that a mutual exchange of goodwill took place between two classes so differently gifted by fate. Inequality and wretchedness were then to be found in society; but the souls of neither rank of men were degraded.

Men are not corrupted by the exercise of power or debased by the habit of obedience; but by the exercise of a power which they believe to be illegal and by obedience to a rule which they consider to be usurped and oppressive.

On one side was wealth, strength, and leisure, accompanied by the refinements of luxury, the elegance of taste, the pleasures of wit, and the religion of art. On the other was labour, and a rude ignorance; but in the midst of this coarse and ignorant multitude, it was not uncommon to meet with energetic passions, generous sentiments, profound religious convictions, and independent virtues.

The body of a State thus organized might boast of its stability, its power, and, above all, of its glory.

But the scene is now changed; and gradually the two ranks mingle; the divisions which once severed mankind are lowered; property is divided, power is held in common, the light of intelligence spreads, and the capacities of all classes are equally cultivated; the State becomes democratic, and the empire of democracy is slowly and peaceably introduced into the institutions and the manners of the nation.

I can conceive a society in which all men would profess an equal attachment and respect for the laws of which they are the common authors; in which the authority of the State would be respected as necessary, though not as divine; and the loyalty of the subject to the chief magistrate would not be a passion, but a quiet and rational persuasion. Every individual being in the possession of rights which he is sure to retain, a kind of manly reliance, and reciprocal courtesy would arise between all classes, alike removed from pride and meanness.

The people, well acquainted with its true interests, would allow, that in order to profit by the advantages of society, it is necessary to satisfy its demands. In this state of things the voluntary association of the citizens might supply the individual exertions of the nobles, and the community would be alike protected from anarchy and from oppression.

I admit that, in a democratic State thus constituted, society will not be stationary; but the impulses of the social body may be regulated and directed forwards; if there be less splendour than in the halls of an aristocracy, the contrast of misery will be less frequent also; the pleasures of enjoyment may be less excessive, but those of comfort will be more general; the sciences may be less perfectly cultivated, but ignorance will be less common; the impetuosity of the feelings will be repressed, and the habits of the nation softened; there will be more vices and fewer crimes.

In the absence of enthusiasm and of an ardent faith, great sacrifices may be obtained from the members of a commonwealth by an appeal to their understandings and their experience; each individual will feel the same necessity for uniting with his fellow-citizens to protect his own weakness; and as he knows that if they are to assist, he must co-operate, he will readily perceive that his personal interest is identified with the interest of the community.

The nation, taken as a whole, will be less brilliant, less glorious, and perhaps less strong; but the majority of the citizens will enjoy a greater degree of prosperity, and the people will remain quiet, not because it despairs of amelioration, but because it is conscious of the advantages of its condition.

If all the consequences of this state of things were not good or useful, society would at least have appropriated all such as were useful and good; and having once and for ever renounced the social advantages of aristocracy, mankind would enter into possession of all the benefits which democracy can afford.

But here it may be asked what we have adopted in the place of those institutions, those ideas, and those customs of our forefathers which we have abandoned.

The spell of royalty is broken, but it has not been succeeded by the majesty of the laws; the people has learned to despise all authority, but fear now extorts a larger tribute of obedience than that which was formerly paid by reverence and by love.

I perceive that we have destroyed those independent beings which were able to cope with tyranny single-handed; but it is the Government that has inherited the privileges of which families, corporations, and individuals have been deprived; the weakness of the whole community has therefore succeeded that influence of a small body of citizens, which, if it was sometimes oppressive, was often conservative.

The division of property has lessened the distance which separated the rich from the poor; but it would seem that the nearer they draw to each other, the greater is their mutual hatred, and the more vehement the envy and the dread with which they resist each other's claims to power; the notion of Right is alike insensible to both classes, and Force affords to both the only argument for the present, and the only guarantee for the future.

The poor man retains the prejudices of his forefathers without their faith, and their ignorance without their virtues; he has adopted the doctrine of self-interest as the rule of his actions, without understanding the science which controls it, and his egotism is no less blind than his devotedness was formerly.

If society is tranquil, it is not because it relies upon its strength and its well-being, but because it knows its weakness and its infirmities; a single effort may cost it its life; everybody feels the evil, but no one has courage or energy enough to seek the cure; the desires, the regret, the sorrows, and the joys of the time produce nothing that is visible or permanent, like the passions of old men which terminate in impotence.

We have, then, abandoned whatever advantages the old state of things afforded, without receiving any compensation from our present condition;

we have destroyed an aristocracy, and we seem inclined to survey its ruins with complacency, and to fix our abode in the midst of them.

The phænomena which the intellectual world presents are not less deplorable. The democracy of France, checked in its course or abandoned to its lawless passions, has overthrown whatever crossed its path, and has shaken all that it has not destroyed. Its empire on society has not been gradually introduced, or peaceably established, but it has constantly advanced in the midst of disorder and the agitation of a conflict. In the heat of the struggle each partisan is hurried beyond the limits of his opinions by the opinions and the excesses of his opponents, until he loses sight of the end of his exertions, and holds a language which disguises his real sentiments or secret instincts. Hence arises the strange confusion which we are witnessing.

I cannot recall to my mind a passage in history more worthy of sorrow and of pity than the scenes which are happening under our eyes; it is as if the natural bond which unites the opinions of man to his tastes, and his actions to his principles, was now broken; the sympathy which has always been acknowledged between the feelings and the ideas of mankind appears to be dissolved, and all the laws of moral analogy to be abolished.

Zealous Christians may be found amongst us, whose minds are nurtured in the love and knowledge of a future life, and who readily espouse the cause of human liberty, as the source of all moral greatness. Christianity, which had declared that all men are equal in the sight of God, will not refuse to acknowledge that all citizens are equal in the eye of the law. But, by a singular concourse of events, religion is entangled in those institutions which democracy assails, and it is not unfrequently brought to reject the equality it loves, and to curse that cause of liberty as a foe, which it might hallow by its alliance.

By the side of these religious men I discern others whose looks are turned to the earth more than to Heaven; they are the partisans of liberty, not only as the source of the noblest virtues, but more especially as the root of all solid advantages; and they sincerely desire to extend its sway, and to impart its blessings to mankind. It is natural that they should hasten to invoke the assistance of religion, for they must know that liberty cannot be established without morality, nor morality without faith; but they have seen religion in the ranks of their adversaries, and they inquire no further; some of them attack it openly, and the remainder are afraid to defend it.

In former ages slavery has been advocated by the venal and slavish-minded, whilst the independent and the warm-hearted were struggling without hope to save the liberties of mankind. But men of high and generous characters are now to be met with, whose opinions are at variance with their inclinations, and who praise that servility which they have themselves never known. Others, on the contrary, speak in the name of liberty, as if they were able to feel its sanctity and its majesty, and loudly claim for humanity those rights which they have always disowned.

There are virtuous and peaceful individuals whose pure morality, quiet habits, affluence, and talents fit them to be the leaders of the surrounding population; their love of their country is sincere, and they are prepared to make the greatest sacrifices to its welfare, but they confound the abuses of civilization with its benefits, and the idea of evil is inseparable in their minds from that of novelty.

Not far from this class is another party, whose object is to materialize mankind, to hit upon what is expedient without heeding what is just, to acquire knowledge without faith, and prosperity apart from virtue; assuming the title of the champions of modern civilization, and placing themselves in a station which they usurp with insolence, and from which they are driven by their own unworthiness.

Where are we then?

The religionists are the enemies of liberty, and the friends of liberty attack religion; the high-minded and the noble advocate subjection, and the meanest and most servile minds preach independence; honest and enlightened citizens are opposed to all progress, whilst men without patriotism and without principles are the apostles of civilization and of intelligence.

Has such been the fate of the centuries which have preceded our own? and has man always inhabited a world, like the present, where nothing is linked together, where virtue is without genius, and genius without honour; where the love of order is confounded with a taste for oppression, and the holy rites of freedom with a contempt of law; where the light thrown by conscience on human actions is dim, and where nothing seems to be any longer forbidden or allowed, honourable or shameful, false or true?

I cannot, however, believe that the Creator made man to leave him in an endless struggle with the intellectual miseries which surround us: God destines a calmer and a more certain future to the communities of Europe; I am unacquainted with his designs, but I shall not cease to believe in them because I cannot fathom them, and I had rather mistrust my own capacity than his justice.

There is a country in the world where the great revolution which I am speaking of seems nearly to have reached its natural limits; it has been effected with ease and simplicity, say rather that this country has attained the consequences of the democratic revolution which we are undergoing, without having experienced the revolution itself.

The emigrants who fixed themselves on the shores of America in the beginning of the seventeenth century, severed the democratic principle from all the principles which repressed it in the old communities of Europe, and transplanted it unalloyed to the New World. It has there been allowed to spread in perfect freedom, and to put forth its consequences in the laws by influencing the manners of the country.

It appears to me beyond a doubt that sooner or later we shall arrive, like the Americans, at an almost complete equality of conditions. But I do not conclude from this, that we shall ever be necessarily led to draw the same political consequences which the Americans have derived from a similar social organization. I am far from supposing that they have chosen the only form of government which a democracy may adopt; but the identity of the efficient cause of laws and manners in the two countries is sufficient to account for the immense interest we have in becoming acquainted with its effects in each of them.

It is not, then, merely to satisfy a legitimate curiosity that I have examined America; my wish has been to find instruction by which we may ourselves profit. Whoever should imagine that I have intended to write a panegyric would be strangely mistaken, and on reading this book he will perceive that such was not my design; nor has it been my object to advocate any form of government in particular, for I am of opinion that absolute excellence is rarely to be found in any legislation; I have not even affected to discuss whether the social revolution, which I believe to be irresistible, is advantageous or prejudicial to mankind; I have acknowledged this revolution as a fact already accomplished or on the eve of its accomplishment; and I have selected the nation, from amongst those which have undergone it, in which its development has been the most peaceful and the most complete, in order to discern its natural consequences, and, if it be possible, to distinguish the means by which it may be rendered profitable. I confess that in America I saw more than America; I sought the image of democracy itself, with its inclinations, its character, its prejudices, and its passions, in order to learn what we have to fear or to hope from its progress.

· · ·

Why Democratic Nations Show a More Ardent and Enduring Love of Equality than of Liberty

The first and most intense passion which is engendered by the equality of conditions is, I need hardly say, the love of that same equality. My readers will therefore not be surprised that I speak of it before all others.

Everybody has remarked, that in our time, and especially in France, this passion for equality is every day gaining ground in the human heart. It has been said a hundred times that our contemporaries are far more ardently and tenaciously attached to equality than to freedom; but, as I do not find that the causes of the fact have been sufficiently analysed, I shall endeavour to point them out.

It is possible to imagine an extreme point at which freedom and equality would meet and be confounded together. Let us suppose that all the members of the community take a part in the government, and that each one of them has an equal right to take a part in it. As none is different from his fellows, none can exercise a tyrannical power: men will be perfectly free, because they will all be entirely equal; and they will all be perfectly equal, because they will be entirely free. To this ideal state democratic nations tend. Such is the completest form that equality can assume upon earth; but there are a thousand others which, without being equally perfect, are not less cherished by those nations.

The principle of equality may be established in civil society, without prevailing in the political world. Equal rights may exist of indulging in the same pleasures, of entering the same professions, of frequenting the same places—in a word, of living in the same manner and seeking wealth by the same means, although all men do not take an equal share in the government.

A kind of equality may even be established in the political world, though there should be no political freedom there. A man may be the equal of all his countrymen save one, who is the master of all without distinction, and who selects equally from among them all the agents of his power.

Several other combinations might be easily imagined, by which very great equality would be united to institutions more or less free, or even to institutions wholly without freedom.

Although men cannot become absolutely equal unless they be entirely free, and consequently equality, pushed to its furthest extent, may be confounded with freedom, yet there is good reason for distinguishing the one from the other. The taste which men have for liberty, and that which they feel for equality, are, in fact, two different things; and I am not afraid to add, that, amongst democratic nations, they are two unequal things.

Upon close inspection, it will be seen that there is in every age some peculiar and preponderating fact with which all others are connected; this fact almost always gives birth to some pregnant idea or some ruling passion, which attracts to itself, and bears away in its course, all the feelings and opinions of the time: it is like a great stream, towards which each of the surrounding rivulets seems to flow.

Freedom has appeared in the world at different times and under various forms; it has not been exclusively bound to any social condition, and it is not confined to democracies. Freedom cannot, therefore, form the distinguishing characteristic of democratic ages. The peculiar and preponderating fact which marks those ages as its own is the equality of conditions; the ruling passion of men in those periods is the love of this equality. Ask not what singular charm the men of democratic ages find in being equal, or what special reason they may have for clinging so tenaciously to equality rather than to the other advantages which society holds out to them: equality is the distinguishing characteristic of the age they live in; that, of itself, is enough to explain that they prefer it to all the rest.

But independently of this reason there are several others, which will at all times habitually lead men to prefer equality to freedom.

If a people could ever succeed in destroying, or even in diminishing, the equality which prevails in its own body, this could only be accomplished by long and laborious efforts. Its social condition must be modified, its laws abolished, its opinions superseded, its habits changed, its manners corrupted. But politically liberty is more easily lost; to neglect to hold it fast is to allow it to escape.

Men therefore not only cling to equality because it is dear to them; they also adhere to it because they think it will last for ever.

That political freedom may compromise in its excesses the tranquillity, the property, the lives of individuals, is obvious to the narrowest and most unthinking minds. But, on the contrary, none but attentive and clear-sighted men perceive the perils with which equality threatens us, and they commonly avoid pointing them out. They know that the calamities they apprehend are remote, and flatter themselves that they will only fall upon future generations, for which the present generation takes but little thought. The evils which freedom sometimes brings with it are immediate; they are apparent to all, and all are more or less affected by them. The evils which extreme equality may produce are slowly disclosed; they creep gradually into the social frame; they are only seen at intervals, and at the moment at which they become most violent, habit already causes them to be no longer felt.

The advantages which freedom brings are only shown by length of time; and it is always easy to mistake the cause in which they originate. The advantages of equality are instantaneous, and they may constantly be traced from their source.

Political liberty bestows exalted pleasures, from time to time, upon a certain number of citizens. Equality every day confers a number of small enjoyments on every man. The charms of equality are every instant felt, and are within the reach of all; the noblest hearts are not insensible to them, and the most vulgar souls exult in them. The passion which equality engenders must therefore be at once strong and general. Men cannot enjoy political liberty unpurchased by some sacrifices, and they never obtain it without great exertions. But the pleasures of equality are self-proffered: each of the petty incidents of life seems to occasion them, and in order to taste them nothing is required but to live.

Democratic nations are at all times fond of equality, but there are certain epochs at which the passion they entertain for it swells to the height of fury. This occurs at the moment when the old social system, long menaced, completes its own destruction after a last intestine struggle, and when the barriers of rank are at length thrown down. At such times men pounce upon equality as their booty, and they cling to it as to some precious treasure which they fear to lose. The passion for equality penetrates on every side into men's hearts, expands there, and fills them entirely. Tell them not that by this blind surrender of themselves to an exclusive passion, they risk their dearest interests: they are deaf. Show them not freedom escaping from their grasp, whilst they are looking another way, they are blind—or rather, they can discern but one sole object to be desired in the universe.

What I have said is applicable to all democratic nations: what I am about to say concerns the French alone. Amongst most modern nations, and especially amongst all those of the continent of Europe, the taste and the idea of freedom only began to exist and to extend itself at the time when social conditions were tending to equality, and as a consequence of that very equality. Absolute kings were the most efficient levellers of ranks amongst their subjects. Amongst these nations equality preceded freedom: equality was therefore a fact of some standing, when freedom was still a novelty: the one had already created customs, opinions, and laws belonging to it, when the other, alone and for the first time, came into actual existence. Thus the latter was still only an affair of opinion and taste, whilst the former had already crept into the habits of the people, possessed itself of their manners, and given a particular turn to the smallest actions in their lives. Can it be wondered that the men of our own time prefer the one to the other?

I think that democratic communities have a natural taste for freedom: left to themselves, they will seek it, cherish it, and view any privation of it with regret. But for equality, their passion is ardent, insatiable, incessant, invincible: they call for equality in freedom; and if they cannot obtain that, they still call for equality in slavery. They will endure poverty, servitude, barbarism,—but they will not endure aristocracy.

This is true of all times, and especially true in our own. All men and all powers seeking to cope with this irresistible passion, will be overthrown and destroyed by it. In our age, freedom cannot be established without it, and despotism itself cannot reign without its support.

Karl Marx,
"Human Equality,"
from *Critique of the Gotha Programme*

Karl Marx (1818–1883) is best known as the author of the Communist
Manifesto *(with Friedrich Engels) and* Capital, *his monumental, un-
finished study of the dynamics of capitalist society, the first volume of which
was published in 1867. Marx believed firmly that human societies are as
amenable to scientific investigation as the workings of nature. He also believed that the capitalist mode of production would inevitably collapse, pav-
ing the way for the eventual emergence of a communist society. The
following selection is excerpted from a critique of the program of a faction of
the German socialist movement, which drew heavily from the ideas of socialist leader Ferdinand Lasalle, whom Marx considered an unscientific and
insufficiently revolutionary socialist. The Lasallean principle of equality
Marx attacks in this passage is sometimes known as the "contribution
principle."*

MARGINAL NOTES TO THE PROGRAMME
OF THE GERMAN WORKERS' PARTY
("Critique of the Gotha Programme")

I

1. "Labour is the source of all wealth and all culture, *and since* useful
labour is possible only in society and through society, the proceeds of labour
belong undiminished with equal right to all members of society."

First Part of the Paragraph: "Labour is the source of all wealth and all
culture."

Labour is *not the source* of all wealth. *Nature* is just as much the source
of use values (and it is surely of such that material wealth consists!) as
labour, which itself is only the manifestation of a force of nature, human
labour power. The above phrase is to be found in all children's primers and
is correct in so far as it is *implied* that labour is performed with the

appurtenant subjects and instruments. But a socialist programme cannot allow such bourgeois phrases to pass over in silence the *conditions* that alone give them meaning. And in so far as man from the beginning behaves towards nature, the primary source of all instruments and subjects of labour, as an owner, treats her as belonging to him, his labour becomes the source of use values, therefore also of wealth. The bourgeois have very good grounds for falsely ascribing *supernatural creative power* to labour; since precisely from the fact that labour depends on nature it follows that the man who possesses no other property than his labour power must, in all conditions of society and culture, be the slave of other men who have made themselves the owners of the material conditions of labour. He can work only with their permission, hence live only with their permission.

Let us now leave the sentence as it stands, or rather limps. What would one have expected in conclusion? Obviously this:

"Since labour is the source of all wealth, no one in society can appropriate wealth except as the product of labour. Therefore, if he himself does not work, he lives by the labour of others and also acquires his culture at the expense of the labour of others."

Instead of this, by means of the verbal rivet "*and since*" a second proposition is added in order to draw a conclusion from this and not from the first one.

Second Part of the Paragraph: "Useful labour is possible only in society and through society."

According to the first proposition, labour was the source of all wealth and all culture, therefore no society is possible without labour. Now we learn, conversely, that no "useful" labour is possible without society.

One could just as well have said that only in society can useless and even socially harmful labour become a branch of gainful occupation, that only in society can one live by being idle, etc., etc.—in short, one could just as well have copied the whole of Rousseau.

And what is "useful" labour? Surely only labour which produces the intended useful result. A savage—and man was a savage after he had ceased to be an ape—who kills an animal with a stone, who collects fruits, etc., performs "useful" labour.

Thirdly, The Conclusion: "And since useful labour is possible only in society and through society, the proceeds of labour belong undiminished with equal right to all members of society."

A fine conclusion! If useful labour is possible only in society and through society, the proceeds of labour belong to society—and only so much therefrom accrues to the individual worker as is not required to maintain the "condition" of labour, society.

In fact, this proposition has at all times been made use of by the champions of the *state of society prevailing at any given time.* First come the claims of the government and everything that sticks to it, since it is the social organ for the maintenance of the social order; then come the claims of the various kinds of private property, for the various kinds of private property are the foundations of society, etc. One sees that such hollow phrases can be twisted and turned as desired.

The first and second parts of the paragraph have some intelligible connection only in the following wording:

"Labour becomes the source of wealth and culture only as social labour," or, what is the same thing, "in and through society."

This proposition is incontestably correct, for although isolated labour (its material conditions presupposed) can create use values, it can create neither wealth nor culture.

But equally incontestable is this other proposition:

"In proportion as labour develops socially, and becomes thereby a source of wealth and culture, poverty and destitution develop among the workers, and wealth and culture among the non-workers."

This is the law of all history hitherto. What, therefore, had to be done here, instead of setting down general phrases about "labour" and "society," was to prove concretely how in present capitalist society the material, etc., conditions have at last been created which enable and compel the workers to lift this social curse.

In fact, however, the whole paragraph, bungled in style and content, is only there in order to inscribe the Lassallean catchword of the "undiminished proceeds of labour" as a slogan at the top of the party banner. I shall return later to the "proceeds of labour," "equal right," etc., since the same thing recurs in a somewhat different form further on.

> 2. "In present-day society, the instruments of labour are the monopoly of the capitalist class; the resulting dependence of the working class is the cause of misery and servitude in all its forms."

This sentence, borrowed from the Rules of the International, is incorrect in this "improved" edition.

In present-day society the instruments of labour are the monopoly of the landowners (the monopoly of property in land is even the basis of the monopoly of capital) *and* the capitalists. In the passage in question, the Rules of the International do not mention either the one or the other class of monopolists. They speak of the *"monopoliser of the means of labour,* that is, *the sources of life."* The addition, *"sources of life,"* makes it sufficiently clear that land is included in the instruments of labour.

The correction was introduced because Lassalle, for reasons now generally known, attacked *only* the capitalist class and not the landowners. In England, the capitalist is usually not even the owner of the land on which his factory stands.

   3. "The emancipation of labour demands the promotion of the instruments of labour to the common property of society and the co-operative
   regulation of the total labour with a fair distribution of the proceeds of
   labour."

"Promotion of the instruments of labour to the common property" ought obviously to read their "conversion into the common property"; but this only in passing.

What are "proceeds of labour"? The product of labour or its value? And in the latter case, is it the total value of the product or only that part of the value which labour has newly added to the value of the means of production consumed?

"Proceeds of labour" is a loose notion which Lassalle has put in the place of definite economic conceptions.

What is "a fair distribution"?

Do not the bourgeois assert that the present-day distribution is "fair"? And is it not, in fact, the only "fair" distribution on the basis of the present-day mode of production? Are economic relations regulated by legal conceptions or do not, on the contrary, legal relations arise from economic ones? Have not also the socialist sectarians the most varied notions about "fair" distribution?

To understand what is implied in this connection by the phrase "fair distribution," we must take the first paragraph and this one together. The latter presupposes a society wherein "the instruments of labour are common property and the total labour is co-operatively regulated," and from the first paragraph we learn that "the proceeds of labour belong undiminished with equal right to all members of society."

"To all members of society"? To those who do not work as well? What remains then of the "undiminished proceeds of labour"? Only to those members of society who work? What remains then of the "equal right" of all members of society?

But "all members of society" and "equal right" are obviously mere phrases. The kernel consists in this, that in this communist society every worker must receive the "undiminished" Lassallean "proceeds of labour."

Let us take first of all the words "proceeds of labour" in the sense of the product of labour; then the co-operative proceeds of labour are the *total social product*.

From this must now be deducted:

First, cover for replacement of the means of production used up.

Secondly, additional portion for expansion of production.

Thirdly, reserve or insurance funds to provide against accidents, dislocations caused by natural calamities, etc.

These deductions from the "undiminished proceeds of labour" are an economic necessity and their magnitude is to be determined according to available means and forces, and partly by computation of probabilities, but they are in no way calculable by equity. *no mathematical equality*

There remains the other part of the total product, intended to serve as means of consumption.

Before this is divided among the individuals, there has to be deducted again, from it:

First, the general costs of administration not belonging to production.

This part will, from the outset, be very considerably restricted in comparison with present-day society and it diminishes in proportion as the new society develops.

Secondly, that which is intended for the common satisfaction of needs, such as schools, health services, etc.

From the outset this part grows considerably in comparison with present-day society and it grows in proportion as the new society develops.

Thirdly, funds for those unable to work, etc., in short, for what is included under so-called official poor relief today.

Only now do we come to the "distribution" which the programme, under Lassallean influence, alone has in view in its narrow fashion, namely, to that part of the means of consumption which is divided among the individual producers of the co-operative society.

The "undiminished proceeds of labour" have already unnoticeably become converted into the "diminished" proceeds, although what the producer is deprived of in his capacity as a private individual benefits him directly or indirectly in his capacity as a member of society.

Just as the phrase of the "undiminished proceeds of labour" has disappeared, so now does the phrase of the "proceeds of labour" disappear altogether.

Within the co-operative society based on common ownership of the means of production, the producers do not exchange their products; just as little does the labour employed on the products appear here *as the value* of these products, as a material quality possessed by them, since now, in contrast to capitalist society, individual labour no longer exists in an indirect fashion but directly as a component part of the total labour. The phrase "proceeds of labour," objectionable also today on account of its ambiguity, thus loses all meaning.

What we have to deal with here is a communist society, not as it has *developed* on its own foundations, but, on the contrary, just as it *emerges* from capitalist society; which is thus in every respect, economically, morally and intellectually, still stamped with the birth marks of the old society from whose womb it emerges. Accordingly, the individual producer receives back from society—after the deductions have been made—exactly what he gives to it. What he has given to it is his individual quantum of labour. For example, the social working day consists of the sum of the individual hours of work; the individual labour time of the individual producer is the part of the social working day contributed by him, his share in it. He receives a certificate from society that he has furnished such and such an amount of labour (after deducting his labour for the common funds), and with this certificate he draws from the social stock of means of consumption as much as costs the same amount of labour. The same amount of labour which he has given to society in one form he receives back in another.

Here obviously the same principle prevails as that which regulates the exchange of commodities, as far as this is exchange of equal values. Content and form are changed, because under the altered circumstances no one can give anything except his labour, and because, on the other hand, nothing can pass to the ownership of individuals except individual means of consumption. But, as far as the distribution of the latter among the individual producers is concerned, the same principle prevails as in the exchange of commodity-equivalents: a given amount of labour in one form is exchanged for an equal amount of labour in another form.

Hence, *equal right* here is still in principle—*bourgeois right*, although principle and practice are no longer at loggerheads, while the exchange of equivalents in commodity exchange only exists *on the average* and not in the individual case.

In spite of this advance, this *equal right* is still constantly stigmatised by a bourgeois limitation. The right of the producers is *proportional* to the labour they supply; the equality consists in the fact that measurement is made with an *equal standard*, labour.

But one man is superior to another physically or mentally and so supplies more labour in the same time, or can labour for a longer time; and labour, to serve as a measure, must be defined by its duration or intensity, otherwise it ceases to be a standard of measurement. This *equal* right is an unequal right for unequal labour. It recognises no class differences, because everyone is only a worker like everyone else; but it tacitly recognises unequal individual endowment and thus productive capacity as natural privileges. *It is, therefore, a right of inequality, in its content, like every right.* Right by its very nature can consist only in the application of an equal standard; but unequal individuals (and they would not be different indi-

necessity of inequality

viduals if they were not unequal) are measurable only by an equal standard in so far as they are brought under an equal point of view, are taken from one *definite* side only, for instance, in the present case, are regarded *only as workers* and nothing more is seen in them, everything else being ignored. Further, one worker is married, another not; one has more children than another, and so on and so forth. Thus, with an equal performance of labour, and hence an equal share in the social consumption fund, one will in fact receive more than another, one will be richer than another, and so on. To avoid all these defects, right instead of being equal would have to be unequal.

But these defects are inevitable in the first phase of communist society as it is when it has just emerged after prolonged birth pangs from capitalist society. Right can never be higher than the economic structure of society and its cultural development conditioned thereby.

In a higher phase of communist society, after the enslaving subordination of the individual to the division of labour, and therewith also the antithesis between mental and physical labour has vanished; after labour has become not only a means of life but life's prime want; after the productive forces have also increased with the all-round development of the individual, and all the springs of co–operative wealth flow more abundantly—only then can the narrow horizon of bourgeois right be crossed in its entirety and society inscribe on its banners: From each according to his ability, to each according to his needs!

— Same argument can be made by capitalists

10

R. H. Tawney,
"Equality in Historical Perspective,"
from *Equality*

Richard H. Tawney (1880–1962) was an influential English economic historian and social critic. Educated at Balliol College, Oxford, he was a professor of economic history at the London School of Economics from 1931. He was also an active social reformer, campaigning with success for fixing a minimum wage, extending worker education, and raising the minimum years of public education. His most famous works include The Acquisitive Society *(1929), in which he argues that the acquisitiveness of capitalist society is morally wrong. The following selection, from his book* Equality, *begins with a discussion of the ideas of legal equality and meritocracy that emerged from the French Revolution in the 1790s.*

The Historical Background

(ii)
Equality of Opportunity

A political doctrine should be judged, in the first place, by its strength, not by its weakness. The transformation effected by the attack on legal privilege was beneficent and profound. It had been the child of economic necessity, and the impetus which it gave to progress in the arts which enrich mankind needs no emphasis. With the abolition of restrictions on freedom of movement, on the choice of occupations, and on the use of land and capital, imprisoned energies were released from the narrow walls of manor and gild and corporate town, from the downward pressure of class status, and from the heavy hand of authoritarian governments, to unite in new forms of association, and by means of them to raise the towering structure of industrial civilization.

It was not only in the stimulus which it supplied to the mobilization of economic power that the movement which levelled legal privilege revealed its magic. Its effect as an agent of social emancipation was not less profound. Few principles have so splendid a record of humanitarian achieve-

From R. H. Tawney, *Equality*, 4th ed. (London: Allen and Unwin, 1952). Reprinted by permission.

ment. The monopoly of political power by corrupt and tyrannical minorities had everywhere been, not merely a practice, but an unquestioned principle of political organization; with the extension of political democracy its legal basis disappeared, and, if it survived as a fact, it lost the respectability of an institution established by law. Careers of profit and distinction had been reserved, as of right, to birth and wealth; now the barriers fell and all employments, at least in theory, were open to all. Slavery and serfdom had survived the exhortations of the Christian Church, the reforms of enlightened despots, and the protests of humanitarian philosophers from Seneca to Voltaire. Before the new spirit, and the practical exigencies of which it was the expression, they disappeared, except from dark backwaters, in three generations. From the time when men first reflected on social problems, the social problem of Europe, tragic, insistent, and unsolved, had been the condition of the peasant. Now, at last, in most parts of the Continent, he came to his own. Increasingly, though by different methods and with varying degrees of completeness—by confiscation, as in France, or the division of estates, as in Germany, or purchase as in Ireland—the nineteenth century saw the end of the system under which the cultivator paid part of his produce to an absentee owner. The last chapter of the story which was begun in 1789 has been written in eastern Europe since 1918.

Reform did not, indeed, bring him economic affluence, but it ended the long nightmare of legal oppression. It turned him from a beast of burden into a human being. It determined that, when science should be invoked to increase the output of the soil, its cultivator, not an absentee owner, should reap the fruits. The principle which released him he described as equality, the destruction of privilege, democracy, the victory of plain people. He understood by it, not the mathematical parity of pecuniary incomes, to proving the impossibility of which so much needless ingenuity has been devoted, but the end of institutions which had made rich men tyrants and poor men slaves.

The movement which equalized legal rights not only released new productive energies, and cut down a forest of ancient abuses; it supplied with their principles the architects who built on the space that it had cleared. It had not attacked all forms of inequality, but only those which had their roots in special advantages conferred on particular groups by custom or law. It was not intolerant of all social gradations, but only of such as rested on legal privilege. The distinctions of wealth and power which survived when these anomalies had been removed, it surrounded with a halo of intellectual prestige and ethical propriety. It condemned the inequalities of the feudal past; it blessed the inequalities of the industrial future.

The second gesture was as important as the first. The great industry, even in its violent youth, had many excellences, but the equalitarian virtues were not conspicuous among them. To the critics in France and England who urged that a new feudalism was arising, in which the contrasts of affluence and misery, of power and helplessness, were not less extreme than in the past, there was an easy answer. It was that such contrasts did, indeed, exist, but that they differed in principle from those which had preceded them.

The inequalities of the old régime had been intolerable because they had been arbitrary, the result not of differences of personal capacity, but of social and political favouritism. The inequalities of industrial society were to be esteemed, for they were the expression of individual achievement or failure to achieve. They were twice blessed. They deserved moral approval, for they corresponded to merit. They were economically beneficial, for they offered a system of prizes and penalties. So it was possible to hate the inequalities most characteristic of the eighteenth century and to applaud those most characteristic of the nineteenth. The distinction between them was that the former had their origin in social institutions, the latter in personal character. The fact of the equality of legal rights could be cited as a reason why any other kind of equality was unnecessary or dangerous.

The abolition of capricious favours and arbitrary restrictions had enlarged the field of economic opportunity. The wider diffusion of economic opportunities secured the selection of individuals according to their capacities, through a social analogue of the biological struggle. If extreme inequality was the final consequence, that result merely meant that men's capacities were unequal. Instead of the class into which he was born determining, as in the past, the position of the individual, the quality of the individual determined his position, and therefore his class. Refined and sublimated by the wholesome acid of free competition, the word "class" itself was purged of the invidious associations which formerly had clung to it. It shed the coarse integuments of status and caste, and emerged as a fluid economic group, which all, if they pleased, were free to enter, and from which all, if they chose, were at liberty to escape. In a world where the law offered no obstacles to aspiring enterprise, class privilege and class tyranny were evidently impossible. A society marked by sharp disparities of wealth and power might properly, nevertheless, be described as classless, since it was open to each man to become wealthy and powerful.

Thus the flank of the criticism of economic inequality was turned by the argument that it was the necessary result of legal equality and economic liberty. Rightly interpreted, equality meant, not the absence of violent contrasts of income and condition, but equal opportunities of becoming unequal. It was true that few could take part in the competition, but no one was forbidden to enter for it, and no handicaps were imposed on those who did. To ensure that it was fair, it was sufficient, it was thought, to insist that the law should neither confer advantages nor impose disabilities.

Most social systems need a lightning-conductor. The formula which supplies it to our own is equality of opportunity. The conception is one to which homage is paid to-day by all, including those who resist most strenuously attempts to apply it. But the rhetorical tribute which it receives appears sometimes to be paid on the understanding that it shall be content with ceremonial honours. It retains its throne, on condition that it refrains from meddling with the profitable business of the factory and market-place. Its credit is good, as long as it does not venture to cash its cheques. Like other respectable principles, it is encouraged to reign, provided that it does not attempt to rule.

The content of the idea has been determined by its history. It was formulated as a lever to overthrow legal inequality and juristic privilege, and from its infancy it has been presented in negative, rather than positive, terms. It has been interpreted rather as freedom from restraints than as the possession of powers. Thus conceived, it has at once the grandeur and the unreality of a majestic phantom. The language in which it is applauded by the powers of this world sometimes leaves it uncertain which would horrify them most, the denial of the principle or the attempt to apply it.

"The law is just. It punishes equally the rich and the poor for stealing bread." It is even generous, for it offers opportunities both to those whom the social system permits to seize them and to those whom it does not. In reality, of course, except in a sense which is purely formal, equality of opportunity is not simply a matter of legal equality. Its existence depends, not merely on the absence of disabilities, but on the presence of abilities. It obtains in so far as, and only in so far as, each member of a community, whatever his birth, or occupation, or social position, possesses in fact, and not merely in form, equal chances of using to the full his natural endowments of physique, of character, and of intelligence. In proportion as the capacities of some are sterilized or stunted by their social environment, while those of others are favoured or pampered by it, equality of opportunity becomes a graceful, but attenuated, figment. It recedes from the world of reality to that of perorations.

Mr. Keynes, in his brilliant sketch of the phase of economic history which ended in 1914, has seized on the avenues which it opened to individual advancement as its most striking feature. "The greater part of the population . . . worked hard and lived at a low standard of comfort . . . But escape was possible, for any man of capacity or character at all exceeding the average, into the middle and upper classes."[1] He is concerned with the set of the current, not with the breakwaters that dammed, or the reefs that diverted, it. In reality, there were then, as there are now, obstacles to the easy movement of ability to new positions, which produced individual frustration of tragic dimensions, and in our own day, of course, the movement towards concentration and amalgamation has made the independent entrepreneur, who fought his way from poverty to wealth, a less plausible hero than in the age when he could be offered by moralists as a golden example to aspiring youth. But, as a picture of the ideals which ruled the nineteenth century, and of the qualities on which it reflected with pride when it had leisure for reflection, Mr. Keynes's words are apt. The tendency and direction of the forces released by the Industrial Revolution, if that phrase is still to be retained, are not open to question. They were those described by Sir Henry Maine, when he wrote of "the beneficent private war which makes one man strive to climb on the shoulders of another and remain there."[2] Compared with that of most earlier periods, the economic system which it created was fluid and elastic. It seemed the social counterpart of natural selection through the struggle for existence.

So the middle classes acquiesced in sharp distinctions of wealth and power, provided that, as individuals, they were free to scale the heights. The upper classes were glad to be reinforced by individuals of means and influence, who sprang from below, provided that, as a class, they remained on their eminence. They were not seriously disturbed by the spectacle of Lazarus in the House of Lords; for they were confident that he would behave like a gentleman in his new surroundings, would ascribe his translation to his own thrift, independence, and piety, would denounce the failings of beggars with the expert knowledge of a professional mendicant, would be an admirable illustration of the virtues of a society in which even the humblest could climb to ease and affluence, and would acquire a reputation for philanthropy for himself and his order by his generosity in financing supplies of cold water for the economically damned. What neither understood nor admired, what, indeed, with rare exceptions, they feared and despised, were the aspirations that found expression, not merely in the claim for an open road to individual advancement, but in collective movements to narrow the space between valley and peak.

Their welcome to individuals was conditional, therefore, on the latter identifying themselves with the sphere which they entered, not with that

1. J. M. Keynes, *The Economic Consequences of the Peace*, 1920, p. 9.
2. Sir H. Maine, *Popular Government*, 1885, p. 50.

which they left. It was accompanied by a not less emphatic conviction of the necessity of preserving the great gulf fixed between Us and Them, the chasm which separated the elect from the mass of the population. This feature of the landscape had always existed, and it was plainly the intention of nature that it should continue to exist. It was an indispensable incentive to economic effort and moral virtue among the poor. It was a guarantee that the civilization of the rich would not be destroyed by its too promiscuous extension to classes incapable of it.

It is possible that intelligent tadpoles reconcile themselves to the inconveniences of their position, by reflecting that, though most of them will live and die as tadpoles and nothing more, the more fortunate of the species will one day shed their tails, distend their mouths and stomachs, hop nimbly on to dry land, and croak addresses to their former friends on the virtues by means of which tadpoles of character and capacity can rise to be frogs. This conception of society may be described, perhaps, as the Tadpole Philosophy, since the consolation which it offers for social evils consists in the statement that exceptional individuals can succeed in evading them. Who has not heard it suggested that the presence of opportunities, by means of which individuals can ascend and get on, relieves economic contrasts of their social poison and their personal sting? Who has not encountered the argument that there is an educational "ladder" up which talent can climb, and that its existence makes the scamped quality of our primary education—the overcrowded classes, and mean surroundings, and absence of amenities—a matter of secondary importance? And what a view of human life such an attitude implies! As though opportunities for talent to rise could be equalized in a society where the circumstances surrounding it from birth are themselves unequal! As though, if they could, it were natural and proper that the position of the mass of mankind should permanently be such that they can attain civilization only by escaping from it! As though the noblest use of exceptional powers were to scramble to shore, undeterred by the thought of drowning companions!

It is true, of course, that a community must draw on a stream of fresh talent, in order to avoid stagnation, and that, unless individuals of ability can turn their powers to account, they are embittered by a sense of defeat and frustration. The existence of opportunities to move from point to point on an economic scale, and to mount from humble origins to success and affluence, is a condition, therefore, both of social well-being and of individual happiness, and impediments which deny them to some, while lavishing them on others, are injurious to both. But opportunities to "rise" are not a substitute for a large measure of practical equality, nor do they make immaterial the existence of sharp disparities of income and social condition. On the contrary, it is only the presence of a high degree of practical equality which can diffuse and generalize opportunities to rise. The existence of such opportunities in fact, and not merely in form, depends, not only upon an open road, but upon an equal start. It is precisely, of course, when capacity is aided by a high level of general well-being in the *milieu* surrounding it, that its ascent is most likely to be regular and rapid, rather than fitful and intermittent.

It is not surprising, therefore, that in England, where that condition does not exist, a large proportion of persons of eminence in different professions should be found to have been drawn from a minute group of comparatively well-to-do strata.

. . .

If a high degree of practical equality is necessary to social well-being, because without it ability cannot find its way to its true vocation, it is necessary also for another and more fundamental reason. It is necessary because a community requires unity as well as diversity, and because, important as it is to discriminate between different powers, it is even more important to provide for common needs. Clever people, who possess exceptional gifts themselves, are naturally impressed by exceptional gifts in others, and desire, when they consider the matter at all, that society should be organized to offer a career to exceptional talent, though they rarely understand the full scope and implications of the revolution they are preaching. But, in the conditions characteristic of large-scale economic organization, in which ninety per cent. of the population are wage-earners, and not more than ten per cent. employers, farmers, independent workers or engaged in professions, it is obviously, whatever the level of individual intelligence and the degree of social fluidity, a statistical impossibility for more than a small fraction of the former to enter the ranks of the latter; and a community cannot be built upon exceptional talent alone, though it would be a poor thing without it. Social well-being does not only depend upon intelligent leadership; it also depends upon cohesion and solidarity. It implies the existence, not merely of opportunities to ascend, but of a high level of general culture, and a strong sense of common interests, and the diffusion throughout society of a conviction that civilization is not the business of an élite alone, but a common enterprise which is the concern of all. And individual happiness does not only require that men should be free to rise to new positions of comfort and distinction; it also requires that they should be able to lead a life of dignity and culture, whether they rise or not, and that, whatever their position on the economic scale may be, it shall be such as is fit to be occupied by men.

Human nature demands, no doubt, space and elbow-room. But there is an excellence of repose and contentment, as well as of effort; and, happily, the mass of mankind are not all elbows. If they possess powers which call for the opportunity to assert themselves in the contests of the market-place, and to reap the reward of successful rivalry, they have also qualities which, though no less admirable, do not find their perfection in a competitive struggle, and the development of which is not less indispensable to social health. Equality of opportunity implies the establishment of conditions which favour the expansion, not, as societies with a strong economic bent are disposed to believe, of the former alone, but of both. Rightly interpreted, it means, not only that what are commonly regarded as the prizes of life should be open to all, but that none should be subjected to arbitrary penalties; not only that exceptional men should be free to exercise their exceptional powers, but that common men should be free to make the most of their common humanity. If a community which is indifferent to the need of facilitating the upward movement of ability becomes torpid and inert, a community which is indifferent to all else but that movement becomes hardened and materialized, and is in the end disillusioned with the idol that it has itself created. It confuses changes with progress. It sacrifices the cultivation of spiritual excellences, which is possible for all, to the acquisition of riches, which is possible, happily, only for the few. It lives in an interminable series of glittering to-morrows, which it discovers to be tinsel when they become to-day.

So the doctrine which throws all its emphasis on the importance of opening avenues to individual advancement is partial and one-sided. It is right in insisting on the necessity of opening a free career to aspiring talent; it is wrong in suggesting that opportunities to rise, which can, of their very nature, be seized only by the few, are a substitute for a general diffusion of the means of civilization, which are needed by all men, whether they rise or not, and which those who cannot climb the economic ladder, and who sometimes, indeed, do not desire to climb it, may turn to as good account as those who can. It is right in attaching a high significance to social mobility; it is wrong in implying that effective mobility can be secured merely through the absence of legal restraints, or that, if it could, economic liberty would be a sufficient prophylactic against the evils produced by social stratification. Men live in the present and future, not in the past. The outlook of individuals is normally determined by the group which they have entered, not by that which they have left, and the relations between classes have been less softened than was expected by the opening of avenues from one class to another.

It was natural, indeed, in the mood of exhilaration produced by swiftly expanding economic horizons—the mood of England during much of the nineteenth century, and of the United States when the tone of its economic life was still set by free land—that opinion should be hypnotized by the absorbing spectacle of a world in motion. It was natural to argue that the position of the proletarian was a secondary problem, since the proletarian of to-day was the capitalist of to-morrow, and that it was unnecessary to be perturbed by the existence of a chasm dividing classes, since the individuals composing them were free to cross it. As far as most parts of Europe, with its historic tradition of social stratification, were concerned, such an attitude was always a piece of economic romanticism. To-day it has long lost whatever plausibility it may once have possessed.

The antidote which it had prescribed for economic evils had been freedom to move, freedom to rise, freedom to buy and sell and invest—the emancipation, in short, of property and enterprise from the restraints which fettered them. But property protects those who own it, not those who do not; and enterprise opens new vistas to those who can achieve independence, not to those who are dependent on weekly wages; and the emancipation of property and enterprise produces different effects in a society where the ownership of land and capital is widely diffused, from those which are caused by it where ownership is centralized. In the former, such property is an instrument of liberation. It enables the mass of mankind to control their own lives. It is, as philosophers say, an extension of their personalities. In the latter, until it has been bridled and tamed, it is a condition of constraint, and, too often, of domination. It enables a minority of property-owners to control the lives of the unpropertied majority. And the personalities which it extends are sometimes personalities which are already too far extended, and which, for the sake both of themselves and of their fellows, it would be desirable to contract.

Thus, in conditions in which ownership is decentralized and diffused, the institution of property is a principle of unity. It confers a measure of security and independence on poor as well as on rich, and softens the harshness of economic contrasts by a common similarity of social status. But, in the conditions most characteristic of industrial societies, its effect is the opposite. It is a principle, not of unity, but of division. It sharpens the edge of economic disparities with humiliating contrasts of power and helplessness—with differences, not merely of income, but of culture, and civilization, and manner of life. For, in such conditions, the mass of mankind are life-long wage-earners; and, though no barriers of caste limit their opportunities, though each is free to assume the risks and responsibilities of independent enterprise, what is possible for each is not possible for all, or for the great majority.

Economic realities make short work of legal abstractions, except when they find them a convenient mask to conceal their own features. The character of a society is determined less by abstract rights than by practical powers. It depends not upon what its members *may* do, if they can, but upon what they *can* do, if they will. All careers may be equally open to all, and the wage-earner, like the property-owner, may be free to use such powers as he possesses, in such ways as he is able, on such occasions as are open to him, to achieve such results as he is capable of achieving. But, in the absence of measures which prevent the exploitation of groups in a weak economic position by those in a strong, and make the external conditions of health and civilization a common possession, the phrase equality of opportunity is obviously a jest, to be described as amusing or heartless according to taste. It is the impertinent courtesy of an invitation offered to unwelcome guests, in the certainty that circumstances will prevent them from accepting it.

Sir Fitzjames Stephen, writing when the individualist movement of the preceding half-century was as yet unexhausted, and the forces which later were to sap it were still hardly disclosed, touched its ethical pretensions with a realist's indiscretion. Whatever its other achievements, he observed, it had produced a society marked by "inequality in its harshest and least sympathetic form", in which "the power of particular persons over their neighbours has never, in any age of the world, been so well defined and so easily and safely exerted."[3] Privilege rested, it was true, not on legal principles, but on economic facts, and no man was debarred from aspiring to its prizes. But the most seductive of optical illusions does not last for ever. The day when a thousand donkeys could be induced to sweat by the prospect of a carrot that could be eaten by one was, even when Stephen wrote, drawing to its close, and by the present century was obviously long over. The miner or railwayman or engineer may not have mastered the intricacies of the theory of chances, but he possesses enough arithmetic to understand the absurdity of staking his happiness on the possibility of his promotion, and to realize that, if he is to attain well-being at all, he must attain it, not by personal advancement, but as the result of a collective effort, the fruits of which he will share with his fellows. The inequalities which he resents are but little mitigated, therefore, by the fact that individuals who profit by them have been born in the same social stratum as himself, or that families who suffer from them in one generation may gain by them in the next.

Slavery did not become tolerable because some slaves were manumitted and became slave-owners in their turn; nor, even if it were possible for the units composing a society to be periodically reshuffled, would that make it a matter of indifference that some among them at any moment should be condemned to frustration while others were cosseted. What matters to a nation is not merely the composition and origins of its different groups,

3. Sir J. Fitzjames Stephen, *Liberty, Equality, Fraternity,* 1873, pp. 233, 234.

but their opportunities and circumstances. It is the powers and advantages
which different classes in practice enjoy, not the social antecedents of the
varying individuals by whom they may happen, from time to time, to be
acquired. Till such powers and advantages have been equalized in fact, not
merely in form, by the extension of communal provision and collective
control, the equality established by the removal of restrictions on property
and enterprise resembles that produced by turning an elephant loose in
the crowd. It offers everyone, except the beast and his rider, equal opportunities of being trampled to death. Caste is deposed, but class succeeds to
the vacant throne. The formal equality of rights between wage-earner and
property-owner becomes the decorous drapery for a practical relationship
of mastery and subordination.

(iii)
The Old Problem in a New Guise

"Thanks to capitalism", writes Professor Sée, in comparing the social
system of the old régime with that which succeeded it, "economic divisions between men take the place of legal ones."[4] The forces which cut
deepest the rifts between classes in modern society are obvious and un-
mistakable. There is inequality of power, in virtue of which certain economic groups exercise authority over others. And there is inequality of
circumstance or condition, such as arises when some social groups are
deprived of the necessaries of civilization which others enjoy. The first is
specially characteristic of the relations between the different classes engaged in production, and finds its most conspicuous expression in the
authority wielded by those who direct industry, control economic enterprise, and administer the resources of land, capital or credit, on which the
welfare of their fellows depends. The second is associated with the enjoyment and consumption of wealth, rather than with its production, and is
revealed in sharp disparities, not only of income, but of environment,
health and education.

Inequality of power is inherent in the nature of organized society, since
action is impossible, unless there is an authority to decide what action shall
be taken, and to see that its decisions are applied in practice. Some
measure, at least, of inequality of circumstance is not to be avoided, since
functions differ, and differing functions require different scales of provision to elicit and maintain them. In practice, therefore, though inequality
of power and inequality of circumstance are the fundamental evils, there

4. H. Sée, *Les Origines du Capitalisme moderne*, 1926, p. 183.

arc forms of each which are regarded, not merely with tolerance, but with active approval. The effect of inequality depends, in short, upon the principles upon which it reposes, the credentials to which it appeals, and the sphere of life which it embraces.

It is not difficult to state the principles which cause certain kinds of inequality to win indulgence, however difficult it may be to apply them in practice. Inequality of power is tolerated, when the power is used for a social purpose approved by the community, when it is not more extensive than that purpose requires, when its exercise is not arbitrary, but governed by settled rules, and when the commission can be revoked, if its terms are exceeded. Inequality of circumstance is regarded as reasonable, in so far as it is the necessary condition of securing the services which the community requires—in so far as, in the words of Professor Ginsberg, it is "grounded in differences in the power to contribute to, and share in, the common good."[5]

No one complains that captains give orders and that the crews obey them, or that engine-drivers must work to a time-table laid down by railway-managers. For, if captains and managers command, they do so by virtue of their office, and it is by virtue of their office that their instructions are obeyed. They are not the masters, but the fellow-servants, of those whose work they direct. Their power is not conferred upon them by birth or wealth, but by the position which they occupy in the productive system, and, though their subordinates may grumble at its abuses, they do not dispute the need for its existence.

No one thinks it inequitable that, when a reasonable provision has been made for all, exceptional responsibilities should be compensated by exceptional rewards, as a recognition of the service performed and an inducement to perform it. For different kinds of energy need different conditions to evoke them, and the sentiment of justice is satisfied, not by offering to every man identical treatment, but by treating different individuals in the same way in so far as, being human, they have requirements which are the same, and in different ways in so far as, being concerned with different services, they have requirements which differ. What is repulsive is not that one man should earn more than others, for where community of environment, and a common education and habit of life, have bred a common tradition of respect and consideration, these details of the counting-house are forgotten or ignored. It is that some classes should be excluded from the heritage of civilization which others enjoy,

5. M. Ginsberg, *The Problem of Colour, in relation to the idea of Equality* (Journal of Philosophical Studies, 1926), p. 15.

and that the fact of human fellowship, which is ultimate and profound, should be obscured by economic contrasts, which are trivial and superficial. What is important is not that all men should receive the same pecuniary income. It is that the surplus resources of society should be so husbanded and applied that it is a matter of minor significance whether they receive it or not.

The enthusiasts, therefore, for true aristocracy, by which appears to be meant an aristocracy of a kind that has never existed, and all others who suppose that they would enjoy being governed by an intellectual élite, can calm the apprehensions which the demand for equality sometimes seems to arouse in them. They need not dread it as the uncreating word, whose utterance presages the return of chaos, while the curtain falls on universal darkness. The criticism which suggests that the effect of conceding it must be to submerge diversities of authority and office beneath a welter of undifferentiated atoms is, in reality, extravagantly *mal-à-propos*. Men do not necessarily desire disorder because what passes for order seems to them, not order, but anarchy. A society which is conscious of the importance of maintaining gradations of authority and varieties of function is no more committed to the preservation of the plutocratic class system of to-day than to the reestablishment of the aristocratic class system of the eighteenth century, which also was defended in its day as the indispensable bulwark of social stability and economic efficiency.

The phenomenon which provokes exasperation, in short, is not power and inequality, but capricious inequality and irresponsible power; and in this matter the sentiments of individuals correspond, it may be observed, with the needs of society. What a community requires is that its work should be done, and done with the minimum of friction and maximum of co-operation. Gradations of authority and income derived from differences of office and function promote that end; distinctions based, not on objective facts, but on personal claims—on birth, or wealth, or social position—impede its attainment. They sacrifice practical realities to meaningless conventions. They stifle creative activity in an elegant drapery of irrelevant futilities. They cause the position of individuals and the relation of classes to reflect the influence, not primarily of personal quality and social needs, but of external conditions, which offer special advantages to some and impose adventitious disabilities upon others.

Such advantages and disabilities are, in some measure, inevitable. Nor need it be denied that the area of life covered by them is narrower to-day than in most past societies. It would be difficult to argue, however, that their influence on the destinies of individuals is trivial, or their effect on the temper of society other than deplorable. Dr. Irving Fisher has described the distribution of wealth as depending "on inheritance, constantly modified by thrift, ability, industry, luck and fraud."[6] It is needless to labour the part which social forces play in determining the condition and prospects of different groups, since it is a truism expounded at length in the pages of economists. "A poor widow is gathering nettles for her children's dinner. A courtly seigneur, delicately lounging in the *Œil-de-Bœuf,* has an alchemy by which he will extract the third nettle and call it rent and law." The inequalities arising from the receipt by private persons of monopoly profits, urban ground-rents, mineral royalties, financial windfalls and the other surpluses accruing when the necessary costs of production and expansion have been met, are a modern and more lucrative species of the picturesque genus pilloried by Carlyle. They resemble the predatory property of the old régime, in being a form of private taxation, the effects of which are partially corrected to-day by public taxation, but which remain mischievous. They create an inequality which, so far from arising from differences of service, is maintained in spite of them. They do not increase the real income of the nation, but diminish it. For they cause the less urgent needs of the minority to be met before the more urgent needs of the majority.

Incomes from personal work obviously stand in a different category from incomes from property. But, even in such incomes, there is normally an element which is due less to the qualities of the individual than to the overruling force of social arrangements. We are all, it is a commonplace to say, disposed to believe that our failures are due to our circumstances, and our successes to ourselves. It is natural, no doubt, for the prosperous professional or business man, who has made his way in the face of difficulties, to regard his achievements as the result of his own industry and ability. When he compares those who have succeeded in his own walk of life with those who have failed, he is impressed by the fact that the former are, on the whole, more enterprising, or forcible, or resourceful, than the latter, and he concludes that the race is to the swift and the battle to the strong.

· · ·

In so far as the individuals between whom comparison is made belong to a homogeneous group, whose members have had equal opportunities of health and education, of entering remunerative occupations, and of obtaining access to profitable financial knowledge, it is plausible, no doubt, if all questions of chance and fortune are excluded, to treat the varying positions which they ultimately occupy as the expression of differences in their personal qualities. But, the less homogeneous the group, and the

6. Irving Fisher, *Elementary Principles of Economics,* 1912, p. 513.

greater the variety of conditions to which its members have been exposed, the more remote from reality does such an inference become. If the rules of a game give a permanent advantage to some of the players, it does not become fair merely because they are scrupulously observed by all who take part in it. When the contrast between the circumstances of different social strata is so profound as to-day, the argument—if it deserves to be called an argument—which suggests that the incomes they receive bear a close relation to their personal qualities is obviously illusory.

In reality, as has often been pointed out, explanations which are relevant as a clue to differences between the incomes of individuals in the same group lose much of their validity when applied, as they often are, to interpret differences between those of individuals in different groups. It would be as reasonable to hold that the final position of competitors in a race were an accurate indication of their physical endowments, if, while some entered fit and carefully trained, others were half-starved, were exhausted by want of sleep, and were handicapped by the starters. If the weights are unequal, it is not less important, but more important, that the scales should be true. The condition of differences of individual quality finding their appropriate expression is the application of a high degree of social art. It is such a measure of communism as is needed to ensure that inequalities of personal capacity are neither concealed nor exaggerated by inequalities which have their source in social arrangements.

While, therefore, the successful professional or business man may be justified in assuming that, if he has outdistanced his rivals, one cause is possibly his own "application, industry, and honesty," and . . . other admirable qualities . . . that gratifying conclusion is less than half the truth. His talents must be somewhat extraordinary, or his experience of life unusually limited, if he has not on occasion asked himself what his position would have been if his father had been an unemployed miner or a casual labourer; if he had belonged to one of the 9,397 families in Bermondsey—over 30 per cent. of the total number—living in 1927 at the rate of two or more persons to a room, or had been brought up in one of the one-apartment houses in the central division of Glasgow, 41 per cent. of which contained in 1926 three or more persons per room; if he had been one of the million-odd children in the elementary schools of England and Wales who are suffering at any given moment from physical defects;[7]

---

7. E. D. Simon, *How to Abolish the Slums*, 1929, pp. 12–13; *Report of Chief Med. Off. of Bd. of Educ. for 1928*, p. 144. The number of children found in the course of routine inspections to be in need of treatment (excluding dental disease) in 1928 was 395,658 out of 1,912,747 inspected. Assuming the proportion to be the same among the children who were not inspected, the number suffering from defects

and if, having been pitched into full-time industry at the age of fourteen, he had been dismissed at the age of sixteen or eighteen to make room for a cheaper competitor from the elementary school. He may quite rightly be convinced that he gets only what he is worth, and that the forces of the market would pull him up sharply if he stood out for more. What he is worth depends, however, not only upon his own powers, but upon the opportunities which his neighbours have had of developing their powers. Behind the forces of the market stand forces of another kind, which determine that the members of some social groups shall be in a position to render services which are highly remunerated because they are scarce, and to add to their incomes by the acquisition of property, whilst those belonging to others shall supply services which are cheap because they are over-supplied, but which form, nevertheless, their sole means of livelihood.

Such forces are partly, no doubt, beyond human control; but they are largely the result of institutions and policy. There is, for example, the unequal pressure of mere material surroundings, of housing, sanitation, and liability to disease, which decides that social groups shall differ in their ability to make the best use of their natural endowments. There is inequality of educational opportunity, which has as its effect that, while a favoured minority can cultivate their powers till manhood, the great majority of children, being compelled to compete for employment in their early adolescence, must enter occupations in which, because they are overcrowded, the remuneration is low, and later, because their remuneration has been low, must complete the vicious circle by sending their children into overcrowded occupations. There is the nepotism which allots jobs in the family business to sons and relations, and the favouritism which fills them with youths belonging to the same social class as its owners. There is inequality of access to financial information, which yields fortunes of surprising dimensions, if occasionally, also, of dubious repute, to the few who possess it. There is the influence of the institution of inheritance in heightening the effects of all other inequalities, by determining the vantage-ground upon which different groups and individuals shall stand, the range of opportunities which shall be open to them, and the degree of economic stress which they shall undergo.

The wage-earner who reflects on the distribution of wealth is apt, as is natural, to look first at the large dividends or watered capital of the firm by which he is employed. The economist looks at the large blocks of property which are owned by individuals and transmitted to their descendants, and which yield large incomes whether profits per cent. are high or low. He

---

among the total school population of England and Wales (4,981,101) would be 1,030,357.

insists, with Professor Cannan, that "the inequality in the amounts of property which individuals have received by way of bequest and inheritance is by far the most potent cause of inequality in the actual distribution of property." He points out, with Mr. Henderson, that the evil is progressive, since it causes "an initial inequality . . . to perpetuate itself throughout subsequent generations in a cumulative degree." He urges, with Sir Ernest Simon, that "inheritance is responsible, not only for the most excessive, but for the most unjust and indefensible, inequalities." Such statements are confirmed by the valuable researches of Mr. Wedgwood, who has made the economic effects of inheritance, almost for the first time, the subject of inductive investigation. The conclusion which he draws from the examination of a sample of large estates at Somerset House accords with common experience, but is not on that account the less perturbing. It is that, "on the whole, the largest fortunes belong to those with the richest parents. . . . In the great majority of cases the large fortunes of one generation belong to the children of those who possessed the large fortunes of the previous generation . . . *There is in our society an hereditary inequality of economic status which has survived the dissolution of the cruder forms of feudalism."* [8]

The advantages and disabilities which these phenomena create are properly described as social, since they are the result of social institutions, and can by the action of society be maintained or corrected. Experience shows that, when combined, as is normally the case, with extreme disparities of economic power between those who own and direct, and those who execute and are directed, but rarely own, they clog the mechanism of society and corrode its spirit. Except in so far as they are modified by deliberate intervention, they produce results surprisingly similar to those foretold by the genius of Marx. They divide what might have been a community into contending classes, of which one is engaged in a struggle to share in advantages which it does not yet enjoy and to limit the exercise of economic authority, while the other is occupied in a nervous effort to defend its position against encroachments.

8. E. Cannan, *The Economic Outlook*, 1912, p. 249; H. D. Henderson, *Inheritance and Inequality*, 1926, pp. 12–13; E. D. Simon, *The Inheritance of Riches*, 1925, p. 15; J. Wedgwood, "The Influence of Inheritance on the Distribution of Wealth" in *Econ. Jl.*, March 1928, pp. 50, 52, 55 (the italics are mine), and (for a more detailed discussion) his *Economics of Inheritance*, chap. vi.

11

F. A. von Hayek,
"Equality, Value, and Merit,"
from *The Constitution of Liberty*

Friedrich A. von Hayek (1899–1992) studied in Vienna and was a professor at the London School of Economics and the University of Chicago. His early writings dealt with issues that were of interest mainly to professional economists. His work first became known to a large public audience after the publication of The Road to Serfdom *in 1944, and from this time onward his writings covered a wide range of issues in social theory. Hayek was a joint recipient of the Nobel Prize in Economics in 1974.*

Equality, Value, and Merit

I have no respect for the passion for equality, which seems to me merely idealizing envy.

OLIVER WENDELL HOLMES, JR.

1. The great aim of the struggle for liberty has been equality before the law. This equality under the rules which the state enforces may be supplemented by a similar equality of the rules that men voluntarily obey in their relations with one another. This extension of the principle of equality to the rules of moral and social conduct is the chief expression of what is commonly called the democratic spirit—and probably that aspect of it that does most to make inoffensive the inequalities that liberty necessarily produces.

Equality of the general rules of law and conduct, however, is the only kind of equality conducive to liberty and the only equality which we can secure without destroying liberty. Not only has liberty nothing to do with any other sort of equality, but it is even bound to produce inequality in

From Friedrich A. Hayek, *The Constitution of Liberty* (Chicago: University of Chicago Press, 1960). Copyright © 1960 by the University of Chicago. All rights reserved. Reprinted by permission of the University of Chicago Press and the estate of F. A. Hayek.

The quotation at the head of the chapter is taken from *The Holmes-Laski Letters: The Correspondence of Mr. Justice Holmes and Harold J. Laski*, 1916–1935 (Cambridge: Harvard University Press, 1953), II, 942. A German translation of an earlier version of this chapter has appeared in *Ordo*, Vol. X (1958).

many respects. This is the necessary result and part of the justification of individual liberty: if the result of individual liberty did not demonstrate that some manners of living are more successful than others, much of the case for it would vanish.

It is neither because it assumes that people are in fact equal nor because it attempts to make them equal that the argument for liberty demands that government treat them equally. This argument not only recognizes that individuals are very different but in a great measure rests on that assumption. It insists that these individual differences provide no justification for government to treat them differently. And it objects to the differences in treatment by the state that would be necessary if persons who are in fact very different were to be assured equal positions in life.

Modern advocates of a more far-reaching material equality usually deny that their demands are based on any assumption of the factual equality of all men.[1] It is nevertheless still widely believed that this is the main justification for such demands. Nothing, however, is more damaging to the demand for equal treatment than to base it on so obviously untrue an assumption as that of the factual equality of all men. To rest the case for equal treatment of national or racial minorities on the assertion that they do not differ from other men is implicitly to admit that factual inequality would justify unequal treatment; and the proof that some differences do, in fact, exist would not be long in forthcoming. It is of the essence of the demand for equality before the law that people should be treated alike in spite of the fact that they are different.

2. The boundless variety of human nature—the wide range of differences in individual capacities and potentialities—is one of the most distinctive facts about the human species. Its evolution has made it probably the most variable among all kinds of creatures. It has been well said that "biology, with variability as its cornerstone, confers on every human individual a unique set of attributes which give him a dignity he could not otherwise possess. Every newborn baby is an unknown quantity so far as potentialities are concerned because there are many thousands of unknown interrelated genes and gene-patterns which contribute to his makeup. As a result of nature and nurture the newborn infant may become one of the greatest of men or women ever to have lived. In every case he or she has the making of a distinctive individual. . . . If the differences are not very important, then freedom is not very important and the idea of individual worth is not very important."[2] The writer justly adds that the

---

1. See, e.g., R. H. Tawney, *Equality* (London, 1931), p. 47.
2. Roger J. Williams, *Free and Unequal: The Biological Basis of Individual Liberty*

widely held uniformity theory of human nature, "which on the surface appears to accord with democracy . . . would in time undermine the very basic ideals of freedom and individual worth and render life as we know it meaningless."[3]

It has been the fashion in modern times to minimize the importance of congenital differences between men and to ascribe all the important differences to the influence of environment. However important the latter may be, we must not overlook the fact that individuals are very different from the outset. The importance of individual differences would hardly be less if all people were brought up in very similar environments. As a statement of fact, it just is not true that "all men are born equal." We may continue to use this hallowed phrase to express the ideal that legally and morally all men ought to be treated alike. But if we want to understand what this ideal of equality can or should mean, the first requirement is that we free ourselves from the belief in factual equality.

From the fact that people are very different it follows that, if we treat them equally, the result must be inequality in their actual position,[4] and that the only way to place them in an equal position would be to treat them differently. Equality before the law and material equality are therefore not only different but are in conflict with each other; and we can achieve either the one or the other, but not both at the same time. The equality before the law which freedom requires leads to material inequality. Our argument will be that, though where the state must use coercion for other reasons, it should treat all people alike, the desire of making people more alike in their condition cannot be accepted in a free society as a justification for further and discriminatory coercion.

We do not object to equality as such. It merely happens to be the case that a demand for equality is the professed motive of most of those who desire to impose upon society a preconceived pattern of distribution. Our objection is against all attempts to impress upon society a deliberately chosen pattern of distribution, whether it be an order of equality or of inequality. We shall indeed see that many of those who demand an extension of equality do not really demand equality but a distribution that conforms more closely to human conceptions of individual merit and that their desires are as irreconcilable with freedom as the more strictly egalitarian demands.

(Austin: University of Texas Press, 1953), pp. 23 and 70; cf. also J. B. S. Haldane, *The Inequality of Man* (London, 1932), and P. B. Medawar, *The Uniqueness of the Individual* (London, 1957).

3. Williams, *op. cit.*, p. 152.

4. Cf. Plato, *Laws*, vi. 757A: "To unequals equals become unequal."

If one objects to the use of coercion in order to bring about a more even or a more just distribution, this does not mean that one does not regard these as desirable. But if we wish to preserve a free society, it is essential that we recognize that the desirability of a particular object is not sufficient justification for the use of coercion. One may well feel attracted to a community in which there are no extreme contrasts between rich and poor and may welcome the fact that the general increase in wealth seems gradually to reduce those differences. I fully share these feelings and certainly regard the degree of social equality that the United States has achieved as wholly admirable.

There also seems no reason why these widely felt preferences should not guide policy in some respects. Wherever there is a legitimate need for government action and we have to choose between different methods of satisfying such a need, those that incidentally also reduce inequality may well be preferable. If, for example, in the law of intestate succession one kind of provision will be more conducive to equality than another, this may be a strong argument in its favor. It is a different matter, however, if it is demanded that, in order to produce substantive equality, we should abandon the basic postulate of a free society, namely, the limitation of all coercion by equal law. Against this we shall hold that economic inequality is not one of the evils which justify our resorting to discriminatory coercion or privilege as a remedy.

3. Our contention rests on two basic propositions which probably need only be stated to win fairly general assent. The first of them is an expression of the belief in a certain similarity of all human beings: it is the proposition that no man or group of men possesses the capacity to determine conclusively the potentialities of other human beings and that we should certainly never trust anyone invariably to exercise such a capacity. However great the differences between men may be, we have no ground for believing that they will ever be so great as to enable one man's mind in a particular instance to comprehend fully all that another responsible man's mind is capable of.

The second basic proposition is that the acquisition by any member of the community of additional capacities to do things which may be valuable must always be regarded as a gain for that community. It is true that particular people may be worse off because of the superior ability of some new competitor in their field; but any such additional ability in the community is likely to benefit the majority. This implies that the desirability of increasing the abilities and opportunities of any individual does not depend on whether the same can also be done for the others—provided, of course, that others are not thereby deprived of the opportunity of acquiring the same or other abilities which might have been accessible to them had they not been secured by that individual.

Egalitarians generally regard differently those differences in individual capacities which are inborn and those which are due to the influences of environment, or those which are the result of "nature" and those which are the result of "nurture." Neither, be it said at once, has anything to do with moral merit. Though either may greatly affect the value which an individual has for his fellows, no more credit belongs to him for having been born with desirable qualities than for having grown up under favorable circumstances. The distinction between the two is important only because the former advantages are due to circumstances clearly beyond human control, while the latter are due to factors which we might be able to alter. The important question is whether there is a case for so changing our institutions as to eliminate as much as possible those advantages due to environment. Are we to agree that "all inequalities that rest on birth and inherited property ought to be abolished and none remain unless it is an effect of superior talent and industry"?[5]

The fact that certain advantages rest on human arrangements does not necessarily mean that we could provide the same advantages for all or that, if they are given to some, somebody else is thereby deprived of them. The most important factors to be considered in this connection are the family, inheritance, and education, and it is against the inequality which they produce that criticism is mainly directed. They are, however, not the only important factors of environment. Geographic conditions such as climate and landscape, not to speak of local and sectional differences in cultural and moral traditions, are scarcely less important. We can, however, consider here only the three factors whose effects are most commonly impugned.

So far as the family is concerned, there exists a curious contrast between the esteem most people profess for the institution and their dislike of the fact that being born into a particular family should confer on a person special advantages. It seems to be widely believed that, while useful qualities which a person acquires because of his native gifts under conditions which are the same for all are socially beneficial, the same qualities become somehow undesirable if they are the result of environmental advantages not available to others. Yet it is difficult to see why the same

---

5. This is the position of R. H. Tawney as summarized by J. P. Plamenatz, "Equality of Opportunity," in *Aspects of Human Equality*, ed. L. Bryson and others (New York, 1956), p. 100.

useful quality which is welcomed when it is the result of a person's natural endowment should be less valuable when it is the product of such circumstances as intelligent parents or a good home.

The value which most people attach to the institution of the family rests on the belief that, as a rule, parents can do more to prepare their children for a satisfactory life than anyone else. This means not only that the benefits which particular people derive from their family environment will be different but also that these benefits may operate cumulatively through several generations. What reason can there be for believing that a desirable quality in a person is less valuable to society if it has been the result of family background than if it has not? There is, indeed, good reason to think that there are some socially valuable qualities which will be rarely acquired in a single generation but which will generally be formed only by the continuous efforts of two or three. This means simply that there are parts of the cultural heritage of a society that are more effectively transmitted through the family. Granted this, it would be unreasonable to deny that a society is likely to get a better elite if ascent is not limited to one generation, if individuals are not deliberately made to start from the same level, and if children are not deprived of the chance to benefit from the better education and material environment which their parents may be able to provide. To admit this is merely to recognize that belonging to a particular family is part of the individual personality, that society is made up as much of families as of individuals, and that the transmission of the heritage of civilization within the family is as important a tool in man's striving toward better things as is the heredity of beneficial physical attributes.

4. Many people who agree that the family is desirable as an instrument for the transmission of morals, tastes, and knowledge still question the desirability of the transmission of material property. Yet there can be little doubt that, in order that the former may be possible, some continuity of standards, of the external forms of life, is essential, and that this will be achieved only if it is possible to transmit not only immaterial but also material advantages. There is, of course, neither greater merit nor any greater injustice involved in some people being born to wealthy parents than there is in others being born to kind or intelligent parents. The fact is that it is no less of an advantage to the community if at least some children can start with the advantages which at any given time only wealthy homes can offer than if some children inherit great intelligence or are taught better morals at home.

We are not concerned here with the chief argument for private inheritance, namely, that it seems essential as a means to preserve the dispersal in the control of capital and as an inducement for its accumulation. Rather, our concern here is whether the fact that it confers unmerited benefits on some is a valid argument against the institution. It is unquestionably one of the institutional causes of inequality. In the present context we need not inquire whether liberty demands unlimited freedom of bequest. Our problem here is merely whether people ought to be free to pass on to children or others such material possessions as will cause substantial inequality.

Once we agree that it is desirable to harness the natural instincts of parents to equip the new generation as well as they can, there seems no sensible ground for limiting this to non-material benefits. The family's function of passing on standards and traditions is closely tied up with the possibility of transmitting material goods. And it is difficult to see how it would serve the true interest of society to limit the gain in material conditions to one generation.

There is also another consideration which, though it may appear somewhat cynical, strongly suggests that if we wish to make the best use of the natural partiality of parents for their children, we ought not to preclude the transmission of property. It seems certain that among the many ways in which those who have gained power and influence might provide for their children, the bequest of a fortune is socially by far the cheapest. Without this outlet, these men would look for other ways of providing for their children, such as placing them in positions which might bring them the income and the prestige that a fortune would have done; and this would cause a waste of resources and an injustice much greater than is caused by the inheritance of property. Such is the case with all societies in which inheritance of property does not exist, including the Communist. Those who dislike the inequalities caused by inheritance should therefore recognize that, men being what they are, it is the least of evils, even from their point of view.

5. Though inheritance used to be the most widely criticized source of inequality, it is today probably no longer so. Egalitarian agitation now tends to concentrate on the unequal advantages due to differences in education. There is a growing tendency to express the desire to secure equality of conditions in the claim that the best education we have learned to provide for some should be made gratuitously available for all and that, if this is not possible, one should not be allowed to get a better education than the rest merely because one's parents are able to pay for it, but only those and all those who can pass a uniform test of ability should be admitted to the benefits of the limited resources of higher education.

The problem of educational policy raises too many issues to allow of their being discussed incidentally under the general heading of equality. We shall have to devote a separate chapter to them at the end of this book. For the present we shall only point out that enforced equality in this field can hardly avoid preventing some from getting the education they otherwise might. Whatever we might do, there is no way of preventing those advantages which only some can have, and which it is desirable that some should have, from going to people who neither individually merit them nor will make as good a use of them as some other person might have done. Such a problem cannot be satisfactorily solved by the exclusive and coercive powers of the state.

It is instructive at this point to glance briefly at the change that the ideal of equality has undergone in this field in modern times. A hundred years ago, at the height of the classical liberal movement, the demand was generally expressed by the phrase *la carrière ouverte aux talents*. It was a demand that all man-made obstacles to the rise of some should be removed, that all privileges of individuals should be abolished, and that what the state contributed to the chance of improving one's conditions should be the same for all. That so long as people were different and grew up in different families this could not assure an equal start was fairly generally accepted. It was understood that the duty of government was not to ensure that everybody had the same prospect of reaching a given position but merely to make available to all on equal terms those facilities which in their nature depended on government action. That the results were bound to be different, not only because the individuals were different, but also because only a small part of the relevant circumstances depended on government action, was taken for granted.

This conception that all should be allowed to try has been largely replaced by the altogether different conception that all must be assured an equal start and the same prospects. This means little less than that the government, instead of providing the same circumstances for all, should aim at controlling all conditions relevant to a particular individual's prospects and so adjust them to his capacities as to assure him of the same prospects as everybody else. Such deliberate adaptation of opportunities to individual aims and capacities would, of course, be the opposite of freedom. Nor could it be justified as a means of making the best use of all available knowledge except on the assumption that government knows best how individual capacities can be used.

When we inquire into the justification of these demands, we find that they rest on the discontent that the success of some people often produces in those that are less successful, or, to put it bluntly, on envy. The modern tendency to gratify this passion and to disguise it in the respectable garment of social justice is developing into a serious threat to freedom.

Recently an attempt was made to base these demands on the argument that it ought to be the aim of politics to remove all sources of discontent.[6] This would, of course, necessarily mean that it is the responsibility of government to see that nobody is healthier or possesses a happier temperament, a better-suited spouse or more prospering children, than anybody else. If really all unfulfilled desires have a claim on the community, individual responsibility is at an end. However human, envy is certainly not one of the sources of discontent that a free society can eliminate. It is probably one of the essential conditions for the preservation of such a society that we do not countenance envy, not sanction its demands by camouflaging it as social justice, but treat it, in the words of John Stuart Mill, as "the most anti-social and evil of all passions."[7]

6. While most of the strictly egalitarian demands are based on nothing better than envy, we must recognize that much that on the surface appears as a demand for greater equality is in fact a demand for a juster distribution of the good things of this world and springs therefore from much more creditable motives. Most people will object not to the bare fact of inequality but to the fact that the differences in reward do not correspond to any recognizable differences in the merits of those who receive them. The answer commonly given to this is that a free society on the whole achieves this kind of justice. This, however, is an indefensible contention if by justice is meant proportionality of reward to moral merit. Any attempt to found the case for freedom on this argument is very damaging to it, since it concedes that material rewards ought to be made to correspond to recognizable merit and then opposes the conclusion that most people will draw from this by an assertion which is untrue. The proper answer is that in a free system it is neither desirable nor practicable that material rewards should be made generally to correspond to what men recognize as merit and that it is an essential characteristic of a free society that an individual's position should not necessarily depend on the views that his fellows hold about the merit he has acquired.

This contention may appear at first so strange and even shocking that I will ask the reader to suspend judgment until I have further explained the distinction between value and merit. The difficulty in making the point clear is due to the fact that the term "merit," which is the only one available to describe what I mean, is also used in a wider and vaguer sense. It will be used here exclusively to describe the attributes of conduct that

6. C. A. R. Crosland, *The Future of Socialism* (London, 1956), p. 205.
7. J. S. Mill, *On Liberty*, ed. R. B. McCallum (Oxford, 1946), p. 70.

make it deserving of praise, that is, the moral character of the action and not the value of the achievement.

As we have seen throughout our discussion, the value that the performance or capacity of a person has to his fellows has no necessary connection with its ascertainable merit in this sense. The inborn as well as the acquired gifts of a person clearly have a value to his fellows which does not depend on any credit due to him for possessing them. There is little a man can do to alter the fact that his special talents are very common or exceedingly rare. A good mind or a fine voice, a beautiful face or a skilful hand, and a ready wit or an attractive personality are in a large measure as independent of a person's efforts as the opportunities or the experiences he has had. In all these instances the value which a person's capacities or services have for us and for which he is recompensed has little relation to anything that we can call moral merit or deserts. Our problem is whether it is desirable that people should enjoy advantages in proportion to the benefits which their fellows derive from their activities or whether the distribution of these advantages should be based on other men's views of their merits.

Reward according to merit must in practice mean reward according to assessable merit, merit that other people can recognize and agree upon and not merit merely in the sight of some higher power. Assessable merit in this sense presupposes that we can ascertain that a man has done what some accepted rule of conduct demanded of him and that this has cost him some pain and effort. Whether this has been the case cannot be judged by the result: merit is not a matter of the objective outcome but of subjective effort. The attempt to achieve a valuable result may be highly meritorious but a complete failure, and full success may be entirely the result of accident and thus without merit. If we know that a man has done his best, we will often wish to see him rewarded irrespective of the result; and if we know that a most valuable achievement is almost entirely due to luck or favorable circumstances, we will give little credit to the author.

We may wish that we were able to draw this distinction in every instance. In fact, we can do so only rarely with any degree of assurance. It is possible only where we possess all the knowledge which was at the disposal of the acting person, including a knowledge of his skill and confidence, his state of mind and his feelings, his capacity for attention, his energy and persistence, etc. The possibility of a true judgment of merit thus depends on the presence of precisely those conditions whose general absence is the main argument for liberty. It is because we want people to use knowledge which we do not possess that we let them decide for themselves. But insofar as we want them to be free to use capacities and knowledge of facts which we do not have, we are not in a position to judge the merit of their achievements. To decide on merit presupposes that we can judge whether people have made such use of their opportunities as they ought to have made and how much effort of will or self-denial this has cost them; it presupposes also that we can distinguish between that part of their achievement which is due to circumstances within their control and that part which is not.

7. The incompatibility of reward according to merit with freedom to choose one's pursuit is most evident in those areas where the uncertainty of the outcome is particularly great and our individual estimates of the chances of various kinds of effort very different. In those speculative efforts which we call "research" or "exploration," or in economic activities which we commonly describe as "speculation," we cannot expect to attract those best qualified for them unless we give the successful ones all the credit or gain, though many others may have striven as meritoriously. For the same reason that nobody can know beforehand who will be the successful ones, nobody can say who has earned greater merit. It would clearly not serve our purpose if we let all who have honestly striven share in the prize. Moreover, to do so would make it necessary that somebody have the right to decide who is to be allowed to strive for it. If in their pursuit of uncertain goals people are to use their own knowledge and capacities, they must be guided, not by what other people think they ought to do, but by the value others attach to the result at which they aim.

What is so obviously true about those undertakings which we commonly regard as risky is scarcely less true of any chosen object we decide to pursue. Any such decision is beset with uncertainty, and if the choice is to be as wise as it is humanly possible to make it, the alternative results anticipated must be labeled according to their value. If the remuneration did not correspond to the value that the product of a man's efforts has for his fellows, he would have no basis for deciding whether the pursuit of a given object is worth the effort and risk. He would necessarily have to be told what to do, and some other person's estimate of what was the best use of his capacities would have to determine both his duties and his remuneration.[8]

8. It is often maintained that justice requires that remuneration be proportional to the unpleasantness of the job and that for this reason the street cleaner or the sewage worker ought to be paid more than the doctor or office worker. This, indeed, would seem to be the consequence of the principle of remuneration according to merit (or "distributive justice"). In a market such a result would come about only if all people were equally skilful in all jobs so that those who could earn as much as others in the more pleasant occupations would have to be paid more to

The fact is, of course, that we do not wish people to earn a maximum of merit but to achieve a maximum of usefulness at a minimum of pain and sacrifice and therefore a minimum of merit. Not only would it be impossible for us to reward all merit justly, but it would not even be desirable that people should aim chiefly at earning a maximum of merit. Any attempt to induce them to do this would necessarily result in people being rewarded differently for the same service. And it is only the value of the result that we can judge with any degree of confidence, not the different degrees of effort and care that it has cost different people to achieve it.

The prizes that a free society offers for the result serve to tell those who strive for them how much effort they are worth. However, the same prizes will go to all those who produce the same result, regardless of effort. What is true here of the remuneration for the same services rendered by different people is even more true of the relative remuneration for different services requiring different gifts and capacities: they will have little relation to merit. The market will generally offer for services of any kind the value they will have for those who benefit from them; but it will rarely be known whether it was necessary to offer so much in order to obtain these services, and often, no doubt, the community could have had them for much less. The pianist who was reported not long ago to have said that he would perform even if he had to pay for the privilege probably described the position of many who earn large incomes from activities which are also their chief pleasure.

8. Though most people regard as very natural the claim that nobody should be rewarded more than he deserves for his pain and effort, it is nevertheless based on a colossal presumption. It presumes that we are able to judge in every individual instance how well people use the different opportunities and talents given to them and how meritorious their achievements are in the light of all the circumstances which have made them possible. It presumes that some human beings are in a position to determine conclusively what a person is worth and are entitled to determine what he may achieve. It presumes, then, what the argument for liberty specifically rejects: that we can and do know all that guides a person's action.

---

undertake the distasteful ones. In the actual world those unpleasant jobs provide those whose usefulness in the more attractive jobs is small an opportunity to earn more than they could elsewhere. That persons who have little to offer their fellows should be able to earn an income similar to that of the rest only at a much greater sacrifice is inevitable in any arrangement under which the individual is allowed to choose his own sphere of usefulness.

A society in which the position of the individuals was made to correspond to human ideas of moral merit would therefore be the exact opposite of a free society. It would be a society in which people were rewarded for duty performed instead of for success, in which every move of every individual was guided by what other people thought he ought to do, and in which the individual was thus relieved of the responsibility and the risk of decision. But if nobody's knowledge is sufficient to guide all human action, there is also no human being who is competent to reward all efforts according to merit.

In our individual conduct we generally act on the assumption that it is the value of a person's performance and not his merit that determines our obligation to him. Whatever may be true in more intimate relations, in the ordinary business of life we do not feel that, because a man has rendered us a service at a great sacrifice, our debt to him is determined by this, so long as we could have had the same service provided with ease by somebody else. In our dealings with other men we feel that we are doing justice if we recompense value rendered with equal value, without inquiring what it might have cost the particular individual to supply us with these services. What determines our responsibility is the advantage we derive from what others offer us, not their merit in providing it. We also expect in our dealings with others to be remunerated not according to our subjective merit but according to what our services are worth to them. Indeed, so long as we think in terms of our relations to particular people, we are generally quite aware that the mark of the free man is to be dependent for his livelihood not on other people's views of his merit but solely on what he has to offer them. It is only when we think of our position or our income as determined by "society" as a whole that we demand reward according to merit.

Though moral value or merit is a species of value, not all value is moral value, and most of our judgments of value are not moral judgments. That this must be so in a free society is a point of cardinal importance; and the failure to distinguish between value and merit has been the source of serious confusion. We do not necessarily admire all activities whose product we value; and in most instances where we value what we get, we are in no position to assess the merit of those who have provided it for us. If a man's ability in a given field is more valuable after thirty years' work than it was earlier, this is independent of whether these thirty years were most profitable and enjoyable or whether they were a time of unceasing sacrifice and worry. If the pursuit of a hobby produces a special skill or an accidental invention turns out to be extremely useful to others, the fact that there is little merit in it does not make it any less valuable than if the result had been produced by painful effort.

This difference between value and merit is not peculiar to any one type of society—it would exist anywhere. We might, of course, attempt to make rewards correspond to merit instead of value, but we are not likely to succeed in this. In attempting it, we would destroy the incentives which enable people to decide for themselves what they should do. Moreover, it is more than doubtful whether even a fairly successful attempt to make rewards correspond to merit would produce a more attractive or even a tolerable social order. A society in which it was generally presumed that a high income was proof of merit and a low income of the lack of it, in which it was universally believed that position and remuneration corresponded to merit, in which there was no other road to success than the approval of one's conduct by the majority of one's fellows, would probably be much more unbearable to the unsuccessful ones than one in which it was frankly recognized that there was no necessary connection between merit and success.

It would probably contribute more to human happiness if, instead of trying to make remuneration correspond to merit, we made clearer how uncertain is the connection between value and merit. We are probably all much too ready to ascribe personal merit where there is, in fact, only superior value. The possession by an individual or a group of a superior civilization or education certainly represents an important value and con-stitutes an asset for the community to which they belong; but it usually constitutes little merit. Popularity and esteem do not depend more on merit than does financial success. It is, in fact, largely because we are so used to assuming an often non-existent merit wherever we find value that we balk when, in particular instances, the discrepancy is too large to be ignored.

There is every reason why we ought to endeavor to honor special merit where it has gone without adequate reward. But the problem of rewarding action of outstanding merit which we wish to be widely known as an example is different from that of the incentives on which the ordinary functioning of society rests. A free society produces institutions in which, for those who prefer it, a man's advancement depends on the judgment of some superior or of the majority of his fellows. Indeed, as organizations grow larger and more complex, the task of ascertaining the individual's contribution will become more difficult; and it will become increasingly necessary that, for many, merit in the eyes of the managers rather than the ascertainable value of the contribution should determine the rewards. So long as this does not produce a situation in which a single comprehensive scale of merit is imposed upon the whole society, so long as a multiplicity of organizations compete with one another in offering different prospects, this is not merely compatible with freedom but extends the range of choice open to the individual.

9. Justice, like liberty and coercion, is a concept which, for the sake of clarity, ought to be confined to the deliberate treatment of men by other men. It is an aspect of the intentional determination of those conditions of people's lives that are subject to such control. Insofar as we want the efforts of individuals to be guided by their own views about prospects and chances, the results of the individual's efforts are necessarily unpredictable, and the question as to whether the resulting distribution of incomes is just has no meaning. Justice does require that those conditions of people's lives that are determined by government be provided equally for all. But equality of those conditions must lead to inequality of results. Neither the equal provision of particular public facilities nor the equal treatment of different partners in our voluntary dealings with one another will secure reward that is proportional to merit. Reward for merit is reward for obeying the wishes of others in what we do, not compensation for the benefits we have conferred upon them by doing what we thought best.

It is, in fact, one of the objections against attempts by government to fix income scales that the state must attempt to be just in all it does. Once the principle of reward according to merit is accepted as the just foundation for the distribution of incomes, justice would require that all who desire it should be rewarded according to that principle. Soon it would also be demanded that the same principle be applied to all and that incomes not in proportion to recognizable merit not be tolerated. Even an attempt merely to distinguish between those incomes or gains which are "earned" and those which are not will set up a principle which the state will have to try to apply but cannot in fact apply generally. And every such attempt at deliberate control of some remunerations is bound to create further demands for new controls. The principle of distributive justice, once introduced, would not be fulfilled until the whole of society was organized in accordance with it. This would produce a kind of society which in all essential respects would be the opposite of a free society—a society in which authority decided what the individual was to do and how he was to do it.

10. In conclusion we must briefly look at another argument on which the demands for a more equal distribution are frequently based, though it is rarely explicitly stated. This is the contention that membership in a particular community or nation entitles the individual to a particular material standard that is determined by the general wealth of the group to

which he belongs. This demand is in curious conflict with the desire to base distribution on personal merit. There is clearly no merit in being born into a particular community, and no argument of justice can be based on the accident of a particular individual's being born in one place rather than another. A relatively wealthy community in fact regularly confers advantages on its poorest members unknown to those born in poor communities. In a wealthy community the only justification its members can have for insisting on further advantages is that there is much private wealth that the government can confiscate and redistribute and that men who constantly see such wealth being enjoyed by others will have a stronger desire for it than those who know of it only abstractly, if at all.

There is no obvious reason why the joint efforts of the members of any group to ensure the maintenance of law and order and to organize the provision of certain services should give the members a claim to a particular share in the wealth of this group. Such claims would be especially difficult to defend where those who advanced them were unwilling to concede the same rights to those who did not belong to the same nation or community. The recognition of such claims on a national scale would in fact only create a new kind of collective (but not less exclusive) property right in the resources of the nation that could not be justified on the same grounds as individual property. Few people would be prepared to recognize the justice of these demands on a world scale. And the bare fact that within a given nation the majority had the actual power to enforce such demands, while in the world as a whole it did not yet have it, would hardly make them more just.

There are good reasons why we should endeavor to use whatever political organization we have at our disposal to make provision for the weak or infirm or for the victims of unforeseeable disaster. It may well be true that the most effective method of providing against certain risks common to all citizens of a state is to give every citizen protection against those risks. The level on which such provisions against common risks can be made will necessarily depend on the general wealth of the community.

It is an entirely different matter, however, to suggest that those who are poor, merely in the sense that there are those in the same community who are richer, are entitled to a share in the wealth of the latter or that being born into a group that has reached a particular level of civilization and comfort confers a title to a share in all its benefits. The fact that all citizens have an interest in the common provision of some services is no justification for anyone's claiming as a right a share in all the benefits. It may set a standard for what some ought to be willing to give, but not for what anyone can demand.

National groups will become more and more exclusive as the acceptance of this view that we have been contending against spreads. Rather than admit people to the advantages that living in their country offers, a nation will prefer to keep them out altogether; for, once admitted, they will soon claim as a right a particular share in its wealth. The conception that citizenship or even residence in a country confers a claim to a particular standard of living is becoming a serious source of international friction. And since the only justification for applying the principle within a given country is that its government has the power to enforce it, we must not be surprised if we find the same principle being applied by force on an international scale. Once the right of the majority to the benefits that minorities enjoy is recognized on a national scale, there is no reason why this should stop at the boundaries of the existing states.

John Rawls, "Justice and Equality," from *A Theory of Justice*

John Rawls is James Bryant Conant University Professor Emeritus at Harvard University. The following selections are drawn from his most important and influential work, A Theory of Justice. *In that book, Rawls offers an alternative, which he calls the theory of justice as fairness, to classical utilitarianism, which holds that the most just society is one which achieves the greatest aggregate happiness. This alternative is encapsulated in Rawls's two principles of justice as fairness, which are explained in this reading.*

The Subject of Justice

Many different kinds of things are said to be just and unjust: not only laws, institutions, and social systems, but also particular actions of many kinds, including decisions, judgments, and imputations. We also call the attitudes and dispositions of persons, and persons themselves, just and unjust. Our topic, however, is that of social justice. For us the primary subject of justice is the basic structure of society, or more exactly, the way in which the major social institutions distribute fundamental rights and duties and determine the division of advantages from social cooperation. By major institutions I understand the political constitution and the principal economic and social arrangements. Thus the legal protection of freedom of thought and liberty of conscience, competitive markets, private property in the means of production, and the monogamous family are examples of major social institutions. Taken together as one scheme, the major institutions define men's rights and duties and influence their life-prospects, what they can expect to be and how well they can hope to do. The basic structure is the primary subject of justice because its effects are so profound and present from the start. The intuitive notion here is that this structure contains various social positions and that men born into different positions have different expectations of life determined, in part, by the political system as well as by economic and social circumstances. In this way the institutions of society favor certain starting places over others. These are especially deep inequalities. Not only are they pervasive, but they affect men's initial chances in life; yet they cannot possibly be justified by an appeal to the notions of merit or desert. It is these inequalities, presumably inevitable in the basic structure of any society, to which the principles of social justice must in the first instance apply. These principles, then, regulate the choice of a political constitution and the main elements of the economic and social system. The justice of a social scheme depends essentially on how fundamental rights and duties are assigned and on the economic opportunities and social conditions in the various sectors of society.

. . .

The Main Idea of the Theory of Justice

My aim is to present a conception of justice which generalizes and carries to a higher level of abstraction the familiar theory of the social contract as found, say, in Locke, Rousseau, and Kant.[1] In order to do this we are not to think of the original contract as one to enter a particular society or to set up a particular form of government. Rather, the guiding idea is that the principles of justice for the basic structure of society are the object of the original agreement. They are the principles that free and rational persons concerned to further their own interests would accept in an initial position of equality as defining the fundamental terms of their association. These principles are to regulate all further agreements; they specify the kinds of social cooperation that can be entered into and the forms of government that can be established. This way of regarding the principles of justice I shall call justice as fairness.

Thus we are to imagine that those who engage in social cooperation choose together, in one joint act, the principles which are to assign basic rights and duties and to determine the division of social benefits. Men are to decide in advance how they are to regulate their claims against one another and what is to be the foundation charter of their society. Just as each person must decide by rational reflection what constitutes his good, that is, the system of ends which it is rational for him to pursue, so a group of persons must decide once and for all what is to count among them as just and unjust. The choice which rational men would make in this hypo-

1. As the text suggests, I shall regard Locke's *Second Treatise of Government,* Rousseau's *The Social Contract,* and Kant's ethical works beginning with *The Foundations of the Metaphysics of Morals* as definitive of the contract tradition.

hypo thetical situation of equal liberty, assuming for the present that this choice problem has a solution, determines the principles of justice.

. . .

arrangement of inequalities so as to be advantageous ## Two Principles of Justice

I shall now state in a provisional form the two principles of justice that I believe would be chosen in the original position. . . .[2]

First: each person is to have an equal right to the most extensive basic liberty compatible with a similar liberty for others.

Second: social and economic inequalities are to be arranged so that they are both (a) reasonably expected to be to everyone's advantage, and (b) attached to positions and offices open to all. . . .[3]

By way of general comment, these principles primarily apply, as I have said, to the basic structure of society. They are to govern the assignment of rights and duties and to regulate the distribution of social and economic advantages. As their formulation suggests, these principles presuppose that the social structure can be divided into two more or less distinct parts, the first principle applying to the one, the second to the other. They distinguish between those aspects of the social system that define and secure the equal liberties of citizenship and those that specify and establish social and economic inequalities. The basic liberties of citizens are, roughly speaking, political liberty (the right to vote and to be eligible for public office) together with freedom of speech and assembly; liberty of conscience and freedom of thought; freedom of the person along with the right to hold (personal) property; and freedom from arbitrary arrest and seizure as defined by the concept of the rule of law. These liberties are all required to be equal by the first principle, since citizens of a just society are to have the same basic rights. *no inhibition*

The second principle applies, in the first approximation, to the distribution of income and wealth and to the design of organizations that make use of differences in authority and responsibility, or chains of command. While the distribution of wealth and income need not be equal, it must be to everyone's advantage, and at the same time, positions of author-

2. [The original position is the hypothetical situation Rawls asks us (in the immediately preceding paragraph, pp. 125–126) to imagine. In it, as he explains elsewhere, individuals are unaware of their social positions, economic standing, and personal identities. Rawls argues that the fairest principles of justice must be whatever principles individuals in the original position would choose.—D. J.]

3. [Later, Rawls calls part (a) of his second principle of justice the "difference principle." The difference principle is one of the most distinctive components of Rawls's theory of justice.]

ity and offices of command must be accessible to all. One applies the second principle by holding positions open, and then, subject to this constraint, arranges social and economic inequalities so that everyone benefits.

These principles are to be arranged in a serial order with the first principle prior to the second. This ordering means that a departure from the institutions of equal liberty required by the first principle cannot be justified by, or compensated for, by greater social and economic advantages.[1] The distribution of wealth and income, and the hierarchies of authority, must be consistent with both the liberties of equal citizenship and equality of opportunity.

It is clear that these principles are rather specific in their content, and their acceptance rests on certain assumptions that I must eventually try to explain and justify. A theory of justice depends upon a theory of society in ways that will become evident as we proceed. For the present, it should be observed that the two principles (and this holds for all formulations) are a special case of a more general conception of justice that can be expressed as follows.

> All social values—liberty and opportunity, income and wealth, and the bases of self-respect—are to be distributed equally unless an unequal distribution of any, or all, of these values is to everyone's advantage.

Injustice, then, is simply inequalities that are not to the benefit of all. Of course, this conception is extremely vague and requires interpretation.

As a first step, suppose that the basic structure of society distributes certain primary goods, that is, things that every rational man is presumed to want. These goods normally have a use whatever a person's rational plan of life. For simplicity, assume that the chief primary goods at the disposition of society are rights and liberties, powers and opportunities, income and wealth (. . . [T]he primary good of self-respect [also] has a central place.) These are the social primary goods. Other primary goods such as health and vigor, intelligence and imagination, are natural goods; although their possession is influenced by the basic structure, they are not so directly under its control. Imagine, then, a hypothetical initial arrange-

---

4. [Usually, Rawls uses the term "lexical order" to describe the relationship between his two principles of justice. That the two principles are lexically ordered means the first principle must be satisfied fully before the second principle comes into play. In other words, according to Rawls's theory, a basic structure that guarantees equal rights to liberty is more just than one that fails to do so, even if the latter basic structure is vastly more successful at meeting the conditions for social and economic inequalities prescribed by Rawls's second principle.]

ment in which all the social primary goods are equally distributed: every-one has similar rights and duties, and income and wealth are evenly shared. This state of affairs provides a benchmark for judging improve-ments. If certain inequalities of wealth and organizational powers would make everyone better off than in this hypothetical starting situation, then they accord with the general conception.

Now it is possible, at least theoretically, that by giving up some of their fundamental liberties men are sufficiently compensated by the resulting social and economic gains. The general conception of justice imposes no restrictions on what sort of inequalities are permissible; it only requires that everyone's position be improved. We need not suppose anything so drastic as consenting to a condition of slavery. Imagine instead that men forego certain political rights when the economic returns are significant and their capacity to influence the course of policy by the exercise of these rights would be marginal in any case. It is this kind of exchange which the two principles as stated rule out; being arranged in serial order they do not permit exchanges between basic liberties and economic and social gains. The serial ordering of principles expresses an underlying preference among primary social goods. When this preference is rational so likewise is the choice of these principles in this order.

In developing justice as fairness I shall, for the most part, leave aside the general conception of justice and examine instead the special case of the two principles in serial order. The advantage of this procedure is that from the first the matter of priorities is recognized and an effort made to find principles to deal with it. One is led to attend throughout to the conditions under which the acknowledgment of the absolute weight of liberty with respect to social and economic advantages, as defined by the lexical order of the two principles, would be reasonable. Offhand, this ranking appears extreme and too special a case to be of much interest; but there is more justification for it than would appear at first sight. . . . Furthermore, the distinction between fundamental rights and liberties and economic and social benefits marks a difference among primary social goods that one should try to exploit. It suggests an important division in the social system. Of course, the distinctions drawn and the ordering proposed are bound to be at best only approximations. There are surely circumstances in which they fail. But it is essential to depict clearly the main lines of a reasonable conception of justice; and under many conditions anyway, the two principles in serial order may serve well enough. When necessary we can fall back on the more general conception.

The fact that the two principles apply to institutions has certain conse-quences. Several points illustrate this. First of all, the rights and liberties referred to by these principles are those which are defined by the public rules of the basic structure. Whether men are free is determined by the rights and duties established by the major institutions of society. Liberty is a certain pattern of social forms. The first principle simply requires that certain sorts of rules, those defining basic liberties, apply to everyone equally and that they allow the most extensive liberty compatible with a like liberty for all. The only reason for circumscribing the rights defining liberty and making men's freedom less extensive than it might otherwise be is that these equal rights as institutionally defined would interfere with one another.

Another thing to bear in mind is that when principles mention persons, or require that everyone gain from an inequality, the reference is to representative persons holding the various social positions, or offices, or whatever, established by the basic structure. Thus in applying the second principle I assume that it is possible to assign an expectation of well-being to representative individuals holding these positions. This expectation indicates their life prospects as viewed from their social station. In general, the expectations of representative persons depend upon the distribution of rights and duties throughout the basic structure. When this changes, expectations change. I assume, then, that expectations are connected: by raising the prospects of the representative man in one position we presumably increase or decrease the prospects of representative men in other positions. Since it applies to institutional forms, the second principle (or rather the first part of it) refers to the expectations of representative individuals. As I shall discuss below, neither principle applies to distributions of particular goods to particular individuals who may be identified by their proper names. The situation where someone is considering how to allocate certain commodities to needy persons who are known to him is not within the scope of the principles. They are meant to regulate basic institutional arrangements. We must not assume that there is much similarity from the standpoint of justice between an administrative allotment of goods to specific persons and the appropriate design of society. Our common sense intuitions for the former may be a poor guide to the latter.

Now the second principle insists that each person benefit from permissible inequalities in the basic structure. This means that it must be reasonable for each relevant representative man defined by this structure, when he views it as a going concern, to prefer his prospects with the inequality to his prospects without it. One is not allowed to justify differences in income or organizational powers on the ground that the disadvantages of those in one position are outweighed by the greater advantages of those in another. Much less can infringements of liberty be counterbalanced in this way. Applied to the basic structure, the principle of utility would have us maximize the sum of expectations of representative men (weighted by the number of persons they represent, on the classical view); and this would permit us to compensate for the losses of some by the gains of others. Instead, the two principles require that everyone benefit from economic and social inequalities.

. . .

Fair Equality of Opportunity and Pure Procedural Justice

I should now like to comment upon the second part of the second principle, henceforth to be understood as the liberal principle of fair equality of opportunity. It must not then be confused with the notion of careers open to talents; nor must one forget that since it is tied in with the difference principle its consequences are quite distinct from the liberal interpretation of the two principles taken together. In particular, I shall try to show further on that this principle is not subject to the objection that it leads to a meritocratic society. Here I wish to consider a few other points, especially its relation to the idea of pure procedural justice.

First, though, I should note that the reasons for requiring open positions are not solely, or even primarily, those of efficiency. I have not maintained that offices must be open if in fact everyone is to benefit from an arrangement. For it may be possible to improve everyone's situation by assigning certain powers and benefits to positions despite the fact that certain groups are excluded from them. Although access is restricted, perhaps these offices can still attract superior talent and encourage better performance. But the principle of open positions forbids this. It expresses the conviction that if some places were not open on a basis fair to all, those kept out would be right in feeling unjustly treated even though they benefited from the greater efforts of those who were allowed to hold them. They would be justified in their complaint not only because they were excluded from certain external rewards of office such as wealth and privilege, but because they were debarred from experiencing the realization of self which comes from a skillful and devoted exercise of social duties. They would be deprived of one of the main forms of human good.

Now I have said that the basic structure is the primary subject of justice. This means, as we have seen, that the first distributive problem is the assignment of fundamental rights and duties and the regulation of social and economic inequalities and of the legitimate expectations founded on these. Of course, any ethical theory recognizes the importance of the basic structure as a subject of justice, but not all theories regard its importance in the same way. In justice as fairness society is interpreted as a cooperative venture for mutual advantage. The basic structure is a public system of rules defining a scheme of activities that leads men to act together so as to produce a greater sum of benefits and assigns to each certain recognized claims to a share in the proceeds. What a person does depends upon what the public rules say he will be entitled to, and what a person is entitled to depends on what he does. The distribution which results is arrived at by honoring the claims determined by what persons undertake to do in the light of these legitimate expectations. social contract

These considerations suggest the idea of treating the question of distributive shares as a matter of pure procedural justice. The intuitive idea is to design the social system so that the outcome is just whatever it happens to be, at least so long as it is within a certain range. The notion of pure procedural justice is best understood by a comparison with perfect and imperfect procedural justice. To illustrate the former, consider the simplest case of fair division. A number of men are to divide a cake: assuming that the fair division is an equal one, which procedure, if any, will give this outcome? Technicalities aside, the obvious solution is to have one man divide the cake and get the last piece, the others being allowed their pick before him. He will divide the cake equally, since in this way he assures for himself the largest share possible. This example illustrates the two characteristic features of perfect procedural justice. First, there is an independent criterion for what is a fair division, a criterion defined separately from and prior to the procedure which is to be followed. And second, it is possible to devise a procedure that is sure to give the desired outcome. Of course, certain assumptions are made here, such as that the man selected can divide the cake equally, wants as large a piece as he can get, and so on. But we can ignore these details. The essential thing is that there is an independent standard for deciding which outcome is just and a procedure guaranteed to lead to it. Pretty clearly, perfect procedural justice is rare, if not impossible, in cases of much practical interest.

Imperfect procedural justice is exemplified by a criminal trial. The desired outcome is that the defendant should be declared guilty if and only if he has committed the offense with which he is charged. The trial procedure is framed to search for and to establish the truth in this regard. But it seems impossible to design the legal rules so that they always lead to the correct result. The theory of trials examines which procedures and rules of evidence, and the like, are best calculated to advance this purpose consistent with the other ends of the law. Different arrangements for hearing cases may reasonably be expected in different circumstances to yield the right results, not always but at least most of the time. A trial, then, is an instance of imperfect procedural justice. Even though the law is carefully followed, and the proceedings fairly and properly conducted, it may reach the wrong outcome. An innocent man may be found guilty, a guilty man may be set free. In such cases we speak of a miscarriage of justice: the injustice springs from no human fault but from a fortuitous combination of circumstances which defeats the purpose of the legal rules. The characteristic mark of imperfect procedural justice is that while there is an independent criterion for the correct outcome, there is no feasible procedure which is sure to lead to it.

By contrast, pure procedural justice obtains when there is no independent criterion for the right result: instead there is a correct or fair procedure such that the outcome is likewise correct or fair, whatever it is, provided that the procedure has been properly followed. This situation is illustrated by gambling. If a number of persons engage in a series of fair bets, the distribution of cash after the last bet is fair, or at least not unfair, whatever this distribution is. I assume here that fair bets are those having a zero expectation of gain, that the bets are made voluntarily, that no one cheats, and so on. The betting procedure is fair and freely entered into under conditions that are fair. Thus the background circumstances define a fair procedure. Now any distribution of cash summing to the initial stock held by all individuals could result from a series of fair bets. In this sense all of these particular distributions are equally fair. A distinctive feature of pure procedural justice is that the procedure for determining the just result must actually be carried out; for in these cases there is no independent criterion by reference to which a definite outcome can be known to be just. Clearly we cannot say that a particular state of affairs is just because it could have been reached by following a fair procedure. This would permit far too much and would lead to absurdly unjust consequences. It would allow one to say that almost any distribution of goods is just, or fair, since it could have come about as a result of fair gambles. What makes the final outcome of betting fair, or not unfair, is that it is the one which has arisen after a series of fair gambles. A fair procedure translates its fairness to the outcome only when it is actually carried out.

In order, therefore, to apply the notion of pure procedural justice to distributive shares it is necessary to set up and to administer impartially a just system of institutions. Only against the background of a just basic structure, including a just political constitution and a just arrangement of economic and social institutions, can one say that the requisite just procedure exists. In Part Two I shall describe in some detail a basic structure that has the necessary features.[5] Its various institutions are explained and connected with the two principles of justice. The intuitive idea is familiar. Suppose that law and government act effectively to keep markets competitive, resources fully employed, property and wealth (especially if private ownership of the means of production is allowed) widely distributed by the appropriate forms of taxation, or whatever, and to guarantee a reason-

---

5. [The discussion to which Rawls refers is not included in this selection.]

able social minimum. Assume also that there is fair equality of opportunity underwritten by education for all; and that the other equal liberties are secured. Then it would appear that the resulting distribution of income and the pattern of expectations will tend to satisfy the difference principle. In this complex of institutions, which we think of as establishing social justice in the modern state, the advantages of the better situated improve the condition of the least favored. Or when they do not, they can be adjusted to do so, for example, by setting the social minimum at the appropriate level. As these institutions presently exist they are riddled with grave injustices. But there presumably are ways of running them compatible with their basic design and intention so that the difference principle is satisfied consistent with the demands of liberty and fair equality of opportunity. It is this fact which underlies our assurance that these arrangements can be made just.

It is evident that the role of the principle of fair opportunity is to insure that the system of cooperation is one of pure procedural justice. Unless it is satisfied, distributive justice could not be left to take care of itself, even within a restricted range. Now the great practical advantage of pure procedural justice is that it is no longer necessary in meeting the demands of justice to keep track of the endless variety of circumstances and the changing relative positions of particular persons. One avoids the problem of defining principles to cope with the enormous complexities which would arise if such details were relevant. It is a mistake to focus attention on the varying relative positions of individuals and to require that every change, considered as a single transaction viewed in isolation, be in itself just. It is the arrangement of the basic structure which is to be judged, and judged from a general point of view. Unless we are prepared to criticize it from the standpoint of a relevant representative man in some particular position, we have no complaint against it. Thus the acceptance of the two principles constitutes an understanding to discard as irrelevant as a matter of social justice much of the information and many of the complications of everyday life.

In pure procedural justice, then, distributions of advantages are not appraised in the first instance by confronting a stock of benefits available with given desires and needs of known individuals. The allotment of the items produced takes place in accordance with the public system of rules, and this system determines what is produced, how much is produced, and by what means. It also determines legitimate claims the honoring of which yields the resulting distribution. Thus in this kind of procedural justice the correctness of the distribution is founded on the justice of the scheme of cooperation from which it arises and on answering the claims of individuals engaged in it. A distribution cannot be judged in isolation from the system of which it is the outcome or from what individuals have done in good faith in the light of established expectations. If it is asked in the abstract whether one distribution of a given stock of things to definite individuals with known desires and preferences is better than another, then there is simply no answer to this question. The conception of the two principles does not interpret the primary problem of distributive justice as one of allocative justice.

By contrast the allocative conception of justice seems naturally to apply when a given collection of goods is to be divided among definite individuals with known desires and needs. The goods to be allotted are not produced by these individuals, nor do these individuals stand in any existing cooperative relations. Since there are no prior claims on the things to be distributed, it is natural to share them out according to desires and needs, or even to maximize the net balance of satisfaction. Justice becomes a kind of efficiency, unless equality is preferred. Suitably generalized, the allocative conception leads to the classical utilitarian view. For as we have seen, this doctrine assimilates justice to the benevolence of the impartial spectator and the latter in turn to the most efficient design of institutions to promote the greatest balance of satisfaction. As I observed earlier,[6] on this conception society is thought of as so many separate individuals each defining a separate line along which rights and duties are to be assigned and scarce means of satisfaction allocated in accordance with rules so as to give the most complete fulfillment of desire. I shall put aside consideration of the other aspects of this notion until later. The point to note here is that utilitarianism does not interpret the basic structure as a scheme of pure procedural justice. For the utilitarian has, in principle anyway, an independent standard for judging all distributions, namely, whether they produce the greatest net balance of satisfaction. In his theory, institutions are more or less imperfect arrangements for bringing about this end. Thus given existing desires and preferences, and the natural continuations into the future which they allow, the statesman's aim is to set up those social schemes that will best approximate an already specified goal. Since these arrangements are subject to the unavoidable constraints and hindrances of everyday life, the basic structure is a case of imperfect procedural justice.

· · ·

Primary Social Goods as the Basis of Expectations

So much, then, for a brief statement and explanation of the two principles of justice and of the procedural conception which they express. . . . I begin with a discussion of expectations and how they are to be estimated.

6. [Rawls's earlier discussion of classical utilitarianism is omitted from this selection.]

The significance of this question can be brought out by a comparison with utilitarianism. When applied to the basic structure the principle of utility requires us to maximize the algebraic sum of expectations taken over all relevant positions. (The classical principle weights these expectations by the number of persons in these positions, the average principle by the fraction of persons.) Leaving aside for the next section the question as to what defines a relevant position, it is clear that utilitarianism assumes some fairly accurate measure of these expectations. Not only is it necessary to have a cardinal measure for each representative individual but these measures must make sense in interpersonal comparisons. Some method of correlating the scales of different persons is presupposed if we are to say that the gains of some are to outweigh the losses of others. It is unreasonable to demand great precision, yet these estimates cannot be left to our unguided intuition. For judgments of a greater balance of interests leave too much room for conflicting claims. Moreover, these judgments may be based on ethical and other notions, not to mention bias and self-interest, which puts their validity in question. Simply because we do in fact make what we call interpersonal comparisons of well-being does not mean that we understand the basis of these comparisons or that we should accept them as sound. To settle these matters we need to give an account of these judgments, to set out the criteria that underlie them. For questions of social justice we should try to find some objective grounds for these comparisons, ones that men can recognize and agree to. At the present time, there appears to be no satisfactory answer to these difficulties from a utilitarian point of view. Therefore it seems that, for the time being at least, the principle of utility makes such heavy demands on our ability to estimate the balance of advantages that it defines at best an ambiguous court of appeal for questions of justice.

I do not assume, though, that a satisfactory solution to these problems is impossible. While these difficulties are real, and the difference principle is framed to circumvent them, I do not wish to stress its relative merits on this score. For one thing, skepticism about interpersonal comparisons is often based on questionable views: for example, that the intensity of pleasure or of the enjoyment which indicates well-being is the intensity of pure sensation; and that while the intensity of such sensations can be experienced and known by the subject, it is impossible for others to know it or to infer it with reasonable certainty. Both these contentions seem wrong. Indeed, the second is simply part of a skepticism about the existence of other minds, unless it is shown why judgments of well-being present special problems which cannot be overcome. I believe that the real difficulties with utilitarianism lie elsewhere. The main point is that even if interpersonal comparisons of satisfaction can be made, these comparisons must reflect values which it makes sense to pursue. It is irrational to advance one end rather than another simply because it can be more accurately estimated. The controversy about interpersonal comparisons tends to obscure the real question, namely, whether the total (or average) happiness is to be maximized in the first place.

The difference principle meets some of the difficulties in making interpersonal comparisons. This it does in two ways. First of all, as long as we can identify the least advantaged representative man, only ordinal judgments of well-being are required from then on. We know from what position the social system is to be judged. It does not matter how much worse off this representative individual is than the others. If positions can be ranked as better or worse, the lowest can be found. The further difficulties of cardinal measurement do not arise since no other interpersonal comparisons are necessary. And, of course, in maximizing with respect to the least favored representative man, we need not go beyond ordinal judgments. If we can decide whether a change in the basic structure makes him better or worse off, we can determine his best situation. We do not have to know how much he prefers one situation to another. The difference principle, then, asks less of our judgments of welfare. We never have to calculate a sum of advantages involving a cardinal measure. While qualitative interpersonal comparisons are made in finding the bottom position, for the rest the ordinal judgments of one representative man suffice.

The difference principle also avoids difficulties by introducing a simplification for the basis of interpersonal comparisons. These comparisons are made in terms of expectations of primary social goods. In fact, I define these expectations simply as the index of these goods which a representative individual can look forward to. One man's expectations are greater than another's if this index for some one in his position is greater. Now primary goods, as I have already remarked, are things which it is supposed a rational man wants whatever else he wants. Regardless of what an individual's rational plans are in detail, it is assumed that there are various things which he would prefer more of rather than less. With more of these goods men can generally be assured of greater success in carrying out their intentions and in advancing their ends, whatever these ends may be. The primary social goods, to give them in broad categories, are rights and liberties, opportunities and powers, income and wealth. (A very important primary good is a sense of one's own worth; but for simplicity I leave this aside until much later.) It seems evident that in general these things fit the description of primary goods. They are social goods in view of their connection with the basic structure; liberties and powers are defined by the rules of major institutions and the distribution of income and wealth is regulated by them.

The theory of the good adopted to account for primary goods. . . . is not in dispute between the contract doctrine and utilitarianism. The main idea is that a person's good is determined by what is for him the most rational long-term plan of life given reasonably favorable circumstances. A man is happy when he is more or less successfully in the way of carrying out this plan. To put it briefly, the good is the satisfaction of rational desire. We are to suppose, then, that each individual has a rational plan of life drawn up subject to the conditions that confront him. This plan is designed to permit the harmonious satisfaction of his interests. It schedules activities so that various desires can be fulfilled without interference. It is arrived at by rejecting other plans that are either less likely to succeed or do not provide for such an inclusive attainment of aims. Given the alternatives available, a rational plan is one which cannot be improved upon; there is no other plan which, taking everything into account, would be preferable.

Now the assumption is that though men's rational plans do have different final ends, they nevertheless all require for their execution certain primary goods, natural and social. Plans differ since individual abilities, circumstances, and wants differ; rational plans are adjusted to these contingencies. But whatever one's system of ends, primary goods are necessary means. Greater intelligence, wealth and opportunity, for example, allow a person to achieve ends he could not rationally contemplate otherwise. The expectations of representative men are, then, to be defined by the index of primary social goods available to them. While the persons in the original position do not know their conception of the good, they do know, I assume, that they prefer more rather than less primary goods. And this information is sufficient for them to know how to advance their interests in the initial situation.

Let us consider several difficulties. One problem clearly is the construction of the index itself. How are the different primary social goods to be weighed? Assuming that the two principles of justice are serially ordered, this problem is greatly simplified. The fundamental liberties are always equal, and there is fair equality of opportunity; one does not need to balance these liberties and rights against other values. The primary social goods that vary in their distribution are the powers and prerogatives of authority, and income and wealth. But the difficulties are not so great as they might seem at first because of the nature of the difference principle. The only index problem that concerns us is that for the least advantaged group. The primary goods enjoyed by other representative individuals are adjusted to raise this index, subject of course to the usual constraints. It is unnecessary to define weights for the more favored positions in any detail, as long as we are sure that they are more favored. But often this is easy since they frequently have more of every primary good, greater powers and wealth tending to go together. If we know how the distribution of goods to the more favored affects the expectations of the most disfavored, this is sufficient. The index problem largely reduces, then, to that of weighting primary goods for the least advantaged, for those with the least authority and the lowest income, since these also tend to be associated. We try to do this by taking up the standpoint of the representative individual from this group and asking which combination of primary social goods it would be rational for him to prefer. In doing this we admittedly rely upon our intuitive capacities. This cannot be avoided entirely, however. The aim is to replace moral judgments by those of rational prudence and to make the appeal to intuition more limited in scope, more sharply focused.

Another difficulty is this. It may be objected that expectations should not be defined as an index of primary goods anyway but rather as the satisfactions to be expected when plans are executed using these goods. After all, it is in the fulfillment of these plans that men gain happiness, and therefore the estimate of expectations should not be founded on the available means. Justice as fairness, however, takes a different view. For it does not look behind the use which persons make of the rights and opportunities available to them in order to measure, much less to maximize, the satisfactions they achieve. Nor does it try to evaluate the relative merits of different conceptions of the good. Instead, it is assumed that the members of society are rational persons able to adjust their conceptions of the good to their situation. There is no necessity to compare the worth of the conceptions of different persons once it is supposed they are compatible with the principles of justice. Everyone is assured an equal liberty to pursue whatever plan of life he pleases as long as it does not violate what justice demands. Men share in primary goods on the principle that some can have more if they are acquired in ways which improve the situation of those who have less. Once the whole arrangement is set up and going no questions are asked about the totals of satisfaction or perfection. Things work themselves out according to the principles that would be chosen in the original position. On this conception of social justice, then, expectations are defined as the index of primary goods that a representative man can reasonably look forward to. A person's prospects are improved when he can anticipate a preferred collection of these goods.

It is worth noting that this interpretation of expectations represents, in effect, an agreement to compare men's situations solely by reference to things which it is assumed they all prefer more of. This seems the most feasible way to establish a publicly recognized objective measure, that is, a common measure that reasonable persons can accept. Whereas there cannot be a similar agreement on how to estimate happiness as defined, say, by men's success in executing their rational plans, much less on the intrinsic value of these plans. Now founding expectations on primary goods is another simplifying device. I should like to comment in passing that this and other simplifications are accompanied by some sort of philosophical explanation, though this is not strictly necessary. Theoretical assumptions must, of course, do more than simplify; they must identify essential elements that explain the facts we want to understand. Similarly, the parts of a theory of justice must represent basic moral features of the social structure, and if it appears that some of these are being left aside, it is desirable to assure ourselves that such is not the case. I shall try to follow this rule. But even so, the soundness of the theory of justice is shown as much in its consequences as in the prima facie acceptability of its premises.

· · ·

The Tendency to Equality

I wish to conclude this discussion of the two principles by explaining the sense in which they express an egalitarian conception of justice. Also I should like to forestall the objection to the principle of fair opportunity that it leads to a callous meritocratic society. In order to prepare the way for doing this, I note several aspects of the conception of justice that I have set out.

First we may observe that the difference principle gives some weight to the considerations singled out by the principle of redress. This is the principle that undeserved inequalities call for redress; and since inequalities of birth and natural endowment are undeserved, these inequalities are to be somehow compensated for. Thus the principle holds that in order to treat all persons equally, to provide genuine equality of opportunity, society must give more attention to those with fewer native assets and to those born into the less favorable social positions. The idea is to redress the bias of contingencies in the direction of equality. In pursuit of this principle greater resources might be spent on the education of the less rather than the more intelligent, at least over a certain time of life, say the earlier years of school.

Now the principle of redress has not to my knowledge been proposed as the sole criterion of justice, as the single aim of the social order. It is plausible as most such principles are only as a prima facie principle, one that is to be weighed in the balance with others. For example, we are to weigh it against the principle to improve the average standard of life, or to advance the common good. But whatever other principles we hold, the claims of redress are to be taken into account. It is thought to represent one of the elements in our conception of justice. Now the difference principle is not of course the principle of redress. It does not require society to try to even out handicaps as if all were expected to compete on a fair basis in the same race. But the difference principle would allocate resources in education, say, so as to improve the long-term expectation of the least favored. If this end is attained by giving more attention to the better endowed, it is permissible; otherwise not. And in making this decision, the value of education should not be assessed solely in terms of economic efficiency and social welfare. Equally if not more important is the role of education in enabling a person to enjoy the culture of his society and to take part in its affairs, and in this way to provide for each individual a secure sense of his own worth.

Thus although the difference principle is not the same as that of redress, it does achieve some of the intent of the latter principle. It transforms the aims of the basic structure so that the total scheme of institutions no longer emphasizes social efficiency and technocratic values. We see then that the difference principle represents, in effect, an agreement to regard the distribution of natural talents as a common asset and to share in the benefits of this distribution whatever it turns out to be. Those who have been favored by nature, whoever they are, may gain from their good fortune only on terms that improve the situation of those who have lost out. The naturally advantaged are not to gain merely because they are more gifted, but only to cover the costs of training and education and for using their endowments in ways that help the less fortunate as well. No one deserves his greater natural capacity nor merits a more favorable starting place in society. But it does not follow that one should eliminate these distinctions. There is another way to deal with them. The basic structure can be arranged so that these contingencies work for the good of the least fortunate. Thus we are led to the difference principle if we wish to set up the social system so that no one gains or loses from his arbitrary place in the distribution of natural assets or his initial position in society without giving or receiving compensating advantages in return.

In view of these remarks we may reject the contention that the ordering of institutions is always defective because the distribution of natural talents and the contingencies of social circumstance are unjust, and this injustice must inevitably carry over to human arrangements. Occasionally this reflection is offered as an excuse for ignoring injustice, as if the refusal to acquiesce in injustice is on a par with being unable to accept death. The natural distribution is neither just nor unjust; nor is it unjust that persons are born into society at some particular position. These are simply natural facts. What is just and unjust is the way that institutions deal with these facts. Aristocratic and caste societies are unjust because they make these contingencies the ascriptive basis for belonging to more or less enclosed and privileged social classes. The basic structure of these societies incorporates the arbitrariness found in nature. But there is no necessity for men to resign themselves to these contingencies. The social system is not an unchangeable order beyond human control but a pattern of human action. In justice as fairness men agree to share one another's fate. In designing institutions they undertake to avail themselves of the accidents of nature and social circumstance only when doing so is for the common benefit. The two principles are a fair way of meeting the arbitrariness of fortune; and while no doubt imperfect in other ways, the institutions which satisfy these principles are just.

A further point is that the difference principle expresses a conception of reciprocity. It is a principle of mutual benefit. We have seen that, at least when chain connection holds, each representative man can accept the basic structure as designed to advance his interests. The social order can be justified to everyone, and in particular to those who are least favored; and in this sense it is egalitarian. But it seems necessary to consider in an intuitive way how the condition of mutual benefit is satisfied. Consider any two representative men A and B, and let B be the one who is less favored. Actually, since we are most interested in the comparison with the least favored man, let us assume that B is this individual. Now B can accept A's being better off since A's advantages have been gained in ways that improve B's prospects. If A were not allowed his better position, B would be even worse off than he is. The difficulty is to show that A has no grounds for complaint. Perhaps he is required to have less than he might since his having more would result in some loss to B. Now what can be said to the more favored man? To begin with, it is clear that the well-being of each depends on a scheme of social cooperation without which no one could have a satisfactory life. Secondly, we can ask for the willing cooperation of everyone only if the terms of the scheme are reasonable. The difference principle, then, seems to be a fair basis on which those better endowed, or more fortunate in their social circumstances, could expect others to collaborate with them when some workable arrangement is a necessary condition of the good of all.

There is a natural inclination to object that those better situated deserve their greater advantages whether or not they are to the benefit of others. At this point it is necessary to be clear about the notion of desert. It is perfectly true that given a just system of cooperation as a scheme of public rules and the expectations set up by it, those who, with the prospect of improving their condition, have done what the system announces that it

will reward are entitled to their advantages. In this sense the more fortunate have a claim to their better situation; their claims are legitimate
expectations established by social institutions, and the community is obli-
gated to meet them. But this sense of desert presupposes the existence of
the cooperative scheme; it is irrelevant to the question whether in the first
place the scheme is to be designed in accordance with the difference
principle or some other criterion.

Perhaps some will think that the person with greater natural endowments deserves those assets and the superior character that made their
development possible. Because he is more worthy in this sense, he deserves
the greater advantages that he could achieve with them. This view, however, is surely incorrect. It seems to be one of the fixed points of our
considered judgments that no one deserves his place in the distribution of
native endowments, any more than one deserves one's initial starting place
in society. The assertion that a man deserves the superior character that
enables him to make the effort to cultivate his abilities is equally problem-
atic; for his character depends in large part upon fortunate family and
social circumstances for which he can claim no credit. The notion of
desert seems not to apply to these cases. Thus the more advantaged
representative man cannot say that he deserves and therefore has a right to
a scheme of cooperation in which he is permitted to acquire benefits in
ways that do not contribute to the welfare of others. There is no basis for
his making this claim. From the standpoint of common sense, then, the
difference principle appears to be acceptable both to the more advantaged
and to the less advantaged individual.

. . .

A further merit of the difference principle is that it provides an interpretation of the principle of fraternity. In comparison with liberty and
equality, the idea of fraternity has had a lesser place in democratic theory.
It is thought to be less specifically a political concept, not in itself defining
any of the democratic rights but conveying instead certain attitudes of
mind and forms of conduct without which we would lose sight of the
values expressed by these rights. Or closely related to this, fraternity is
held to represent a certain equality of social esteem manifest in various
public conventions and in the absence of manners of deference and servility. No doubt fraternity does imply these things, as well as a sense of
civic friendship and social solidarity, but so understood it expresses no
definite requirement. We have yet to find a principle of justice that
matches the underlying idea. The difference principle, however, does
seem to correspond to a natural meaning of fraternity: namely, to the idea
of not wanting to have greater advantages unless this is to the benefit of

others who are less well off. The family, in its ideal conception and often in practice, is one place where the principle of maximizing the sum of advantages is rejected. Members of a family commonly do not wish to gain unless they can do so in ways that further the interests of the rest. Now wanting to act on the difference principle has precisely this consequence. Those better circumstanced are willing to have their greater advantages only under a scheme in which this works out for the benefit of the less fortunate.

The ideal of fraternity is sometimes thought to involve ties of sentiment and feeling which it is unrealistic to expect between members of the wider society. And this is surely a further reason for its relative neglect in democratic theory. Many have felt that it has no proper place in political affairs. But if it is interpreted as incorporating the requirements of the difference principle, it is not an impracticable conception. It does seem that the institutions and policies which we most confidently think to be just satisfy its demands, at least in the sense that the inequalities permitted by them contribute to the well-being of the less favored. On this interpretation, then, the principle of fraternity is a perfectly feasible standard. Once we accept it we can associate the traditional ideas of liberty, equality, and fraternity with the democratic interpretation of the two principles of justice as follows: liberty corresponds to the first principle, equality to the idea of equality in the first principle together with equality of fair opportunity, and fraternity to the difference principle. In this way we have found a place for the conception of fraternity in the democratic interpretation of the two principles, and we see that it imposes a definite requirement on the basic structure of society. The other aspects of fraternity should not be forgotten, but the difference principle expresses its fundamental meaning from the standpoint of social justice.

Now it seems evident in the light of these observations that the democratic interpretation of the two principles will not lead to a meritocratic society. This form of social order follows the principle of careers open to talents and uses equality of opportunity as a way of releasing men's energies in the pursuit of economic prosperity and political dominion. There exists a marked disparity between the upper and lower classes in both means of life and the rights and privileges of organizational authority. The culture of the poorer strata is impoverished while that of the governing and technocratic elite is securely based on the service of the national ends of power and wealth. Equality of opportunity means an equal chance to leave the less fortunate behind in the personal quest for influence and social position. Thus a meritocratic society is a danger for the other interpretations of the principles of justice but not for the democratic conception. For, as we have just seen, the difference principle transforms the aims of society in fundamental respects. This consequence is even more obvious once we note that we must when necessary take into account the essential primary good of self-respect and the fact that a well-ordered society is a social union of social unions. It follows that the confident sense of their own worth should be sought for the least favored and this limits the forms of hierarchy and the degrees of inequality that justice permits. Thus, for example, resources for education are not to be allotted solely or necessarily mainly according to their return as estimated in productive trained abilities, but also according to their worth in enriching the personal and social life of citizens, including here the less favored. As a society progresses the latter consideration becomes increasingly more important.

These remarks must suffice to sketch the conception of social justice expressed by the two principles for institutions.

·   ·   ·

[The final and fullest statement of Rawls's two principles of justice in his book is as follows:]

First Principle
   Each person is to have an equal right to the most extensive total system of equal basic liberties compatible with a similar system of liberty for all.
Second Principle
   Social and economic inequalities are to be arranged so that they are both:
      (a) to the greatest benefit of the least advantaged, consistent with the just savings principle, and
      (b) attached to offices and positions open to all under conditions of fair equality of opportunity.
First Priority Rule (The Priority of Liberty)
   The principles of justice are to be ranked in lexical order and therefore liberty can be restricted only for the sake of liberty. There are two cases:
      (a) a less extensive liberty must strengthen the total system of liberty shared by all;
      (b) a less than equal liberty must be acceptable to those with the lesser liberty.
Second Priority Rule (The Priority of Justice over Efficiency and Welfare)
   The second principle of justice is lexically prior to the principle of efficiency and to that of maximizing the sum of advantages; and fair opportunity is prior to the difference principle. There are two cases:

(a) an inequality of opportunity must enhance the opportunities of those with the lesser opportunity;

(b) an excessive rate of saving must on balance mitigate the burden of those bearing this hardship.

General Conception

All social primary goods—liberty and opportunity, income and wealth, and the bases of self-respect—are to be distributed equally unless an unequal distribution of any or all of these goods is to the advantage of the least favored.

13

Robert Nozick,
"Equality versus Entitlement,"
from *Anarchy, State, and Utopia*

Robert Nozick is Pellegrino University Professor at Harvard University. In addition to political philosophy, he has written on a wide range of issues including the theory of knowledge and the meaning of life. In this selection from Anarchy, State, and Utopia, *his major work of political philosophy, Nozick argues against what he calls "patterned" principles of justice, of which John Rawls's two principles of justice as fairness are a prominent example. Nozick's own view, the entitlement theory of justice, is that individuals have a right to their "holdings" as long as they acquired those holdings fairly, regardless of the overall pattern of holdings.*

Patterning

The entitlement principles of justice in holdings that we have sketched are historical principles of justice. To better understand their precise character, we shall distinguish them from another subclass of the historical principles. Consider, as an example, the principle of distribution according to moral merit. This principle requires that total distributive shares vary directly with moral merit; no person should have a greater share than anyone whose moral merit is greater. (If moral merit could be not merely ordered but measured on an interval or ratio scale, stronger principles could be formulated.) Or consider the principle that results by substituting "usefulness to society" for "moral merit" in the previous principle. Or instead of "distribute according to moral merit," or "distribute according to usefulness to society," we might consider "distribute according to the weighted sum of moral merit, usefulness to society, and need," with the weights of the different dimensions equal. Let us call a principle of distribution *patterned* if it specifies that a distribution is to vary along with some natural dimension, weighted sum of natural dimensions, or lexicographic ordering of natural dimensions. And let us say a distribution is patterned if it accords with some patterned principle. (I speak of natural dimensions, admittedly without a general criterion for them, because for any set of holdings some artificial dimensions can be gimmicked up to vary along with the distribution of the set.) The principle of distribution in accordance with moral merit is a patterned historical principle, which specifies a patterned distribution. "Distribute according to I.Q." is a patterned principle that looks to information not contained in distributional matrices. It is not historical, however, in that it does not look to any past actions creating differential entitlements to evaluate a distribution; it requires only distributional matrices whose columns are labeled by I.Q. scores. The distribution in a society, however, may be composed of such simple patterned distributions, without itself being simply patterned. Different sectors may operate different patterns, or some combination of patterns may operate in different proportions across a society. A distribution composed in this manner, from a small number of patterned distributions, we also shall term "patterned." And we extend the use of "pattern" to include the overall designs put forth by combinations of end-state principles.

Almost every suggested principle of distributive justice is patterned: to each according to his moral merit, or needs, or marginal product, or how hard he tries, or the weighted sum of the foregoing, and so on. The principle of entitlement we have sketched is *not* patterned.* There is no one natural dimension or weighted sum or combination of a small number of natural dimensions that yields the distributions generated in accordance with the principle of entitlement. The set of holdings that results when some persons receive their marginal products, others win at gambling, others receive a share of their mate's income, others receive gifts from foundations, others receive interest on loans, others receive gifts from admirers, others receive returns on investment, others make for them-

---

*One might try to squeeze a patterned conception of distributive justice into the framework of the entitlement conception, by formulating a gimmicky obligatory "principle of transfer" that would lead to the pattern. For example, the principle that if one has more than the mean income one must transfer everything one holds above the mean to persons below the mean so as to bring them up to (but not over) the mean. We can formulate a criterion for a "principle of transfer" to rule out such obligatory transfers, or we can say that no correct principle of transfer, no principle of transfer in a free society will be like this. The former is probably the better course, though the latter also is true.

Alternatively, one might think to make the entitlement conception instantiate a pattern, by using matrix entries that express the relative strength of a person's entitlements as measured by some real-valued function. But even if the limitation to natural dimensions failed to exclude this function, the resulting edifice would *not* capture our system of entitlements to *particular* things.

selves much of what they have, others find things, and so on, will not be
patterned. Heavy strands of patterns will run through it; significant portions of the variance in holdings will be accounted for by pattern-variables.
If most people most of the time choose to transfer some of their entitlements to others only in exchange for something from them, then a large
part of what many people hold will vary with what they held that others
wanted. More details are provided by the theory of marginal productivity.
But gifts to relatives, charitable donations, bequests to children, and the
like, are not best conceived, in the first instance, in this manner. Ignoring
the strands of pattern, let us suppose for the moment that a distribution
actually arrived at by the operation of the principle of entitlement is
random with respect to any pattern. Though the resulting set of holdings
will be unpatterned, it will not be incomprehensible, for it can be seen as
arising from the operation of a small number of principles. These principles specify how an initial distribution may arise (the principle of acquisition of holdings) and how distributions may be transformed into others
(the principle of transfer of holdings). The process whereby the set of
holdings is generated will be intelligible, though the set of holdings itself
that results from this process will be unpatterned.

The writings of F. A. Hayek focus less than is usually done upon what
patterning distributive justice requires. Hayek argues that we cannot know
enough about each person's situation to distribute to each according to his
moral merit (but would justice demand we do so if we did have this
knowledge?); and he goes on to say, "our objection is against all attempts to
impress upon society a deliberately chosen pattern of distribution,
whether it be an order of equality or of inequality."[1] However, Hayek
concludes that in a free society there will be distribution in accordance
with value rather than moral merit; that is, in accordance with the perceived value of a person's actions and services to others. Despite his
rejection of a patterned conception of distributive justice, Hayek himself
suggests a pattern he thinks justifiable: distribution in accordance with the
perceived benefits given to others, leaving room for the complaint that a
free society does not realize exactly this pattern. Stating this patterned
strand of a free capitalist society more precisely, we get "To each according
to how much he benefits others who have the resources for benefiting
those who benefit them." This will seem arbitrary unless some acceptable
initial set of holdings is specified, or unless it is held that the operation of
the system over time washes out any significant effects from the initial set
of holdings. As an example of the latter, if almost anyone would have

1. F. A. Hayek, *The Constitution of Liberty* (Chicago: University of Chicago Press,
1960), p. 87 [p. 109 in this anthology].

bought a car from Henry Ford, the supposition that it was an arbitrary matter who held the money then (and so bought) would not place Henry Ford's earnings under a cloud. In any event, *his* coming to hold it is not arbitrary. Distribution according to benefits to others *is* a major patterned strand in a free capitalist society, as Hayek correctly points out, but it is only a strand and does not constitute the whole pattern of a system of entitlements (namely, inheritance, gifts for arbitrary reasons, charity, and so on) or a standard that one should insist a society fit. Will people tolerate for long a system yielding distributions that they believe are unpatterned? No doubt people will not long accept a distribution they believe is *unjust*. People want their society to be and to look just. But must the look of justice reside in a resulting pattern rather than in the underlying generating principles? We are in no position to conclude that the inhabitants of a society embodying an entitlement conception of justice in holdings will find it unacceptable. Still, it must be granted that were people's reasons for transferring some of their holdings to others always irrational or arbitrary, we would find this disturbing. (Suppose people always determined what holdings they would transfer, and to whom, by using a random device.) We feel more comfortable upholding the justice of an entitlement system if most of the transfers under it are done for reasons. This does not mean necessarily that all deserve what holdings they receive. It means only that there is a purpose or point to someone's transferring a holding to one person rather than to another; that usually we can see what the transferrer thinks he's gaining, what cause he thinks he's serving, what goals he thinks he's helping to achieve, and so forth. Since in a capitalist society people often transfer holdings to others in accordance with how much they perceive these others benefiting them, the fabric constituted by the individual transactions and transfers is largely reasonable and intelligible.* (Gifts to loved ones, bequests to children, charity to the needy also are nonarbitrary components of the fabric.) In stressing the large strand of distribution in accordance with benefit to others, Hayek shows the point of many transfers, and so shows that the system of transfer of entitlements is

---

*We certainly benefit because great economic incentives operate to get others to spend much time and energy to figure out how to serve us by providing things we will want to pay for. It is not mere paradox mongering to wonder whether capitalism should be criticized for most rewarding and hence encouraging, not individualists like Thoreau who go about their own lives, but people who are occupied with serving others and winning them as customers. But to defend capitalism one need not think businessmen are the finest human types. (I do not mean to join here the general maligning of businessmen, either.) Those who think the finest should acquire the most can try to convince their fellows to transfer resources in accordance with *that* principle.

not just spinning its gears aimlessly. The system of entitlements is defensible when constituted by the individual aims of individual transactions. No overarching aim is needed, no distributional pattern is required.

To think that the task of a theory of distributive justice is to fill in the blank in "to each according to his ———" is to be predisposed to search for a pattern; and the separate treatment of "from each according to his ———" treats production and distribution as two separate and independent issues. On an entitlement view these are *not* two separate questions. Whoever makes something, having bought or contracted for all other held resources used in the process (transferring some of his holdings for these cooperating factors), is entitled to it. The situation is *not* one of something's getting made, and there being an open question of who is to get it. Things come into the world already attached to people having entitlements over them. From the point of view of the historical entitlement conception of justice in holdings, those who start afresh to complete "to each according to his ———" treat objects as if they appeared from nowhere, out of nothing. A complete theory of justice might cover this limit case as well; perhaps here is a use for the usual conceptions of distributive justice.

So entrenched are maxims of the usual form that perhaps we should present the entitlement conception as a competitor. Ignoring acquisition and rectification, we might say:

> From each according to what he chooses to do, to each according to what he makes for himself (perhaps with the contracted aid of others) and what others choose to do for him and choose to give him of what they've been given previously (under this maxim) and haven't yet expended or transferred.

This, the discerning reader will have noticed, has its defects as a slogan. So as a summary and great simplification (and not as a maxim with any independent meaning) we have:

> *From each as they choose, to each as they are chosen.*

How Liberty Upsets Patterns

It is not clear how those holding alternative conceptions of distributive justice can reject the entitlement conception of justice in holdings. For suppose a distribution favored by one of these non-entitlement conceptions is realized. Let us suppose it is your favorite one and let us call this distribution D_1; perhaps everyone has an equal share, perhaps shares vary in accordance with some dimension you treasure. Now suppose that Wilt Chamberlain is greatly in demand by basketball teams, being a great gate attraction. (Also suppose contracts run only for a year, with players being free agents.) He signs the following sort of contract with a team: In each home game, twenty-five cents from the price of each ticket of admission goes to him. (We ignore the question of whether he is "gouging" the owners, letting them look out for themselves.) The season starts, and people cheerfully attend his team's games; they buy their tickets, each time dropping a separate twenty-five cents of their admission price into a special box with Chamberlain's name on it. They are excited about seeing him play; it is worth the total admission price to them. Let us suppose that in one season one million persons attend his home games, and Wilt Chamberlain winds up with $250,000, a much larger sum than the average income and larger even than anyone else has. Is he entitled to this income? Is this new distribution D_2, unjust? If so, why? There is *no* question about whether each of the people was entitled to the control over the resources they held in D_1; because that was the distribution (your favorite) that (for the purposes of argument) we assumed was acceptable. Each of these persons *chose* to give twenty-five cents of their money to Chamberlain. They could have spent it on going to the movies, or on candy bars, or on copies of *Dissent* magazine, or of *Monthly Review*. But they all, at least one million of them, converged on giving it to Wilt Chamberlain in exchange for watching him play basketball. If D_1 was a just distribution, and people voluntarily moved from it to D_2, transferring parts of their shares they were given under D_1 (what was it for if not to do something with?), isn't D_2 also just? If the people were entitled to dispose of the resources to which they were entitled (under D_1), didn't this include their being entitled to give it to, or exchange it with, Wilt Chamberlain? Can anyone else complain on grounds of justice? Each other person already has his legitimate share under D_1. Under D_1, there is nothing that anyone has that anyone else has a claim of justice against. After someone transfers something to Wilt Chamberlain, third parties *still* have their legitimate shares; *their* shares are not changed. By what process could such a transfer among two persons give rise to a legitimate claim of distributive justice on a portion of what was transferred, by a third party who had no claim of justice on any holding of the others *before* the transfer?* To cut off objections irrelevant

*Might not a transfer have instrumental effects on a third party, changing his feasible options? (But what if the two parties to the transfer independently had used their holdings in this fashion?) . . . Note here that this question concedes the point for distributions of ultimate intrinsic noninstrumental goods (pure utility

here, we might imagine the exchanges occurring in a socialist society, after hours. After playing whatever basketball he does in his daily work, or doing whatever other daily work he does, Wilt Chamberlain decides to put in *overtime* to earn additional money. (First his work quota is set; he works time over that.) Or imagine it is a skilled juggler people like to see, who puts on shows after hours.

Why might someone work overtime in a society in which it is assumed their needs are satisfied? Perhaps because they care about things other than needs. I like to write in books that I read, and to have easy access to books for browsing at odd hours. It would be very pleasant and convenient to have the resources of Widener Library in my back yard. No society, I assume, will provide such resources close to each person who would like them as part of his regular allotment (under D_1). Thus, persons either must do without some extra things that they want, or be allowed to do something extra to get some of these things. On what basis could the inequalities that would eventuate be forbidden? Notice also that small factories would spring up in a socialist society, unless forbidden. I melt down some of my personal possessions (under D_1) and build a machine out of the material. I offer you, and others, a philosophy lecture once a week in exchange for your cranking the handle on my machine, whose products I exchange for yet other things, and so on. (The raw materials used by the machine are given to me by others who possess them under D_1, in exchange for hearing lectures.) Each person might participate to gain things over and above their allotment under D_1. Some persons even might want to leave their job in socialist industry and work full time in this private sector. I shall say something more about these issues in the next chapter. Here I wish merely to note how private property even in means of production would occur in a socialist society that did not forbid people to

---

experiences, so to speak) that are transferable. It also might be objected that the transfer might make a third party more envious because it worsens his position relative to someone else. I find it incomprehensible how this can be thought to involve a claim of justice.

Here and elsewhere in this chapter, a theory which incorporates elements of pure procedural justice might find what I say acceptable, *if* kept in its proper place; that is, if background institutions exist to ensure the satisfaction of certain conditions on distributive shares. But if these institutions are not themselves the sum or invisible-hand result of people's voluntary (nonaggressive) actions, the constraints they impose require justification. At no point does *our* argument assume any background institutions more extensive than those of the minimal nightwatchman state, a state limited to protecting persons against murder, assault, theft, fraud, and so forth.

use as they wished some of the resources they are given under the socialist distribution D_1. The socialist society would have to forbid capitalist acts between consenting adults.

The general point illustrated by the Wilt Chamberlain example and the example of the entrepreneur in a socialist society is that no end-state principle or distributional patterned principle of justice can be continuously realized without continuous interference with people's lives. Any favored pattern would be transformed into one unfavored by the principle, by people choosing to act in various ways; for example, by people exchanging goods and services with other people, or giving things to other people, things the transferrers are entitled to under the favored distributional pattern. To maintain a pattern one must either continually interfere to stop people from transferring resources as they wish to, or continually (or periodically) interfere to take from some persons resources that others for some reason chose to transfer to them. (But if some time limit is to be set on how long people may keep resources others voluntarily transfer to them, why let them keep these resources for *any* period of time? Why not have immediate confiscation?) It might be objected that all persons voluntarily will choose to refrain from actions which would upset the pattern. This presupposes unrealistically (1) that all will most want to maintain the pattern (are those who don't, to be "reeducated" or forced to undergo "self-criticism"?), (2) that each can gather enough information about his own actions and the ongoing activities of others to discover which of his actions will upset the pattern, and (3) that diverse and far-flung persons can coordinate their actions to dovetail into the pattern. Compare the manner in which the market is neutral among persons' desires, as it reflects and transmits widely scattered information via prices, and coordinates persons' activities.

It puts things perhaps a bit too strongly to say that every patterned (or end-state) principle is liable to be thwarted by the voluntary actions of the individual parties transferring some of their shares they receive under the principle. For perhaps some *very* weak patterns are not so thwarted. Any distributional pattern with any egalitarian component is overturnable by the voluntary actions of individual persons over time; as is every patterned condition with sufficient content so as actually to have been proposed as presenting the central core of distributive justice. Still, given the possibility that some weak conditions or patterns may not be unstable in this way, it would be better to formulate an explicit description of the kind of interesting and contentful patterns under discussion, and to prove a theorem about their instability. Since the weaker the patterning, the more likely it is that the entitlement system itself satisfies it, a plausible conjecture is that any patterning either is unstable or is satisfied by the entitlement system.

. . .

Equality

The legitimacy of altering social institutions to achieve greater equality of material condition is, though often assumed, rarely argued for. Writers note that in a given country the wealthiest *n* percent of the population holds more than that percentage of the wealth, and the poorest *n* percent holds less; that to get to the wealth of the top *n* percent from the poorest, one must look at the bottom *p* percent (where *p* is vastly greater than *n*), and so forth. They then proceed immediately to discuss how this might be altered. On the entitlement conception of justice in holdings, one cannot decide whether the state must do something to alter the situation merely by looking at a distributional profile or at facts such as these. It depends upon how the distribution came about. Some processes yielding these results would be legitimate, and the various parties would be entitled to their respective holdings. If these distributional facts *did* arise by a legitimate process, then they themselves are legitimate. This is, of course, *not* to say that they may not be changed, provided this can be done without violating people's entitlements. Any persons who favor a particular endstate pattern may choose to transfer some or all of their own holdings so as (at least temporarily) more nearly to realize their desired pattern.

The entitlement conception of justice in holdings makes no presumption in favor of equality, or any other overall end state or patterning. It cannot merely be *assumed* that equality must be built into any theory of justice. There is a surprising dearth of arguments for equality capable of coming to grips with the considerations that underlie a nonglobal and nonpatterned conception of justice in holdings. (However, there is no lack of unsupported statements of a presumption in favor of equality.) I shall consider the argument which has received the most attention from philosophers in recent years; that offered by Bernard Williams in his influential essay "The Idea of Equality."[2] (No doubt many readers will feel that all hangs on some other argument; I would like to see *that* argument precisely set out, in detail.)

2. Bernard Williams, "The Idea of Equality," in *Philosophy, Politics, and Society,* 2nd ser., ed. Peter Laslett and W. G. Runciman (Oxford: Blackwell, 1962), pp. 110–131; reprinted in Joel Feinberg, ed., *Moral Concepts* (New York: Oxford University Press, 1969).

Leaving aside preventive medicine, the proper ground of distribution of medical care is ill health: this is a necessary truth. Now in very many societies, while ill health may work as a necessary condition of receiving treatment, it does not work as a sufficient condition, since such treatment costs money, and not all who are ill have the money; hence the possession of sufficient money becomes in fact an additional necessary condition of actually receiving treatment. . . . When we have the situation in which, for instance, wealth is a further necessary condition of the receipt of medical treatment, we can once more apply the notions of equality and inequality: not now in connection with the inequality between the well and the ill, but in connection with the inequality between the rich ill and the poor ill, since we have straightforwardly the situation of those whose needs are the same not receiving the same treatment, though the needs are the ground of the treatment. This is an irrational state of affairs . . . it is a situation in which reasons are insufficiently operative; it is a situation insufficiently controlled by reasons—and hence by reason itself.[3]

Williams seems to be arguing that if among the different descriptions applying to an activity, there is one that contains an "internal goal" of the activity, then (it is a necessary truth that) the only proper grounds for the performance of the activity, or its allocation if it is scarce, are connected with the effective achievement of the internal goal. If the activity is done upon others, the only proper criterion for distributing the activity is their need for it, if any. Thus it is that Williams says (it is a necessary truth that) the only proper criterion for the distribution of medical care is medical need. Presumably, then, the only proper criterion for the distribution of barbering services is barbering need. But why must the internal goal of the activity take precedence over, for example, the person's particular purpose in performing the activity? (We ignore the question of whether one activity can fall under two different descriptions involving different internal goals.) If someone becomes a barber because he likes talking to a variety of different people, and so on, is it unjust of him to allocate his services to those he most likes to talk to? Or if he works as a barber in order to earn money to pay tuition at school, may he cut the hair of only those who pay or tip well? Why may not a barber use exactly the same criteria in allocating his services as someone else whose activities have no internal goal involving others? Need a gardener allocate his services to those lawns which need him most?

In what way does the situation of a doctor differ? Why must his activities be allocated via the internal goal of medical care? (If there was no "shortage," could some *then* be allocated using other criteria as well?) It

3. Williams, "The Idea of Equality," pp. 121–122.

seems clear that *he* needn't do that; just because he has this skill, why should *he* bear the costs of the desired allocation, why is he less entitled to pursue his own goals, within the special circumstances of practicing medicine, than everyone else? So it is *society* that, somehow, is to arrange things so that the doctor, in pursuing his own goals, allocates according to need; for example, the society pays him to do this. But why must the society do this? (Should they do it for barbering as well?) Presumably, because medical care is important, people need it very much. This is true of food as well, though farming does *not* have an internal goal that refers to other people in the way doctoring does. When the layers of Williams's argument are peeled away, what we arrive at is the claim that society (that is, each of us acting together in some organized fashion) should make provision for the important needs of all of its members. This claim, of course, has been stated many times before. Despite appearances, Williams presents no argument for it.* Like others, Williams looks only to questions of allocation. He ignores the question of where the things or actions to be allocated and distributed come from. Consequently, he does not consider whether they come already tied to people who have entitlements over them (surely the case for service activities, which are people's *actions*), people who therefore may decide for themselves to whom they will give the thing and on what grounds.

Equality of Opportunity

Equality of opportunity has seemed to many writers to be the minimal egalitarian goal, questionable (if at all) only for being too weak. (Many writers also have seen how the existence of the family prevents fully achieving this goal.) There are two ways to attempt to provide such equality: by directly worsening the situations of those more favored with opportunity, or by improving the situation of those less well-favored. The latter requires the use of resources, and so it too involves worsening the situation of some: those from whom holdings are taken in order to improve the situation of others. But holdings to which these people are entitled

---

*We have discussed Williams's position without introducing an essentialist view that some activities necessarily involve certain goals. Instead we have tied the goals to *descriptions* of the activities. For essentialist issues only becloud the discussion, and they still leave open the question of why the only proper ground for allocating the activity is its essentialist goal. The motive for making such an essentialist claim would be to avoid someone's saying: let "schmoctoring" be an activity just like doctoring except that *its* goal is to earn money for the practitioner; has Williams presented any reason why *schmoctoring* services should be allocated according to need?

may not be seized, even to provide equality of opportunity for others. In the absence of magic wands, the remaining means toward equality of opportunity is convincing persons each to choose to devote some of their holdings to achieving it.

The model of a race for a prize is often used in discussions of equality of opportunity. A race where some started closer to the finish line than others would be unfair, as would a race where some were forced to carry heavy weights, or run with pebbles in their sneakers. But life is not a race in which we all compete for a prize which someone has established; there is no unified race, with some person judging swiftness. Instead, there are different persons separately giving other persons different things. Those who do the giving (each of us, at times) usually do not care about desert or about the handicaps labored under; they care simply about what they actually get. No centralized process judges people's use of the opportunities they had; that is not what the processes of social cooperation and exchange are *for*.

There is a reason why some inequality of opportunity might seem *unfair*, rather than merely unfortunate in that some do not have every opportunity (which would be true even if no one else had greater advantage). Often the person entitled to transfer a holding has no special desire to transfer it to a particular person; this contrasts with a bequest to a child or a gift to a particular person. He chooses to transfer to someone who satisfies a certain condition (for example, who can provide him with a certain good or service in exchange, who can do a certain job, who can pay a certain salary), and he would be equally willing to transfer to anyone else who satisfied that condition. Isn't it unfair for one party to receive the transfer, rather than another who had less opportunity to satisfy the condition the transferrer used? Since the giver doesn't care to whom he transfers, provided the recipient satisfies a certain general condition, equality of opportunity to be a recipient in such circumstances would violate no entitlement of the giver. Nor would it violate any entitlement of the person with the greater opportunity; while entitled to what he has, he has no entitlement that it be more than another has. Wouldn't it be *better* if the person with less opportunity had an equal opportunity? If one so could equip him without violating anyone else's entitlements (the magic wand?) shouldn't one do so? Wouldn't it be fairer? If it *would* be fairer, can such fairness also justify overriding some people's entitlements in order to acquire the resources to boost those having poorer opportunities into a more equal competitive position?

The process is competitive in the following way. If the person with greater opportunity didn't exist, the transferrer might deal with some person having lesser opportunity who then would be, under those circumstances, the best person available to deal with. This differs from a situation in which unconnected but similar beings living on different planets, confront different difficulties, and have different opportunities to realize various of their goals. There, the situation of one does *not* affect that of another; though it would be better if the worse planet were better endowed than it is (it also would be better if the better planet were better endowed than *it* is), it wouldn't be *fairer*. It also differs from a situation in which a person does not, though he could, choose to *improve* the situation of another. In the particular circumstances under discussion, a person having lesser opportunities would be better off if some particular person having better opportunities didn't exist. The person having better opportunities can be viewed not merely as someone better off, or as someone not choosing to aid, but as someone *blocking* or *impeding* the person having lesser opportunities from becoming better off.[4] Impeding another by being a more alluring alternative partner in exchange is not to be compared to directly *worsening* the situation of another, as by stealing from him. But still, cannot the person with lesser opportunity justifiably complain at being so impeded by another who does not *deserve* his better opportunity to satisfy certain conditions? (Let us ignore any similar complaints another might make about *him*.)

While feeling the power of the questions of the previous two paragraphs (it is *I* who ask them), I do not believe they overturn a thoroughgoing entitlement conception. If the woman who later became my wife rejected another suitor (whom she otherwise would have married) for me, partially because (I leave aside my lovable nature) of my keen intelligence and good looks, neither of which did I earn, would the rejected less intelligent and less handsome suitor have a legitimate complaint about unfairness? Would my thus impeding the other suitor's winning the hand of fair lady justify taking some resources from others to pay for cosmetic surgery for him and special intellectual training, or to pay to develop in him some sterling trait that I lack in order to equalize our chances of being chosen? (I here take for granted the impermissibility of worsening the situation of the person having better opportunities so as to equalize opportunity; in this sort of case by disfiguring him or injecting drugs or playing noises which prevent him from fully using his intelligence.) *No such consequences follow.* (Against whom would the rejected suitor have a legitimate complaint? Against what?) Nor are things different if the differential opportunities arise from the accumulated effects of people's acting or transferring their entitlement

---

4. Perhaps we should understand Rawls's focus on social cooperation as based upon this triadic notion of one person, by dealing with a second, blocking a third person from dealing with the second.

as they choose. The case is even easier for consumption goods which cannot plausibly be claimed to have any such triadic impeding effect. *Is* it unfair that a child be raised in a home with a swimming pool, using it daily even though he is no more *deserving* than another child whose home is without one? Should such a situation be prohibited? Why then should there be objection to the transfer of the swimming pool to an adult by bequest?

The major objection to speaking of everyone's having a right *to* various things such as equality of opportunity, life, and so on, and enforcing this right, is that these "rights" require a substructure of things and materials and actions; and *other* people may have rights and entitlements over these. No one has a right to something whose realization requires certain uses of things and activities that other people have rights and entitlements over. Other people's rights and entitlements to *particular things* (*that* pencil, *their* body, and so on) and how they choose to exercise these rights and entitlements fix the external environment of any given individual and the means that will be available to him. If his goal requires the use of means which others have rights over, he must enlist their voluntary cooperation. Even to *exercise* his right to determine how something he owns is to be used may require other means he must acquire a right to, for example, food to keep him alive; he must put together, with the cooperation of others, a feasible package.

There are particular rights over particular things held by particular persons, and particular rights to reach agreements with others, *if* you and they together can acquire the means to reach an agreement. (No one has to supply you with a telephone so that you may reach an agreement with another.) No rights exist in conflict with this substructure of particular rights. Since no neatly contoured right to achieve a goal will avoid incompatibility with this substructure, no such rights exist. The particular rights over things fill the space of rights, leaving no room for general rights to be in a certain material condition. The reverse theory would place only such universally held general "rights to" achieve goals or to be in a certain material condition into its substructure so as to determine all else; to my knowledge no serious attempt has been made to state this "reverse" theory.

14

Amartya Sen,
"Equality of What?"

Amartya Sen is Master of Trinity College, Cambridge. He was trained as an economist and is a leading expert on social choice theory and famines. He is the author of numerous works, including Collective Choice and Social Welfare; Poverty and Famines: An Essay on Entitlement and Deprivation; Choice, Welfare, and Measurement; *and most recently* Development as Freedom. *He was awarded the Nobel Memorial Prize in Economic Science in 1998. The lecture reprinted here was given at Stanford University in 1979. Some of the discussion is rather technical, especially toward the beginning of the lecture, but no special expertise is necessary to understand his main points.*

Discussions in moral philosophy have offered us a wide menu in answer to the question: equality of what? In this lecture I shall concentrate on three particular types of equality, viz., (i) utilitarian equality, (ii) total utility equality, and (iii) Rawlsian equality. I shall argue that all three have serious limitations, and that while they fail in rather different and contrasting ways, an adequate theory cannot be constructed even on the *combined* grounds of the three. Towards the end I shall try to present an alternative formulation of equality which seems to me to deserve a good deal more attention than it has received, and I shall not desist from doing some propaganda on its behalf.

First a methodological question. When it is claimed that a certain moral principle has shortcomings, what can be the basis of such an allegation? There seem to be at least two different ways of grounding such a criticism, aside from just checking its *direct* appeal to moral intuition. Once is to check the *implications* of the principle by taking up particular cases in which the results of employing that principle can be seen in a rather stark way, and then to examine these implications against our intuition. I shall call such a critique a *case-implication critique*. The other is to move not from the general to the particular, but from the general to the *more*

NOTE: For helpful comments I am most grateful to Derek Parfit, Jim Griffin, and John Perry.

"Equality of What?" was first published in *The Tanner Lectures on Human Values*, ed. by S. M. McMurrin (Salt Lake City: University of Utah Press, 1980). Reprinted by permission.

general. One can examine the consistency of the principle with another principle that is acknowledged to be more fundamental. Such prior principles are usually formulated at a rather abstract level, and frequently take the form of congruence with some very general procedures. For example, what could be reasonably assumed to have been chosen under the *as if* ignorance of the Rawlsian "original position," a hypothetical primordial state in which people decide on what rules to adopt without knowing who they are going to be—as if they could end up being any one of the persons in the community.[1] Or what rules would satisfy Richard Hare's requirement of "universalizability" and be consistent with "giving equal weights to the equal interests of the occupants of all the roles."[2] I shall call a critique based on such an approach a *prior-principle critique*. Both approaches can be used in assessing the moral claims of each type of equality, and will indeed be used here.

1. Utilitarian Equality

Utilitarian equality is the equality that can be derived from the utilitarian concept of goodness applied to problems of distribution. Perhaps the simplest case is the "pure distribution problem": the problem of dividing a given homogeneous cake among a group of persons. Each person gets more utility the larger his share of the cake, and gets utility *only* from his share of the cake; his utility increases at a diminishing rate as the amount of his share goes up. The utilitarian objective is to maximize the sum-total of utility irrespective of distribution, but that requires the *equality* of the *marginal* utility of everyone—marginal utility being the incremental utility each person would get from an additional unit of cake. According to one interpretation, this equality of marginal utility embodies equal treatment of everyone's interests.

The position is a bit more complicated when the total size of the cake is not independent of its distribution. But even then maximization of the total utility sum requires that transfers be carried to the point at which the marginal utility gain of the gainers equals the marginal utility loss of the losers, after taking into account the effect of the transfer on the size and distribution of the cake. It is in this wider context that the special type of equality insisted upon by utilitarianism becomes assertively distinguished. Richard Hare has claimed that "giving equal weight to the equal interests

1. J. Rawls, *A Theory of Justice* (Cambridge: Harvard University Press, 1971), pp. 17–22 [see pp. 125–126 in this anthology].

2. R. M. Hare, *The Language of Morals* (Oxford: Clarendon Press, 1952); "Ethical Theory and Utilitarianism," in H. D. Lewis, ed., *Contemporary British Philosophy* (London: Allen and Unwin, 1976), pp. 116–17.

of all the parties" would "lead to utilitarianism"—thus satisfying the prior-principle requirement of universalizability.[3] Similarly, John Harsanyi shoots down the nonutilitarians (including this lecturer, I hasten to add), by claiming for utilitarianism an exclusive ability to avoid "unfair discrimination" between "one person's and another person's equally urgent human needs."[4]

The moral importance of needs, on this interpretation, is based exclusively on the notion of utility. This is disputable, and having had several occasions to dispute it in the past,[5] I shall not shy away from disputing it in this particular context. But while I will get on to this issue later, I want first to examine the nature of utilitarian equality without— for the time being—questioning the grounding of moral importance entirely on utility. Even when utility is the sole basis of importance there is still the question as to whether the size of *marginal* utility, irrespective of *total* utility enjoyed by the person, is an adequate index of moral importance. It is, of course, possible to define a metric on utility characteristics such that each person's utility scale is coordinated with everyone else's in a way that equal social importance is simply "scaled" as equal marginal utility. If interpersonal comparisons of utility are taken to have no descriptive content, then this can indeed be thought to be a natural approach. No matter how the relative social importances are arrived at, the marginal utilities attributed to each person would then simply reflect these values. This can be done explicitly by appropriate interpersonal scaling, or implicitly through making the utility numbering reflect choices in situations of *as if* uncertainty associated with the "original position" under the additional assumption that ignorance be interpreted as equal probability of being anyone. This is not the occasion to go into the technical details of this type of exercise, but the essence of it consists in using a scaling procedure such that marginal utility measures are automatically identified as indicators of social importance.

This route to utilitarianism may meet with little resistance, but it is non-controversial mainly because it says so little. A problem arises the

3. Hare (1976), pp. 116–17.

4. John Harsanyi, "Non-linear Social Welfare Functions: A Rejoinder to Professor Sen," in R. E. Butts and J. Hintikka, eds., *Foundational Problems in the Special Sciences* (Dordrecht: Reidel, 1977), pp. 294–95.

5. *Collective Choice and Social Welfare* (San Francisco: Holden-Day, 1970), chapter 6 and section 11.4; "On Weights and Measures: Informational Constraints in Social Welfare Analysis," *Econometrica* 45 (1977). See also T. M. Scanlon's arguments against identifying utility with "urgency" in his "Preference and Urgency," *Journal of Philosophy* 72 (1975).

moment utilities and interpersonal comparisons thereof are taken to have some independent descriptive content, as utilitarians have traditionally insisted that they do. There could then be conflicts between these descriptive utilities and the appropriately scaled, essentially normative, utilities in terms of which one is "forced" to be a utilitarian. In what follows I shall have nothing more to say on utilitarianism through appropriate interpersonal scaling, and return to examining the traditional utilitarian position, which takes utilities to have interpersonally comparable descriptive content. How moral importance should relate to these descriptive features must, then, be explicitly faced.

The position can be examined from the prior-principle perspective as well as from the case-implication angle. John Rawls's criticism as a preliminary to presenting his own alternative conception of justice took mostly the prior-principle form. This was chiefly in terms of acceptability in the "original position," arguing that in the postulated situation of *as if* ignorance people would not choose to maximize the utility sum. But Rawls also discussed the violence that utilitarianism does to our notions of liberty and equality. Some replies to Rawls's arguments have reasserted the necessity to be a utilitarian by taking the "scaling" route, which was discussed earlier, and which—I think—is inappropriate in meeting Rawls's critique. But I must confess that I find the lure of the "original position" distinctly resistible since it seems very unclear what precisely would be chosen in such a situation. It is also far from obvious that prudential choice under *as if* uncertainty provides an adequate basis for moral judgment in *unoriginal,* i.e., real life, positions. But I believe Rawls's more direct critiques in terms of liberty and equality do remain powerful.

Insofar as one is concerned with the *distribution* of utilities, it follows immediately that utilitarianism would in general give one little comfort. Even the minutest gain in total utility *sum* would be taken to outweigh distributional inequalities of the most blatant kind. This problem would be avoidable under certain assumptions, notably the case in which everyone has the *same* utility function. In the pure distribution problem, with this assumption the utilitarian best would require absolute equality of everyone's total utilities.[6] This is because when the marginal utilities are equated, so would be the total utilities if everyone has the same utility function. This is, however, egalitarianism by serendipity: just the accidental result of the marginal tail wagging the total dog. More importantly, the

6. The problem is much more complex when the total cake is not fixed, and where the maximization of utility sum need not lead to the equality of total utilities unless some additional assumptions are made, e.g., the absence of incentive arguments for inequality.

assumption would be very frequently violated, since there are obvious and well-discussed variations between human beings. John may be easy to please, but Jeremy not. If it is taken to be an acceptable prior-principle that the equality of the distribution of total utilities has some value, then the utilitarian conception of equality—marginal as it is—must stand condemned.

The recognition of the fundamental diversity of human beings does, in fact, have very deep consequences, affecting not merely the utilitarian conception of social good, but others as well, including (as I shall argue presently) even the Rawlsian conception of equality. If human beings are identical, then the application of the prior-principle of universalizability in the form of "giving equal weight to the equal interest of all parties" simplifies enormously. Equal marginal utilities of all—reflecting one interpretation of the equal treatment of needs—coincides with equal total utilities—reflecting one interpretation of serving their overall interests equally well. With diversity, the two can pull in opposite directions, and it is far from clear that "giving equal weight to the equal interest of all parties" would require us to concentrate only on one of the two parameters—taking no note of the other.

The case-implication perspective can also be used to develop a related critique, and I have tried to present such a critique elsewhere.[7] For example, if person A as a cripple gets half the utility that the pleasure-wizard person B does from any given level of income, then in the pure distribution problem between A and B the utilitarian would end up giving the pleasure-wizard B more income than the cripple A. The cripple would then be doubly worse off: both since he gets less utility from the same level of income, *and* since he will also get less income. Utilitarianism must lead to this thanks to its single-minded concern with maximizing the utility sum. The pleasure-wizard's superior efficiency in producing utility would pull income away from the less efficient cripple.

Since this example has been discussed a certain amount, I should perhaps explain what is being asserted and what is not. First, it is *not* being claimed that anyone who has lower total utility (e.g., the cripple) at any given level of income must of necessity have lower marginal utility also. This must be true for some levels of income, but need not be true everywhere. Indeed, the opposite could be the case when incomes are equally distributed. If that were so, then of course even utilitarianism would give the cripple more income than the non-cripple, since at that point the cripple would be the more efficient producer of utility. My point is that there is no guarantee that this will be the case, and more particularly, if it

7. *On Economic Inequality* (Oxford: Clarendon Press, 1973), pp. 16–20.

were the case that the cripple were not only worse off in terms of total utility but could convert income into utility less efficiently everywhere (or even just at the point of equal income division), then utilitarianism would compound his disadvantage by settling him with less income on top of lower efficiency in making utility out of income. The point, of course, is not about cripples in general, nor about all people with total utility disadvantage, but concerns people—including cripples—with disadvantage in terms of both total *and* marginal utility at the relevant points.

Second, the descriptive content of utility is rather important in this context. Obviously, if utilities were scaled to reflect moral importance, then wishing to give priority to income for the cripple would simply amount to attributing a higher "marginal utility" to the cripple's income; but this—as we have already discussed—is a very special sense of utility—quite devoid of descriptive content. In terms of descriptive features, what is being assumed in our example is that the cripple can be helped by giving him income, but the increase in his utility as a consequence of a marginal increase in income is less—in terms of the accepted descriptive criteria—than giving that unit of income to the pleasure-wizard, when both have initially the same income.

Finally, the problem for utilitarianism in this case-implication argument is not dependent on an implicit assumption that the claim to more income arising from disadvantage must dominate over the claim arising from high marginal utility. A system that gives some weight to both claims would still fail to meet the utilitarian formula of social good, which demands an exclusive concern with the latter claim. It is this narrowness that makes the utilitarian conception of equality such a limited one. Even when utility is accepted as the only basis of moral importance, utilitarianism fails to capture the relevance of overall advantage for the requirements of equality. The prior-principle critiques can be supplemented by case-implication critiques using this utilitarian lack of concern with distributional questions except at the entirely marginal level.

2. Total Utility Equality

Welfarism is the view that the goodness of a state of affairs can be judged entirely by the goodness of the utilities in that state.[8] This is a less demanding view than utilitarianism in that it does not demand—in addition—that the goodness of the utilities must be judged by their sum-total. Utilitarianism is, in this sense, a special case of welfarism, and pro-

8. See Sen (1977), and also my "Welfarism and Utilitarianism," *Journal of Philosophy* 76 (1979).

vides one illustration of it. Another distinguished case is the criterion of judging the goodness of a state by the utility level of the worst-off person in that state—a criterion often attributed to John Rawls. (*Except* by John Rawls! He uses social primary goods rather than utility as the index of advantage, as we shall presently discuss.) One can also take some other function of the utilities—other than the sum-total or the minimal element.

Utilitarian equality is one type of welfarist equality. There are others, notably the equality of total utility. It is tempting to think of this as some kind of an analogue of utilitarianism shifting the focus from marginal utility to total utility. This correspondence is, however, rather less close than it might first appear. First of all, while we economists often tend to treat the marginal and the total as belonging to the same plane of discourse, there is an important difference between them. Marginal is an essentially *counter-factual* notion: marginal utility is the additional utility that *would be* generated if the person had one more unit of income. It contrasts what is observed with what allegedly would be observed if something else were different: in this case if the income had been one unit greater. Total is not, however, an inherently counter-factual concept; whether it is or is not would depend on the variable that is being totalled. In case of utilities, if they are taken to be observed facts, total utility will not be counter-factual. Thus total utility equality is a matter for direct observation, whereas utilitarian equality is not so, since the latter requires hypotheses as to what things would have been under different postulated circumstances. The contrast can be easily traced to the fact that utilitarian equality is essentially a consequence of sum *maximization,* which is itself a counter-factual notion, whereas total utility equality is an equality of some directly observed magnitudes.

Second, utilitarianism provides a complete ordering of all utility distributions—the ranking reflecting the order of the sums of individual utilities—but as specified so far, total utility equality does not do more than just point to the case of absolute equality. In dealing with two cases of non-equal distributions, something more has to be said so that they could be ranked. The ranking can be completed in many different ways.

One way to such a complete ranking is provided by the lexicographic version of the maximin rule, which is associated with the Rawlsian Difference Principle, but interpreted in terms of utilities as opposed to primary goods. Here the goodness of the state of affairs is judged by the level of utility of the worst-off person in that state; but if the worst-off persons in two states respectively have the same level of utility, then the states are ranked according to the utility levels of the second worst-off. If they too tie, then by the utility levels of the third worst-off, and so on. And if two utility distributions are matched at each rank all the way from the worst off to the best off, then the two distributions are equally good. Following a convention established in social choice theory, I shall call this *leximin*.

In what way does total utility equality lead to the leximin? It does this when combined with some other axioms, and in fact the analysis closely parallels the recent axiomatic derivations of the Difference Principle by several authors. Consider four utility levels *a, b, c, d*, in decreasing order of magnitude. One can argue that in an obvious sense the pair of extreme points *(a, d)* displays greater inequality than the pair of intermediate points *(b, c)*. Note that this is a purely *ordinal* comparison based on ranking only, and the exact magnitudes of *a, b, c*, and *d* make no difference to the comparison in question. If one were *solely* concerned with equality, then it could be argued that *(b, c)* is superior—or at least non-inferior—to *(a, d)*. This requirement may be seen as a strong version of preferring equality of utility distributions, and may be called "utility equality preference." It is possible to combine this with an axiom due to Patrick Suppes which captures the notion of *dominance* of one utility distribution over another, in the sense of each element of one distribution being at least as large as the corresponding element in the other distribution.[9] In the two-person case this requires that state *x* must be regarded as at least as good as *y, either* if each person in state *x* has at least as much utility as himself in state *y, or* if each person in state *x* has at least as much utility as the *other* person in state *y. If,* in addition, at least one of them has strictly more, then of course *x* could be declared to be strictly better (and not merely at least as good). If this Suppes principle and the "utility equality preference" are combined, then we are pushed in the direction of leximin. Indeed, leximin can be fully derived from these two principles by requiring that the approach must provide a complete ordering of all possible states no matter what the interpersonally comparable individual utilities happen to be (called "unrestricted domain"), and that the ranking of any two states must depend on utility information concerning *those* states only (called "independence").

Insofar as the requirements other than utility equality preference (i.e., the Suppes principle, unrestricted domain, and independence) are regarded as acceptable—and they have indeed been widely used in the social choice literature—leximin can be seen as the natural concomitant of giving priority to the conception of equality focussing on total utility.

It should be obvious, however, that leximin can be fairly easily criticised

9. P. Suppes, "Some Formal Models of Grading Principles," *Synthese* 6 (1966).

from the prior-principle perspective as well as the case-implication perspective. Just as utilitarianism pays no attention to the force of one's claim arising from one's disadvantage, leximin ignores claims arising from the *intensity* of one's needs. The *ordinal* characteristic that was pointed out while presenting the axiom of utility equality preference makes the approach insensitive to the magnitudes of potential utility gains and losses. While in the critique of utilitarianism that was presented earlier I argued against treating these potential gains and losses as the only basis of moral judgment, it was *not* of course alleged that these have no moral relevance at all. Take the comparison of *(a, d)* vis-à-vis *(b, c)*, discussed earlier, and let *(b, c)* stand for *(3, 2)*. Utility equality preference would assert the superiority of *(3, 2)* over *(10, 1)* as well as *(4, 1)*. Indeed, it would not distinguish between the two cases at all. It is this lack of concern with "how much" questions that makes leximin rather easy to criticise *either* by showing its failure to comply with such prior-principles as "giving equal weight to the equal interest of all parties," *or* by spelling out its rather austere implications in specific cases.

Aside from its indifference to "how much" questions, leximin also has little interest in "how many" questions—paying no attention at all to the number of people whose interests are overridden in the pursuit of the interests of the worst off. The worst-off position rules the roost, and it does not matter whether this goes against the interests of one other person, or against those of a million or a billion other persons. It is sometimes claimed that leximin would not be such an extreme criterion if it could be modified so that this innumeracy were avoided, and if the interests of *one* worse-off position were given priority over the interests of exactly *one* better-off position, but not necessarily against the interests of *more than one* better-off position. In fact, one can define a less demanding version of leximin, which can be called leximin-2, which takes the form of applying the leximin principle *if* all persons other than two are indifferent between the alternatives, but not necessarily otherwise. Leximin-2, as a compromise, will be still unconcerned with "how much" questions on the magnitudes of utilities of the two non-indifferent persons, but need not be blinkered about "how many" questions dealing with numbers of people: the priority applies to one person over exactly one other.[10]

Interestingly enough, a consistency problem intervenes here. It can be

10. Leximin—and maximin—are concerned with conflicts between positional priorities, i.e., between ranks (such as the "worst-off position," "second worst-off position," etc.), and not with interpersonal priorities. When positions coincide with persons (e.g., the *same* person being the worst off in each state), then positional conflicts translate directly into personal conflicts.

proved that given the regularity conditions, viz., unrestricted domain and independence, leximin-2 logically entails leximin in general.[11] That is, given these regularity conditions, there is no way of retaining moral sensitivity to the number of people on each side by choosing the limited requirement of leximin-2 without going all the way to leximin itself. It appears that indifference to *how much* questions concerning utilities implies indifference to *how many* questions concerning the number of people on different sides. One innumeracy begets another.

Given the nature of these critiques of utilitarian equality and total utility equality respectively, it is natural to ask whether some *combination* of the two should not meet both sets of objections. If utilitarianism is attacked for its unconcern with inequalities of the utility distribution, and leximin is criticised for its lack of interest in the magnitudes of utility gains and losses, and even in the numbers involved, then isn't the right solution to choose some mixture of the two? It is at this point that the long-postponed question of the relation between utility and moral worth becomes crucial. While utilitarianism and leximin differ sharply from each other in the use that they respectively make of the utility information, both share an exclusive concern with utility data. If non-utility considerations have any role in either approach, this arises from the part they play in the determination of utilities, or possibly as surrogates for utility information in the absence of adequate utility data. A combination of utilitarianism and leximin would still be confined to the box of welfarism, and it remains to be examined whether welfarism as a general approach is *itself* adequate.

One aspect of the obtuseness of welfarism was discussed clearly by John Rawls.

> In calculating the greatest balance of satisfaction it does not matter, except indirectly, what the desires are for. We are to arrange institutions so as to obtain the greatest sum of satisfactions; we ask no questions about their source or quality but only how their satisfaction would affect the total of well-being. . . . Thus if men take a certain pleasure in discriminating against one another, in subjecting others to a lesser liberty as a means of enhancing their self-respect, then the satisfaction of these desires must be weighed in our deliberations according to their intensity, or whatever, along with other desires. . . . In justice as fairness, on the other hand, persons accept in advance a principle of equal liberty and they do this without a knowledge of their more particular ends. . . . An individual who finds that he enjoys seeing others in positions of lesser liberty understands that he has no claim whatever to this enjoyment. The pleasure he takes in others' deprivation is wrong

11. Theorem 8, Sen (1977).

in itself: it is a satisfaction which requires the violation of a principle to which
he would agree in the original position.[12]

It is easily seen that this is an argument not merely against utilitarianism, but against the adequacy of utility information for moral judgments
of states of affairs, and is, thus, an attack on welfarism in general. Second,
it is clear that as a criticism of welfarism—and *a fortiori* as a critique of
utilitarianism—the argument uses a principle that is unnecessarily strong.
If it were the case that pleasures taken "in other's deprivation" were not
taken to be wrong in itself, but simply *disregarded*, even then the rejection
of welfarism would stand. Furthermore, even if such pleasures were regarded as valuable, but *less* valuable than pleasures arising from other
sources (e.g., enjoying food, work, or leisure), welfarism would still stand
rejected. The issue—as John Stuart Mill had noted—is the lack of "parity" between one source of utility and another.[13] Welfarism requires the
endorsement not merely of the widely shared intuition that any pleasure
has some value—and one would have to be a bit of a kill-joy to dissent
from this—but also the much more dubious proposition that pleasures
must be relatively weighed *only* according to their respective intensities,
irrespective of the source of the pleasure and the nature of the activity that
goes with it. Finally, Rawls's argument takes the form of an appeal to the
prior-principle of equating moral rightness with prudential acceptability
in the original position. Even those who do not accept that prior-principle
could reject the welfarist no-nonsense counting of utility irrespective of all
other information by reference to other prior-principles, e.g., the irreduc-
ible value of liberty.

The relevance of non-utility information to moral judgments is the
central issue involved in disputing welfarism. Libertarian considerations
point towards a particular class of non-utility information, and I have
argued elsewhere that this may require even the rejection of the so-called
Pareto principle based on utility dominance.[14] But there are also other
types of non-utility information which have been thought to be intrin-
sically important. Tim Scanlon has recently discussed the contrast between "urgency" and utility (or intensity of preference). He has also
argued that "the criteria of well-being that we actually employ in making
moral judgments are objective," and a person's level of well-being is taken
to be "independent of that person's tastes and interests."[15] These moral

12. Rawls (1971), pp. 30–31.
13. John Stuart Mill, *On Liberty* (1859), p. 140.
14. Sen (1970), especially chap. 6. Also Sen (1979).
15. T. M. Scanlon (1975), pp. 658–59.

judgments could thus conflict with utilitarian—and more generally (Scanlon could have argued) with welfarist—moralities, no matter whether utility is interpreted as pleasure, or—as is increasingly common recently—as desire-fulfilment.

However, acknowledging the relevance of objective factors does not require that well-being be taken to be independent of tastes, and Scanlon's categories are *too* pure. For example, a lack of "parity" between utility from self-regarding actions and that from other-regarding actions will go beyond utility as an index of well-being and will be fatal to welfarism, but the contrast is not, of course, independent of tastes and subjective features. "Objective" considerations can count along with a person's tastes. What is required is the denial that a person's well-being be judged *exclusively* in terms of his or her utilities. If such judgments take into account a person's pleasures and desire-fulfilments, but also certain objective factors, e.g., whether he or she is hungry, cold, or oppressed, the resulting calculus would still be non-welfarist. Welfarism is an extremist position, and its denial can take many different forms—pure and mixed—so long as totally ignoring non-utility information is avoided.

Second, it is also clear that the notion of urgency need not work only *through* the determinants of personal well-being—however broadly conceived. For example, the claim that one should not be *exploited* at work is not based on making exploitation an additional parameter in the specification of well-being on top of such factors as income and effort, but on the moral view that a person deserves to get what he—according to one way of characterizing production—has produced. Similarly, the urgency deriving from principles such as "equal pay for equal work" hits directly at discrimination without having to redefine the notion of personal well-being to take note of such discriminations. One could, for example, say: "She must be paid just as much as the men working in that job, not primarily because she would otherwise have a lower level of well-being than the others, but simply because she is doing the *same* work as the men there, and why should she be paid less?" These moral claims, based on non-welfarist conceptions of equality, have played important parts in social movements, and it seems difficult to sustain the hypothesis that they are purely "instrumental" claims—ultimately justified by their indirect impact on the fulfilment of welfarist, or other well-being-based, objectives.

Thus the dissociation of urgency from utility can arise from two different sources. One disentangles the notion of personal well-being from utility, and the other makes urgency not a function only of well-being. But, at the same time, the former does not require that well-being be independent of utility, and the latter does not necessitate a notion of urgency that is independent of personal well-being. Welfarism is a purist position and must avoid any contamination from either of these sources.

3. Rawlsian Equality

Rawls's "two principles of justice" characterize the need for equality in terms of—what he has called—"primary social goods."[16] These are "things that every rational man is presumed to want," including "rights, liberties and opportunities, income and wealth, and the social bases of self-respect." Basic liberties are separated out as having priority over other primary goods, and thus priority is given to the principle of liberty which demands that "each person is to have an equal right to the most extensive basic liberty compatible with a similar liberty for others." The second principle supplements this, demanding efficiency and equality, judging advantage in terms of an index of primary goods. Inequalities are condemned unless they work out to everyone's advantage. This incorporates the "Difference Principle" in which priority is given to furthering the interests of the worst-off. And that leads to maximin, or to leximin, defined not on individual utilities but on the index of primary goods. But given the priority of the liberty principle, no trade-offs are permitted between basic liberties and economic and social gain.

Herbert Hart has persuasively disputed Rawls's arguments for the priority of liberty,[17] but with that question I shall not be concerned in this lecture. What is crucial for the problem under discussion is the concentration on bundles of primary social goods. Some of the difficulties with welfarism that I tried to discuss will not apply to the pursuit of Rawlsian equality. Objective criteria of well-being can be directly accommodated within the index of primary goods. So can be Mill's denial of the parity between pleasures from different sources, since the sources can be discriminated on the basis of the nature of the goods. Furthermore, while the Difference Principle is egalitarian in a way similar to leximin, it avoids the much-criticised feature of leximin of giving more income to people who are hard to please and who have to be deluged in champagne and buried in caviar to bring them to a normal level of utility, which you and I get from a sandwich and beer. Since advantage is judged not in terms of utilities at all, but through the index of primary goods, expensive tastes

16. Rawls (1971), pp. 60–65. [pp. 126–130 in this anthology]
17. H. L. A. Hart, "Rawls on Liberty and Its Priority," *University of Chicago Law Review* 40 (1973); reprinted in N. Daniels, ed., *Reading Rawls* (Oxford: Blackwell, 1975).

cease to provide a ground for getting more income. Rawls justifies this in terms of a person's responsibility for his own ends.

But what about the cripple with utility disadvantage, whom we discussed earlier? Leximin will give him more income in a pure distribution problem. Utilitarianism, I had complained, will give him *less*. The Difference Principle will give him neither more nor less on grounds of his being a cripple. His utility disadvantage will be irrelevant to the Difference Principle. This may seem hard, and I think it is. Rawls justifies this by pointing out that "hard cases" can "distract our moral perception by leading us to think of people distant from us whose fate arouses pity and anxiety."[18] This can be so, but hard cases do exist, and to take disabilities, or special health needs, or physical or mental defects, as morally irrelevant, or to leave them out for fear of making a mistake, may guarantee that the *opposite* mistake will be made.

And the problem does not end with hard cases. The primary goods approach seems to take little note of the diversity of human beings. In the context of assessing utilitarian equality, it was argued that if people were fundamentally similar in terms of utility functions, then the utilitarian concern with maximizing the sum total of utilities would push us simultaneously also in the direction of equality of utility levels. Thus utilitarianism could be rendered vastly more attractive if people really were similar. A corresponding remark can be made about the Rawlsian Difference Principle. If people were basically very similar, then an index of primary goods might be quite a good way of judging advantage. But, in fact, people seem to have very different needs varying with health, longevity, climatic conditions, location, work conditions, temperament, and even body size (affecting food and clothing requirements). So what is involved is not merely ignoring a few hard cases, but overlooking very widespread and real differences. Judging advantage purely in terms of primary goods leads to a partially blind morality.

Indeed, it can be argued that there is, in fact, an element of "fetishism" in the Rawlsian framework. Rawls takes primary goods as the embodiment of advantage, rather than taking advantage to be a *relationship* between persons and goods. Utilitarianism, or leximin, or—more generally—welfarism does not have this fetishism, since utilities are reflections of one type of relation between persons and goods. For example, income and wealth are not valued under utilitarianism as physical units, but in terms of their capacity to create human happiness or to satisfy human desires. Even if utility is not thought to be the right focus for the person–good

18. John Rawls, "A Kantian Concept of Equality," *Cambridge Review* (February 1975), p. 96.

ɔ, to have an entirely good-oriented framework provides a pe-
of judging advantage.

also be argued that while utility in the form of happiness or
ulfilment may be an *inadequate* guide to urgency, the Rawlsian
framework asserts it to be *irrelevant* to urgency, which is, of course, a much
stronger claim. The distinction was discussed earlier in the context of
assessing welfarism, and it was pointed out that a rejection of welfarism
need not take us to the point in which utility is given no role whatsoever.
That a person's interest should have nothing directly to do with his
happiness or desire-fulfilment seems difficult to justify. Even in terms of
the prior-principle of prudential acceptability in the "original position," it
is not at all clear why people in that primordial state should be taken to be
so indifferent to the joys and sufferings in occupying particular positions,
or if they are not, why their concern about these joys and sufferings should
be taken to be morally irrelevant.

4. Basic Capability Equality

This leads to the further question: Can we not construct an adequate
theory of equality on the *combined* grounds of Rawlsian equality and
equality under the two welfarist conceptions, with some trade-offs among
them? I would now like to argue briefly why I believe this too may prove to
be informationally short. This can, of course, easily be asserted *if* claims
arising from considerations other than well-being were acknowledged to
be legitimate. Non-exploitation, or non-discrimination, requires the use
of information not fully captured either by utility or by primary goods.
Other conceptions of entitlements can also be brought in going beyond
concern with personal well-being only. But in what follows I shall not
introduce these concepts. My contention is that *even* the concept of *needs*
does not get adequate coverage through the information on primary goods
and utility.

I shall use a case-implication argument. Take the cripple again with
marginal utility disadvantage. We saw that utilitarianism would do nothing
for him; in fact it will give him *less* income than to the physically fit. Nor
would the Difference Principle help him; it will leave his physical disadvantage severely alone. He did, however, get preferential treatment under
leximin, and more generally, under criteria fostering total equality. His low
level of total utility was the basis of his claim. But now suppose that he is
no worse off than others in utility terms despite his physical handicap
because of certain other utility features. This could be because he has a
jolly disposition. Or because he has a low aspiration level and his heart

leaps up whenever he sees a rainbow in the sky. Or because he is religious and feels that he will be rewarded in after-life, or cheerfully accepts what he takes to be just penalty for misdeeds in a past incarnation. The important point is that despite his marginal utility disadvantage, he has no longer a total utility deprivation. Now not even leximin—or any other notion of equality focussing on total utility—will do much for him. If we still think that he has needs as a cripple that should be catered to, then the basis of that claim clearly rests neither in high marginal utility, nor in low total utility, nor—of course—in deprivation in terms of primary goods.

It is arguable that what is missing in all this framework is some notion of "basic capabilities": a person being able to do certain basic things. The ability to move about is the relevant one here, but one can consider others, e.g., the ability to meet one's nutritional requirements, the wherewithal to be clothed and sheltered, the power to participate in the social life of the community. The notion of urgency related to this is not fully captured by either utility or primary goods, or any combination of the two. Primary goods suffers from fetishist handicap in being concerned with goods, and even though the list of goods is specified in a broad and inclusive way, encompassing rights, liberties, opportunities, income, wealth, and the social basis of self-respect, it still is concerned with good things rather than with what these good things *do to human* beings. Utility, on the other hand, *is* concerned with what these things do to human beings, but uses a metric that focusses not on the person's capabilities but on his mental reaction. There is something still missing in the combined list of primary goods and utilities. If it is argued that resources should be devoted to remove or substantially reduce the handicap of the cripple despite there being no marginal utility argument (because it is expensive), despite there being no total utility argument (because he is so contented), and despite there being no primary goods deprivation (because he has the goods that others have), the case must rest on something else. I believe what is at issue is the interpretation of needs in the form of basic capabilities. This interpretation of needs and interests is often implicit in the demand for equality. This type of equality I shall call "basic capability equality."

The focus on basic capabilities can be seen as a natural extension of Rawls's concern with primary goods, shifting attention from goods to what goods do to human beings. Rawls himself motivates judging advantage in terms of primary goods by referring to capabilities, even though his criteria end up focussing on goods as such: on income rather than on what income does, on the "social bases of self-respect" rather than on self-respect itself, and so on. If human beings were very like each other, this would not have mattered a great deal, but there is evidence that the conversion of goods to capabilities varies from person to person substantially, and the equality of the former may still be far from the equality of the latter.

There are, of course, many difficulties with the notion of "basic capability equality." In particular, the problem of indexing the basic capability bundles is a serious one. It is, in many ways, a problem comparable with the indexing of primary good bundles in the context of Rawlsian equality. This is not the occasion to go into the technical issues involved in such an indexing, but it is clear that whatever partial ordering can be done on the basis of broad uniformity of personal preferences must be supplemented by certain established conventions of relative importance.

The ideas of relative importance are, of course, conditional on the nature of the society. The notion of the equality of basic capabilities is a very general one, but any application of it must be rather culture-dependent, especially in the weighting of different capabilities. While Rawlsian equality has the characteristic of being both culture-dependent and fetishist, basic capability equality avoids fetishism, but remains culture-dependent. Indeed, basic capability equality can be seen as essentially an extension of the Rawlsian approach in a non-fetishist direction.

5. Concluding Remarks

I end with three final remarks. First, it is not my contention that basic capability equality can be the sole guide to the moral good. For one thing morality is not concerned only with equality. For another, while it is my contention that basic capability equality has certain clear advantages over other types of equality, I did not argue that the others were morally irrelevant. Basic capability equality is a partial guide to the part of moral goodness that is associated with the idea of equality. I have tried to argue that as a partial guide it has virtues that the other characterisations of equality do not possess.

Second, the index of basic capabilities, like utility, can be used in many different ways. Basic capability equality corresponds to total utility equality, and it can be extended in different directions, e.g., to leximin of basic capabilities. On the other hand, the index can be used also in a way similar to utilitarianism, judging the strength of a claim in terms of incremental contribution to *enhancing* the index value. The main departure is in focussing on a *magnitude* different from utility as well as the primary goods index. The new dimension can be utilised in different ways, of which basic capability equality is only one.

Last, the bulk of this lecture has been concerned with rejecting the claims of utilitarian equality, total utility equality, and Rawlsian equality to provide a sufficient basis for the equality-aspect of morality—indeed, even for that part of it which is concerned with needs rather than deserts. I have argued that none of these three is sufficient, nor is any combination of the three.

This is my main thesis. I have also made the constructive claim that this gap can be narrowed by the idea of basic capability equality, and more generally by the use of basic capability as a morally relevant dimension taking us beyond utility and primary goods. I should end by pointing out that the validity of the main thesis is not conditional on the acceptance of this constructive claim.

15

Ronald Dworkin,
"Equality of Resources"

Ronald Dworkin, an expert on a variety of issues in legal and political the-
ory, is the author of Taking Rights Seriously, Law's Empire, *and* Life's
Dominion, *among other works. The essay excerpted here was originally*
published as Part 2 of a pair of essays. In the first essay, Dworkin criticized
the view, which he called equality of welfare, that the ideal of equality de-
mands that different people be equally happy, or that their desires be satis-
fied to equal degrees. In this excerpt, Dworkin sketches an alternative to
that view.

The economic market . . . has . . . come to be regarded as the enemy of
equality, largely because the forms of economic market systems developed
and enforced in industrial countries have permitted and indeed encouraged vast inequality in property. Both political philosophers and ordinary
citizens have therefore pictured equality as the antagonist or victim of the
values of efficiency and liberty supposedly served by the market, so that
wise and moderate politics consists in striking some balance or trade-off
between equality and these other values, either by imposing constraints on
the market as an economic environment, or by replacing it, in part or
altogether, with a different economic system.

I shall try to suggest, on the contrary, that the idea of an economic
market, as a device for setting prices for a vast variety of goods and
services, must be at the center of any attractive theoretical development of
equality of resources. The main point can be shown most quickly by
constructing a reasonably simple exercise in equality of resources, deliberately artificial so as to abstract from problems we shall later have to
face. Suppose a number of shipwreck survivors are washed up on a desert
island which has abundant resources and no native population, and any
likely rescue is many years away. These immigrants accept the principle
that no one is antecedently entitled to any of these resources, but that they
shall instead be divided equally among them. (They do not yet realize, let
us say, that it might be wise to keep some resources as owned in common
by any state they might create.) They also accept (at least provisionally)

This essay was originally published as "What is Equality? Part 2: Equality of
Resources," in *Philosophy and Public Affairs* 10 (1981): 283–345. Reprinted by
permission of Ronald Dworkin.

the following test of an equal division of resources, which I shall call the envy test. No division of resources is an equal division if, once the division is complete, any immigrant would prefer someone else's bundle of resources to his own bundle.[1]

Now suppose some one immigrant is elected to achieve the division according to that principle. It is unlikely that he can succeed simply by physically dividing the resources of the island into n identical bundles of resources. The number of each kind of the nondivisible resources, like milking cows, might not be an exact multiple of n, and even in the case of divisible resources, like arable land, some land would be better than others, and some better for one use than another. Suppose, however, that by a great deal of trial and error and care the divider could create n bundles of resources, each of which was somewhat different from the others, but was nevertheless such that he could assign one to each immigrant and no one would in fact envy anyone else's bundle.

The distribution might still fail to satisfy the immigrants as an equal distribution, for a reason that is not caught by the envy test. Suppose (to put the point in a dramatic way) the divider achieved his result by transforming all the available resources into a very large stock of plovers' eggs and pre-phylloxera claret (either by magic or trade with a neighboring island that enters the story only for that reason) and divides this glut into identical bundles of baskets and bottles. Many of the immigrants—let us say all but one—are delighted. But if that one hates plovers' eggs and pre-phylloxera claret he will feel that he has not been treated as an equal in the division of resources. The envy test is met—he does not prefer any one's bundle to his own—but he prefers what he would have had under some fairer treatment of the initially available resources.

A similar, though less dramatic, piece of unfairness might be produced even without magic or bizarre trades. For the combination of resources that composes each bundle the divider creates will favor some tastes over others, compared with different combinations he might have composed. That is, different sets of n bundles might be created by trial and error, each of which would pass the envy test, so that for any such set that the divider chooses, someone will prefer that he had chosen a different set, even though that person would not prefer a different bundle within that set. Trades after the initial distribution may, of course, improve that person's position. But they will be unlikely to bring him to the position he would have had under the set of bundles he would have preferred, because some

---

1. D. Foley, "Resource Allocation and the Public Sector," *Yale Economic Essays* 7 (Spring 1967); H. Varian, "Equity, Energy and Efficiency, *Journal of Economic Theory* (Sept. 1974): 63–91.

others will begin with a bundle they prefer to the bundle they would have had in that set, and so will have no reason to trade to that bundle.

So the divider needs a device that will attack two distinct foci of arbitrariness and possible unfairness. The envy test cannot be satisfied by any simple mechanical division of resources. If any more complex division can be found that will satisfy it, many such might be found so that the choice amongst these would be arbitrary. The same solution will by now have occurred to all readers. The divider needs some form of auction or other market procedure in order to respond to these problems. I shall describe a reasonably straightforward procedure that would seem acceptable if it could be made to work, though as I shall describe it it will be impossibly expensive of time. Suppose the divider hands each of the immigrants an equal and large number of clamshells, which are sufficiently numerous and in themselves valued by no one, to use as counters in a market of the following sort. Each distinct item on the island (not including the immigrants themselves) is listed as a lot to be sold, unless someone notifies the auctioneer (as the divider has now become) of his or her desire to bid for some part of an item, including part, for example, of some piece of land, in which case that part becomes itself a distinct lot. The auctioneer then proposes a set of prices for each lot and discovers whether that set of prices clears all markets, that is, whether there is only one purchaser at that price and all lots are sold. If not, then the auctioneer adjusts his prices until he reaches a set that does clear the markets.[2] But the process does not stop then, because each of the immigrants remains free to change his bids even when an initially market-clearing set of prices is reached, or even to propose different lots. But let us suppose that in time even this leisurely process comes to an end, everyone declares himself satisfied, and goods are distributed accordingly.[3]

Now the envy test will have been met. No one will envy another's set of purchases because, by hypothesis, he could have purchased that bundle

2. I mean to describe a Walrasian auction in which all productive resources are sold. I do not assume that the immigrants enter into complete forward contingent claims contracts, but only that markets will remain open and will clear in a Walrasian fashion once the auction of productive resources is completed. I make all the assumptions about production and preferences made in G. Debreu, *Theory of Value* (New Haven: Yale University Press, 1959). In fact the auction I describe here will become more complex in virtue of a tax scheme discussed later.

3. The process does not guarantee that the auction will come to an end in this way, because there may be various equilibria. I am supposing that people will come to understand that they cannot do better by further runs of the auction, and will for practical reasons settle on one equilibrium. If I am wrong, then this fact provides one of the aspects of incompleteness I describe in the next section.

with his clamshells instead of his own bundle. Nor is the choice of sets of bundles arbitrary. Many people will be able to imagine a different set of bundles meeting the no-envy test that might have been established, but the actual set of bundles has the merit that each person played, through his purchases against an initially equal stock of counters, an equal role in determining the set of bundles actually chosen. No one is in the position of the person in our earlier example who found himself with nothing but what he hated. Of course, luck plays a certain role in determining how satisfied anyone is with the outcome, against other possibilities he might envision. If plovers' eggs and old claret were the only resources to auction, then the person who hated these would be as badly off as in our earlier example. He would be unlucky that the immigrants had not washed up on an island with more of what he wanted (though lucky, of course, that it did not have even less). But he could not complain that the division of the actual resources they found was unequal.

He might think himself lucky or unlucky in other ways as well. It would be a matter of luck, for example, how many others shared various of his tastes. If his tastes or ambitions proved relatively popular, this might work in his favor in the auction, if there were economies of scale in the production of what he wanted. Or against him, if what he wanted was scarce. If the immigrants had decided to establish a regime of equality of welfare, instead of equality of resources, then these various pieces of good or bad luck would be shared with others, because distribution would be based, not on any auction of the sort I described, in which luck plays this role, but on a strategy of evening out differences in whatever concept of welfare had been chosen. Equality of resources, however, offers no similar reason for correcting for the contingencies that determine how expensive or frustrating someone's preferences turn out to be.[4]

Under equality of welfare, people are meant to decide what sorts of lives they want independently of information relevant to determining how much their choices will reduce or enhance the ability of others to have what they want.[5] That sort of information becomes relevant only at a second, political level at which administrators then gather all the choices made at the first level to see what distribution will give each of these choices equal success under some concept of welfare taken as the correct

---

4. See, however, the discussion of handicaps below, which recognizes that certain kinds of preferences, which people wish they did not have, may call for compensation as handicaps.
5. See Part 1 of this essay (*Philosophy & Public Affairs* 10, no. 3 [Summer 1981]) for a discussion of whether equality of welfare can be modified so as to make an exception here for "expensive tastes" deliberately cultivated. I argue that it cannot.

dimension of success. Under equality of resources, however, people decide what sorts of lives to pursue against a background of information about the actual cost their choices impose on other people and hence on the total stock of resources that may fairly be used by them. The information left to an independent political level under equality of welfare is therefore brought into the initial level of individual choice under equality of resources. The elements of luck in the auction we have just described are in fact pieces of information of a crucial sort; information that is acquired and used in that process of choice.

So the contingent facts of raw material and the distribution of tastes are not grounds on which someone might challenge a distribution as unequal. They are rather background facts that determine what equality of resources, in these circumstances, is. Under equality of resources, no test for calculating what equality requires can be abstracted from these background facts and used to test them. The market character of the auction is not simply a convenient or ad hoc device for resolving technical problems that arise for equality of resources in very simple exercises like our desert island case. It is an institutionalized form of the process of discovery and adaptation that is at the center of the ethics of that ideal. Equality of resources supposes that the resources devoted to each person's life should be equal. That goal needs a metric. The auction proposes what the envy test in fact assumes, that the true measure of the social resources devoted to the life of one person is fixed by asking how important, in fact, that resource is for others. It insists that the cost, measured in that way, figure in each person's sense of what is rightly his and in each person's judgment of what life he should lead, given that command of justice. Anyone who insists that equality is violated by any particular profile of initial tastes, therefore, must reject equality of resources, and fall back on equality of welfare.

Of course it is sovereign in this argument, and in this connection between the market and equality of resources, that people enter the market on equal terms. The desert island auction would not have avoided envy, and would have no appeal as a solution to the problem of dividing the resources equally, if the immigrants had struggled ashore with different amounts of money in their pocket, which they were free to use in the auction, or if some had stolen clamshells from others. We must not lose sight of that fact, either in the argument that follows or in any reflections on the application of that argument to contemporary economic systems. But neither should we lose sight, in our dismay over the inequities of those systems, of the important theoretical connection between the market and the concept of equality in resources.

There are, of course, other and very different sorts of objection that might be made to the use of an auction, even an equal auction of the sort I described. It might be said, for example, that the fairness of an auction supposes that the preferences people bring to the auction, or form in its course, are authentic—the true preferences of the agent rather than preferences imposed upon him by the economic system itself. Perhaps an auction of any sort, in which one person bids against another, imposes an illegitimate assumption that what is valuable in life is individual ownership of something rather than more cooperative enterprises of the community or some group within it as a whole. Insofar as this (in part mysterious) objection is pertinent here, however, it is an objection against the idea of private ownership over an extensive domain of resources, which is better considered under the title of political equality, not an objection to the claim that a market of some sort must figure in any satisfactory account of what equality in private ownership is.

The Project

Since the device of an equal auction seems promising as a technique for achieving an attractive interpretation of equality of resources in a simple context, like the desert island, the question arises whether it will prove useful in developing a more general account of that ideal. We should ask whether the device could be elaborated to provide a scheme for developing or testing equality of resources in a community that has a dynamic economy, with labor, investment, and trade. What structure must an auction take in such an economy—what adjustments or supplements must be made to the production and trade that would follow such an auction—in order that the results continue to satisfy our initial requirement that an equal share of the resources be available to each citizen?

. . .

Luck and Insurance

If the auction is successful as described, then equality of resources holds for the moment among the immigrants. But perhaps only for the moment, because if they are left alone, once the auction is completed, to produce and trade as they wish, then the envy test will shortly fail. Some may be more skillful than others at producing what others want and will trade to get. Some may like to work, or to work in a way that will produce more to trade, while others like not to work or prefer to work at what will bring them less. Some will stay healthy while others fall sick, or lightning will strike the farms of others but avoid theirs. For any of these and dozens of other reasons some people will prefer the bundle others have in say, five years, to their own.

We must ask whether (or rather how far) such developments are consistent with equality of resources, and I shall begin by considering the character and impact of luck on the immigrants' post-auction fortunes. I shall distinguish, at least for the moment, between two kinds of luck. Option luck is a matter of how deliberate and calculated gambles turn out—whether someone gains or loses through accepting an isolated risk he or she should have anticipated and might have declined. Brute luck is a matter of how risks fall out that are not in that sense deliberate gambles. If I buy a stock on the exchange that rises, then my option luck is good. If I am hit by a falling meteorite whose course could not have been predicted, then my bad luck is brute (even though I could have moved just before it struck if I had any reason to know where it would strike). Obviously the difference between these two forms of luck can be represented as a matter of degree, and we may be uncertain how to describe a particular piece of bad luck. If someone develops cancer in the course of a normal life, and there is no particular decision to which we can point as a gamble risking the disease, then we will say that he has suffered brute bad luck. But if he smoked cigarettes heavily then we may prefer to say that he took an unsuccessful gamble.

Insurance, so far as it is available, provides a link between brute and option luck, because the decision to buy or reject catastrophe insurance is a calculated gamble. Of course, insurance does not erase the distinction. Someone who buys medical insurance and is hit by an unexpected meteorite still suffers brute bad luck, because he is worse off than if he had bought insurance and not needed it. But he has had better option luck than if he had not bought the insurance, because his situation is better in virtue of his not having run the gamble of refusing to insure.

It is consistent with equality of resources that people should have different income or wealth in virtue of differing option luck? Suppose some of the immigrants plant valuable but risky crops while others play it safer, and that some of the former buy insurance against uncongenial weather while others do not. Skill will play a part in determining which of these various programs succeed, of course, and we shall consider the problems this raises later. But option luck will also play a part. Does its role threaten or invade equality of resources?

Consider, first, the differences in wealth between those who play it safe and those who gamble and succeed. Some people enjoy, while others hate, risks; but this particular difference in personality is comprehended in a more general difference between the kinds of lives that different people wish to lead. The life chosen by someone who gambles contains, as an element, the factor of risk; someone who chooses not to gamble has decided that he prefers a safer life. We have already decided that people should pay the price of the life they have decided to lead, measured in what others give up in order that they can do so. That was the point of the auction as a device to establish initial equality of resources. But the price of a safer life, measured in this way, is precisely forgoing any chance of the gains whose prospect induces others to gamble. So we have no reason to object, against the background of our earlier decisions, to a result in which those who decline to gamble have less than some of those who do not.

But we must also compare the situation of those who gamble and win with that of those who gamble and lose. We cannot say that the latter have chosen a different life and must sacrifice gains accordingly; for they have chosen the same lives as those who won. But we can say that the possibility of loss was part of the life they chose—that it was the fair price of the possibility of gain. For we might have designed our initial auction so that people could purchase (for example) lottery tickets with their clamshells. But the price of those tickets would have been some amount of other resources (fixed by the odds and the gambling preferences of others) that the shells would otherwise have bought, and which will be wholly forgone if the ticket does not win.

The same point can be made by considering the arguments for re-distribution from winners to losers after the event. If winners were made to share their winnings with losers, then no one would gamble, as individuals, and the kind of life preferred by both those who in the end win and those who lose would be unavailable. Of course, it is not a good argument, against someone who urges redistribution in order to achieve equality of resources, that redistribution would make some forms of life less attractive or even impossible. For the demands of equality (we assume in this essay) are prior to other desiderata, including variety in the kinds of life available to people. (Equality will in any case make certain kinds of lives—a life of economic and political domination of others, for example—impossible.) In the present case, however, the difference is apparent. For the effect of redistribution from winners to losers in gambles would be to deprive both of lives they prefer, which indicates, not simply that this would produce an unwanted curtailment of available forms of life, but that it would deprive them of an equal voice in the construction of lots to be auctioned, like the man who hated both plovers' eggs and claret but was confronted only with bundles of both. They both want gambles to be in the mix, either origi-nally or as represented by resources with which they can take risks later, and the chance of losing is the correct price, measured on the metric we have been using, of a life that includes gambles with a chance of gain.

We may, of course, have special reasons for forbidding certain forms of gambles. We may have paternalistic reasons for limiting how much any individual may risk, for example. We may also have reasons based in a theory of political equality for forbidding someone to gamble with his freedom or his religious or political rights. The present point is more limited. We have no general reason for forbidding gambles altogether in the bare fact that in the event winners will control more resources than losers, any more than in the fact that winners will have more than those who do not gamble at all. Our initial principle, that equality of resources requires that people pay the true cost of the lives that they lead, warrants rather than condemns these differences.

We may (if we wish) adjust our envy test to record that conclusion. We may say that in computing the extent of someone's resources over his life, for the purpose of asking whether anyone else envies those resources, any resources gained through a successful gamble should be represented by the opportunity to take the gamble at the odds in force, and comparable adjustments made to the resources of those who have lost through gambles. The main point of this artificial construction of the envy test, however, would be to remind us that the argument in favor of allowing differences in option luck to affect income and wealth assumes that everyone has in principle the same gambles available to him. Someone who never had the opportunity to run a similar risk, and would have taken the opportunity had it been available, will still envy some of those who did have it.

Nor does the argument yet confront the case of brute bad luck. If two people lead roughly the same lives, but one goes suddenly blind, then we cannot explain the resulting differences in their incomes either by saying that one took risks that the other chose not to take, or that we could not redistribute without denying both the lives they prefer. For the accident has (we assume) nothing to do with choices in the pertinent sense. It is not necessary to the life either has chosen that he run the risk of going blind without redistribution of funds from the other. This is a fortiori so if one is born blind and the other sighted.

But the possibility of insurance provides, as I suggested, a link between the two kinds of luck. For suppose insurance against blindness is available, in the initial auction, at whatever level of coverage the policy holder chooses to buy. And also suppose that two sighted people have, at the time of the auction, equal chance of suffering an accident that will blind them, and know that they have. Now if one chooses to spend part of his initial resources for such insurance and the other does not, or if one buys more coverage than the other, then this difference will reflect their different opinions about the relative value of different forms or components of their prospective lives. It may reflect the fact that one puts more value on sight than the other. Or, differently, that one would count monetary compensation for the loss of his sight as worthless in the face of such a tragedy while the other, more practical, would fix his mind on the aids and special training that such money might buy. Or simply that one minds or values risk differently from the other, and would, for example, rather try for a brilliant life that would collapse under catastrophe than a life guarded at the cost of resources necessary to make it brilliant.

But in any case the bare idea of equality of resources, apart from any paternalistic additions, would not argue for redistribution from the person who had insured to the person who had not if, horribly, they were both blinded in the same accident. For the availability of insurance would mean that, though they had both had brute bad luck, the difference between them was a matter of option luck, and the arguments we entertained against disturbing the results of option luck under conditions of equal antecedent risk hold here as well. But then the situation cannot be different if the person who decided not to insure is the only one to be blinded. For once again the difference is a difference in option luck against a background of equal opportunity to insure or not. If neither had been blinded, the man who had insured against blindness would have been the loser. His option luck would have been bad—though it seems bizarre to put it this way—because he spent resources that, as things turned out, would have been better spent otherwise. But he would have no claim, in that event, from the man who did not insure and also survived unhurt.

So if the condition just stated were met—if everyone had an equal risk of suffering some catastrophe that would leave him or her handicapped, and everyone knew roughly what the odds were and had ample opportunity to insure—then handicaps would pose no special problem for equality of resources. But of course that condition is not met. Some people are born with handicaps, or develop them before they have either sufficient knowledge or funds to insure on their own behalf. They cannot buy insurance after the event. Even handicaps that develop later in life, against which people do have the opportunity to insure, are not randomly distributed through the population, but follow genetic tracks, so that sophisticated insurers would charge some people higher premiums for the same coverage before the event. Nevertheless the idea of a market in insurance provides a counterfactual guide through which equality of resources might face the problem of handicaps in the real world.

Suppose we can make sense of and even give a rough answer to the following question. If (contrary to fact) everyone had at the appropriate age the same risk of developing physical or mental handicaps in the future (which assumes that no one has developed these yet) but that the total number of handicaps remained what it is, how much insurance coverage against these handicaps would the average member of the community purchase? We might then say that but for (uninsurable) brute luck that has altered these equal odds, the average person would have purchased insurance at that level, and compensate those who do develop handicaps accordingly, out of some fund collected by taxation or other compulsory process but designed to match the fund that would have been provided through premiums if the odds had been equal. Those who develop handicaps will then have more resources at their command than others, but the extent of their extra resources will be fixed by the market decisions that people would supposedly have made if circumstances had been more equal than they are. Of course, this argument does involve the fictitious assumption that everyone who suffers handicaps would have bought the average amount of insurance, and we may wish to refine the argument and the strategy so that that no longer holds.[6] But it does not seem an unreasonable assumption for this purpose as it stands.

Can we answer the counterfactual question with sufficient confidence to develop a program of compensation of that sort? We face a threshold difficulty of some importance. People can decide how much of their resources to devote to insurance against a particular catastrophe only with some idea of the life they hope to lead, because only then can they decide how serious a particular catastrophe would be, how far additional resources would alleviate the tragedy, and so forth. But people who are born with a particular handicap, or develop one in childhood, will of course take that circumstance into account in the plans they make. So in order to decide how much insurance such a person would have bought without the handicap we must decide what sort of life he would have planned in that case. But there may be no answer, even in principle, to that question.

We do not need, however, to make counterfactual judgments that are so personalized as to embarrass us for that reason. Even if people did all have equal risk of all catastrophes, and evaluated the value and importance of insurance differently entirely due to their different ambitions and plans, the insurance market would nevertheless be structured through categories designating the risks against which most people would insure in a general way. After all, risks of most catastrophes are now regarded by the actual insurance market as randomly distributed, and so we might follow actual

---

6. The averaging assumption is a simplifying assumption only, made to provide a result in the absence of the detailed (and perhaps, for reasons described in the text, indeterminate) information that would enable us to decide how much each handicapped person would have purchased in the hypothetical market. If we had such full information, so that we could tailor compensation to what a particular individual in fact would have bought, the accuracy of the program would be improved. But in the absence of such information averaging is second best, or in any case better than nothing.

insurance practice, modified to remove the discriminations insurers make when they know that one group is more likely, perhaps for genetic reasons, to suffer a particular kind of brute bad luck. It would make sense to suppose, for example, that most people would make roughly the same assessment of the value of insurance against general handicaps, such as blindness or the loss of a limb, that affect a wide spectrum of different sorts of lives. (We might look to the actual market to discover the likelihood and the contours of more specialized insurance we might decide to use in more complex schemes, like the insurance of musicians against damage to their hands, and so forth.)

We would, in any case, pay great attention to matters of technology, and be ready to adjust our sums as technology changed. People purchase insurance against catastrophes, for example, against a background of assumptions about the remedial medical technology, or special training, or mechanical aids that are in fact available, and about the cost of these remedies. People would seek insurance at a higher level against blindness, for example, if the increased recovery would enable them to purchase a newly discovered sight-substitute technology, than they would if that increased recovery simply swelled a bank account they could not, in any case, use with much satisfaction.

Of course, any judgments that the officials of a community might make about the structure of the hypothetical insurance market would be speculative and open to a variety of objections. But there is no reason to think, certainly in advance, that a practice of compensating the handicapped on the basis of such speculation would be worse, in principle, than the alternatives, and it would have the merit of aiming in the direction of the theoretical solution most congenial to equality of resources.

We might now remind ourselves of what these alternatives are. I said in Part 1 of this essay that the regime of equality of welfare, contrary to initial impressions, does a poor job of either explaining or guiding our impulse to compensate the severely handicapped with extra resources. It provides, in particular, no upper bound to compensation so long as any further payment would improve the welfare of the wretched; but this is not, as it might seem, generous, because it leaves the standard for actual compensation to the politics of selfishness broken by sympathy, politics that we know will supply less than any defensible hypothetical insurance market would offer.

Consider another approach to the problem of handicaps under equality of resources. Suppose we say that any person's physical and mental powers must count as part of his resources, so that someone who is born handicapped starts with less by way of resources than others have, and should be allowed to catch up, by way of transfer payments, before what remains is auctioned off in any equal market.[7] People's powers are indeed resources, because these are used, together with material resources, in making something valuable out of one's life. Physical powers are resources for that purpose in the way that aspects of one's personality, like one's conception of what is valuable in life, are not. Nevertheless the suggestion, that a design of equality of resources should provide for an initial compensation to alleviate differences in physical or mental resources, is troublesome in a variety of ways. It requires, for example, some standard of "normal" powers to serve as the benchmark for compensation.[8] But whose powers should be taken as normal for this purpose? It suffers, moreover, from the same defect as the parallel recommendation under equality of welfare. In fact, no amount of initial compensation could make someone born blind or mentally incompetent equal in physical or mental resources with someone taken to be "normal" in these ways. So the argument provides no upper bound to initial compensation, but must leave this to a political compromise likely to be less generous, again, than what the hypothetical insurance market would command.

Quite apart from these practical and theoretical inadequacies, the suggestion is troublesome for another reason. Though powers are resources, they should not be considered resources whose ownership is to be determined through politics in accordance with some interpretation of equality of resources. They are not, that is, resources for the theory of equality in exactly the sense in which ordinary material resources are. They cannot be manipulated or transferred, even so far as technology might permit. So in this way it misdescribes the problem of handicaps to say that equality of resources must strive to make people equal in physical and mental constitution so far as this is possible. The problem is, rather, one of determining how far the ownership of independent material resources should be affected by differences that exist in physical and mental powers, and the response of our theory should speak in that vocabulary.

It might be wise (if for no other reason than as a convenient summary of the argument from time to time) to bring our story of the immigrants up to date. By way of supplement to the auction, they now establish a hypothetical insurance market which they effectuate through compulsory insurance at a fixed premium for everyone based on speculations about what

7. Cf. Amartya Sen, "Equality of What?," *The Tanner Lectures on Human Values,* Vol. 1 (Salt Lake City: University of Utah Press, 1980), pp. 197, 218 [pp. 160, 175 in this anthology].

8. The hypothetical insurance approach does not require any stipulation of "normal" powers, because it allows the hypothetical market to determine which infirmities are compensable.

the average immigrant would have purchased by way of insurance had the antecedent risk of various handicaps been equal. . . .

But now a question arises. Does this decision place too much weight on the distinction between handicaps, which the immigrants treat in this compensatory way, and accidents touching preferences and ambitions (like the accident of what material resources are in fact available, and of how many other people share a particular person's taste)? The latter will also affect welfare, but they are not matters for compensation under our scheme. Would it not now be fair to treat as handicaps eccentric tastes, or tastes that are expensive or impossible to satisfy because of scarcity of some good that might have been common? We might compensate those who have these tastes by supposing that everyone had an equal chance of being in that position and then establishing a hypothetical insurance market against that possibility.

A short answer is available. Someone who is born with a serious handicap faces his life with what we concede to be fewer resources, just on that account, than others do. This justifies compensation, under a scheme devoted to equality of resources, and though the hypothetical insurance market does not right the balance—nothing can—it seeks to remedy one aspect of the resulting unfairness. But we cannot say that the person whose tastes are expensive, for whatever reason, therefore has fewer resources at his command. For we cannot state (without falling back on some version of equality of welfare) what equality in the distribution of tastes and preferences would be. Why is there less equality of resources when someone has an eccentric taste that makes goods cheaper for others, than when he shares a popular taste and so makes goods more expensive for them? The auction, bringing to bear information about the resources that actually exist and the competing preferences actually in play, is the only true measure of whether any particular person commands equal resources. If the auction has in fact been an equal auction, then the man of eccentric tastes has no less than equal material resources, and the argument that justifies a compensatory hypothetical auction in the case of handicaps has no occasion even to begin. It is true that this argument produces a certain view of the distinction between a person and his circumstances, and assigns his tastes and ambitions to his person, and his physical and mental powers to his circumstances. That is the view of a person I sketched in the introductory section, of someone who forms his ambitions with a sense of their cost to others against some presumed initial equality of economic power, and though this is different from the picture assumed by equality of welfare, it is a picture at the center of equality of resources.

In one way, however, my argument might well be thought to overstate the distinction between handicaps and at least certain sorts of what are often considered preferences. Suppose someone finds he has a craving (or obsession or lust or, in the words of an earlier psychology, a "drive") that he wishes he did not have, because it interferes with what he wants to do with his life and offers him frustration or even pain if it is not satisfied. This might indeed be some feature of his physical needs that other people would not consider a handicap at all: for example, a generous appetite for sex. But it is a "preference" (if that is the right word) that he does not want, and it makes perfect sense to say that he would be better off without it. For some people these unwanted tastes include tastes they have (perhaps unwittingly) themselves cultivated, such as a taste for a particular sport or for music of a sort difficult to obtain. They regret that they have these tastes, and believe they would be better off without them, but nevertheless find it painful to ignore them. These tastes are handicaps; though for other people they are rather an essential part of what gives value to their lives.

Now these cases do not present, for particular people, borderline cases between ambitions and handicaps (though no doubt other sorts of borderline cases could be found). The distinction required by equality of resources is the distinction between those beliefs and attitudes that define what a successful life would be like, which the ideal assigns to the person, and those features of body or mind or personality that provide means or impediments to that success, which the ideal assigns to the person's circumstances. Those who see their sexual desires or their taste for opera as unwanted disadvantages will class these features of their body or mind or personality firmly as the latter. These are, for them, handicaps, and are therefore suitable for the regime proposed for handicaps generally. We may imagine that everyone has an equal chance of acquiring such a craving by accident. (Of course, for each person the content of a craving that would have that consequence would be different. We are supposing here, not the risk of any particular craving, but the risk of whatever craving would interfere with set goals in that way.) We may then ask—with as much or as little intelligibility as in the case of blindness—whether people generally would purchase insurance against that risk, and if so at what premium and what level of coverage. It seems unlikely that many people would purchase such insurance, at the rates of premium likely to govern if they sought it, except in the case of cravings so severe and disabling as to fall under the category of mental disease. But that is a different matter. The important point, presently, is that the idea of an insurance market is available here, because we can imagine people who have such a craving not having it, without thereby imagining them to have a different conception of what they want from life than what in fact they do want. So the idea of the imaginary insurance auction provides at once a device for identifying cravings and distinguishing them from positive features of personality, and also for bringing these cravings within the general regime designed for handicaps.

Labor and Wages

Equality of resources, once established by the auction, and corrected to provide for handicaps, would be disturbed by production and trade. If one of the immigrants, for example, was specially proficient at producing tomatoes, he might trade his surplus for more than anyone else could acquire, in which case others would begin to envy his bundle of resources. Suppose we wished to create a society in which the division of resources would be continuously equal, in spite of different kinds and degrees of production and trade. Can we adapt our auction so as to produce such a society?

We should begin by considering a different sequence after which people would envy each other's resources, and the division might be thought no longer to be equal. Suppose all the immigrants are in fact sufficiently equal in talent at the few modes of production that the resources allow so that each could produce roughly the same goods from the same set of resources. Nevertheless they wish to lead their lives in different ways, and they in fact acquire different bundles of resources in the initial auction and use them differently thereafter. Adrian chooses resources and works them with the single-minded ambition of producing as much of what others value as possible; and so, at the end of a year, his total stock of goods is larger than anyone else's. Each of the other immigrants would now prefer Adrian's stock to his own; but by hypothesis none of them would have been willing to lead his life so as to produce them. If we look for envy at particular points in time, then each envies Adrian's resources at the end of the year, and the division is therefore not equal. But if we look at envy differently, as a matter of resources over an entire life, and we include a person's occupation as part of the bundle of his goods, then no one envies Adrian's bundle, and the distribution cannot be said to be unequal on that account.

Surely we should take the second, synoptic, point of view. Our final aim is that an equal share of resources should be devoted to the lives of each person, and we have chosen the auction as the right way to measure the value of what is made available to a person, through his decision, for that purpose. If Bruce chooses to acquire land for use as a tennis court, then the question is raised how much his account should be charged, in the reckoning whether an equal share has been put to his use, in virtue of that choice, and it is right that his account should be charged the amount that others would have been willing to pay had the land been devoted to their purposes instead. The appeal of the auction, as a device for picturing equality of resources, is precisely that it enforces that metric. But this scheme will fail, and the device disappoint us, unless Adrian is able to bid a price for the same land that reflects his intention to work rather than play on it and so to acquire whatever gain would prompt him to make that decision. For unless this is permitted, those who want tomatoes and would pay Adrian his price for them will not be able to bid indirectly, through Adrian's decision, against Bruce, who will then secure his tennis court at a price that, because it is too low, defeats equality of resources. This is not, I should add, an argument from efficiency as distinct from fairness; but rather an argument that in the circumstances described, in which talents are equal, efficiency simply is fairness, at least as fairness is conceived under equality of resources. If Adrian is willing to spend his life at drudgery, in return for the profit he will make at prices that others will pay for what he produces, then the land on which he would drudge should not be used for a tennis court instead, unless its value as a tennis court is greater as measured by someone's willingness to invade an initially equal stock of abstract resources.

Now this is to look at the matter entirely from the standpoint of those who want Adrian's tomatoes, a standpoint that treats Adrian only as a means. But we reach the same conclusion if we look at the matter from his point of view as well. If someone chooses to have something inexpensive in his life, under a regime of equality of resources, then he will have more left over for the rest of what he wants. Someone who accepts Algerian wine may use it to wash down plovers' eggs. But a decision to produce one thing rather than another with land, or to use the land for leisure rather than production, is also the choice of something for one's life, and this may be inexpensive as well. Suppose Adrian is desperate for plovers' eggs but would rather work hard at tilling his land than settle for less than champagne. The total may be no more expensive, measured in terms of what his decisions cost others, than a life of leisure and grape juice. If he earns enough by working hard, or by working at work that no one else wants to do, to satisfy all his expensive tastes, then his choice for his own life costs the rest of the community no more than if his tastes were simpler and his industry less. So we have no more reason to deny him hard work and high consumption than less work and frugality. The choice should be indifferent under equality of resources, so long as no one envies the total package of work plus consumption that he chooses. So long as no one envies, that is, his life as a whole. Of course, Adrian might actually enjoy his hard work, so that he makes no sacrifice. He prefers working hard to anything else. But this cannot provide any argument, under equality of resources, that he should gain less in money or other goods by his work than if he hated every minute of it, any more than it argues against charging someone a low price for lettuce, which he actually prefers to truffles.

So we must apply the envy test diachronically: it requires that no one envy the bundle of occupation and resources at the disposal of anyone else over time, though someone may envy another's bundle at any particular time. It would therefore violate equality of resources if the community were to redistribute Adrian's wealth, say, at the end of each year. If everyone had equal talents (as we have been assuming just now), the initial auction would produce continuing equality of resources even though bank-account wealth became more and more unequal as years passed.

Is that unlikely condition—that everyone has equal talent—absolutely necessary to that conclusion? Would the auction produce continuing equality of resources if (as in the real world) talents for production differed sharply from person to person? Now the envy test would fail, even interpreted diachronically. Claude (who likes farming but has a black thumb) would not bid enough for farming land to take that land from Adrian. Or, if he did, he would have to settle for less in the rest of his life. But he would then envy the package of Adrian's occupation and wealth. If we interpret occupation in a manner sensitive to the joys of craft, then Adrian's occupation, which must then be described as skillful, craftsmanlike farming, is simply unavailable to Claude. If we interpret occupation in a more census-like fashion, then Claude may undertake Adrian's occupation, but he cannot have the further resources that Adrian has along with it. So if we continue to insist that the envy test is a necessary condition of equality of resources, then our initial auction will not insure continuing equality, in the real world of unequal talents for production.

But it may now be objected that we should not insist on the envy test at this point, even in principle, for the following reason. We are moving too close to a requirement that people must not envy each other, which is different from the requirement that they must not envy each other's bundles of resources. People may envy each other for a variety of reasons: some are physically more attractive, some more easily satisfied with their condition, some better liked by others, some more intelligent or able in different ways, and so on. Of course, under a regime of equality of welfare each of these differences would be taken into account, and transfers made to erase their welfare consequences so far as possible or feasible. But the point of equality of resources is fundamentally different: it is that people should have the same external resources at their command to make of them what, given these various features and talents, they can. That point is satisfied by an initial auction, but since people are different it is neither necessary nor desirable that resources should remain equal thereafter, and quite impossible that all envy should be eliminated by political distribution. If one person, by dint of superior effort or talent, uses his equal share to create more than another, he is entitled to profit thereby, because his gain is not made at the expense of someone else who does less with his share. We recognized that, just now, when we conceded that superior industry should be rewarded, so that Adrian, who worked hard, should be allowed to keep the rewards of his effort.

Now this objection harbors many mistakes, but they all come to this: it confuses equality of resources with the fundamentally different idea sometimes called equality of opportunity. It is not true, in the first place, that someone who does more with his initial share does not, in so doing, lessen the value of what others have. If Adrian were not so successful at agriculture, then Claude's own efforts would be rewarded more, because people would buy his inferior produce having no better alternative. If Adrian were not so successful and hence so rich he would not be able to pay so much for wine, and Claude, with his smaller fortune, would be able to buy more at a cheaper price. These are simply the most obvious consequences of the fact that the immigrants form one economy, after the initial auction, rather than a set of distinct economies. Of course these consequences also follow from the situation we discussed a moment ago. If Adrian and Bruce have the same talents, but Adrian chooses to work harder or differently and acquires more money, then this may also decrease the value of Claude's share to him. The difference between these two circumstances, if there is one, lies elsewhere; but it is important to reject the claim, instinct in some arguments for equality of opportunity, that if people start with equal shares the prosperity of one does no damage to the other.

Nor is it true that if we aim at a result in which those with less talent do not envy the circumstances of those with more talent we have destroyed the distinction between envying others and envying what they have. For Adrian has two things that Claude would prefer to have which belong to Adrian's circumstances rather than his person. The desires and needs of other people provide Adrian but not Claude with a satisfying occupation, and Adrian has more money than Claude can have. Perhaps nothing can be done, by way of political structure or distribution, to erase these differences and remove the envy entirely. We cannot, for example, alter the tastes of other people by electrical means so as to make them value what Claude can produce more and what Adrian can produce less. But this provides no argument against other schemes, like schemes of education that would allow Claude to find satisfaction in his work or of taxation that would redistribute some of Adrian's wealth to him, and we could fairly describe these schemes as aiming to remove Claude's envy of what Adrian has rather than of what Adrian is.

Important as these points are, it is more important still to identify and correct another mistake that the present objection makes. It misunderstands our earlier conclusion, that when talents are roughly equal the auction provides continuing equality of resources, and so misses the important distinction between that case and the present argument. The objection supposes that we reached that conclusion because we accept, as the basis of equality of resources, what we might call the starting-gate theory of fairness: that if people start in the same circumstances, and do not cheat or steal from one another, then it is fair that people keep what they gain through their own skill. But the starting-gate theory of fairness is very far from equality of resources. Indeed it is hardly a coherent political theory at all.

The starting-gate theory holds that justice requires equal initial resources. But it also holds that justice requires laissez-faire thereafter, in accordance, presumably, with some version of the Lockean theory that people acquire property by mixing their labor with goods or something of that sort. But these two principles cannot live comfortably together. Equality can have no greater force in justifying initial equal holdings when the immigrants land—against the competing [claim] that all property should be available for Lockean acquisition at that time—than later in justifying redistributions when wealth becomes unequal because people's productive talents are different. The same point may be put the other way around. The theory of Lockean acquisition (or whatever other theory of justice in acquisition is supposed to justify the laissez-faire component in a starting-gate theory) can have no less force in governing the initial distribution than it has in justifying title through talent and effort later. If the theory is sound later, then why does it not command a Lockean process of acquisition in the first instance, rather than an equal distribution of all there is? The moment when the immigrants first land is, after all, an arbitrary point in their lives at which to locate any one-shot requirement that they each have an equal share of any available resources. If that requirement holds then, it must also hold on the tenth anniversary of that date, which is, in the words of the banal and important cliché, the first day in the rest of their lives. So if justice requires an equal auction when they land, it must require a fresh, equal auction from time to time thereafter; and if justice requires laissez-faire thereafter, it must require it when they land.

Suppose someone replies that there is an important difference between the initial distribution of resources and any later redistribution. When the immigrants land, no one owns any of the resources, and the principle of equality therefore dictates equal initial shares. But later, after the initial resources have been auctioned, they are each owned in some way by someone, so that the principle of equality is superceded by respect for people's rights in property or something of that sort. This reply begs the question straightway. For we are considering precisely the question whether a system of ownership should be established in the first instance that has that consequence, or, rather, whether a different system of ownership should be chosen that explicitly makes any acquisition subject to schemes of redistribution later. If the latter sort of system is chosen, at the outset, then no one can later complain that redistribution is ruled out by his property rights alone. I do not mean that no theory of justice can consistently distinguish between justice in initial acquisition and justice in transfer on the ground that anyone may do what he wants with property that is already his. Nozick's theory, for example, does just that. This is consistent, because his theory of justice in initial acquisition purports to justify a system of property rights which have that consequence: justice in transfer, that is, flows from the rights the theory of acquisition claims are acquired in acquiring property. But the theory of initial acquisition on which the starting-gate theory relies, which is equality of resources, does not even purport to justify a characterization of property that necessarily includes absolute control without limit of time thereafter.

So the starting-gate theory, that the immigrants should start off equal in resources but grow prosperous or lean through their own efforts thereafter, is an indefensible combination of very different theories of justice. Something like that combination makes sense in games, such as Monopoly, whose point is to allow luck and skill to play a highly circumscribed and, in the last analysis, arbitrary, role; but it cannot hold together a political theory. Our own principle, that if people of equal talent choose different lives it is unfair to redistribute halfway through those lives, makes no appeal to the starting-gate theory at all. It is based on the very different idea that the equality in question is equality of resources devoted to whole lives. This principle offers a clear answer to the question that embarrasses the present objection. Our theory does not suppose that an equal division of resources is appropriate at one moment in someone's life but not at any other. It argues only that resources available to him at any moment must be a function of resources available or consumed by him at others, so that the explanation of why someone has less money now may be that he has consumed expensive leisure earlier. Nothing like that explanation is available to explain why Claude, who has worked as hard and in the same way as Adrian, should have less in virtue of the fact that he is less skillful.

So we must reject the starting-gate theory, and recognize that the

requirements of equality (in the real world at least) pull in opposite directions. On the one hand we must, on pain of violating equality, allow the
distribution of resources at any particular moment to be (as we might say)
ambition-sensitive. It must, that is, reflect the cost or benefit to others of
the choices people make so that, for example, those who choose to invest
rather than consume, or to consume less expensively rather than more, or
to work in more rather than less profitable ways, must be permitted to
retain the gains that flow from these decisions in an equal auction followed
by free trade. But on the other hand, we must not allow the distribution of
resources at any moment to be endowment-sensitive, that is, to be affected
by differences in ability of the sort that produce income differences in a
laissez-faire economy among people with the same ambitions. Can we
devise some formula that offers a practical, or even a theoretical, compromise between these two, apparently competing, requirements?

We might mention, but only to dismiss, one possible response. Suppose
we allow our initial auction to include, as resources to be auctioned, the
labor of the immigrants themselves, so that each immigrant can bid for the
right to control part or all of his own or other people's labor. Special skills
would accrue to the benefit, not of the laborer himself, but of the community as a whole, like any other valuable resource the immigrants found
when they landed. Except in unusual cases, since people begin with equal
resources for bidding, each agent would bid enough to secure his own
labor. But the result would be that each would have to spend his life in
close to the commercially most profitable manner he could, or, at least if he
is talented, suffer some very serious deprivation if he did not. For since
Adrian, for example, is able to produce prodigious income from farming,
others would be willing to bid a large amount to have the right to his labor
and the vegetables thereof, and if he outbids them, but chooses to write
indifferent poetry instead of farming full time, he will have spent a large
part of his initial endowment on a right that will bring him little financial
benefit. This is indeed the slavery of the talented.

We cannot permit this, but it is worth pausing to ask what grounds we
have for barring it. Shall we say that since a person owns his own mind and
body, he owns the talents that are only capacities thereof, and therefore
owns the fruits of those talents? This is, of course, a series of nonsequiturs.
It is also a familiar argument in favor of the laissez-faire labor market we
have decided is a violation of equality of resources when people are unequal in talent. But we could not accept it in any case, because it uses the
idea of pre-political entitlement based on something other than equality,
and that is inconsistent with the premise of the scheme of equality of
resources we have developed.

So we must look elsewhere for the ground of our objection to taking people's labor as a resource for the auction. We need not, in fact, look very far; for the principle that people should not be penalized for talent is simply part of the same principle we relied on in rejecting the apparently opposite idea, that people should be allowed to retain the benefits of superior talent. The envy test forbids both of these results. If Adrian is treated as owning whatever his talents enable him to produce, then Claude envies the package of resources, including occupation, that Adrian has over his life considered as a whole. But if Adrian is required to purchase leisure time or the right to a less productive occupation at the cost of other resources, then Adrian will envy Claude's package. If equality of resources is understood to include some plausible version of the envy test, as a necessary condition of an equal distribution, then the role of talent must be neutralized in a way that no simple addition to the stock of goods to be auctioned can accomplish.

We should turn, therefore, to a more familiar idea: the periodic redistribution of resources through some form of income tax.[9] We want to develop a scheme of redistribution, so far as we are able, that will neutralize the effects of differential talents, yet preserve the consequences of one person choosing an occupation, in response to his sense of what he wants to do with his life, that is more expensive for the community than the choice another makes. An income tax is a plausible device for this purpose because it leaves intact the possibility of choosing a life in which sacrifices are constantly made and discipline steadily imposed for the sake of financial success and the further resources it brings, though of course it neither endorses nor condemns that choice. But it also recognizes the role of genetic luck in such a life. The accommodation it makes is a compromise;

---

9. Notice that our analysis of the problem that differential talents presents to equality of resources calls for an income tax, rather than either a wealth or a consumption tax. If people begin with equal resources, then we wish to tax to adjust for different skills so far as these produce different income, because it is only in that way that they threaten equality of resources. Someone's decision to spend rather than save what he has earned is precisely the kind of decision whose impact should be determined by the market uncorrected for tax under this analysis. Of course, there might be technical or other reasons why a society dedicated to equality of welfare would introduce taxes other than income taxes. Such a society might want to encourage savings, for example. But these taxes would not be responses to the problem now under consideration. Should unearned (investment) income be taxed under the present argument? I assume that unearned income reflects skill in investment as well as preferences for later consumption, in which case that argument would extend to taxing such income. Since I am not considering, in this essay, the problem of later generations, I do not consider inheritance or estate taxes at all.

but it is a compromise of two requirements of equality, in the face of both practical and conceptual uncertainty how to satisfy these requirements, not a compromise of equality for the sake of some independent value such as efficiency.

. . .

[In a portion of the text that is omitted from this excerpt, Dworkin extends his discussion of insurance to the case of underemployment insurance and considers the question of insurance premiums in the form of taxation.]

I shall try to say something, finally, about the connections and differences between our conception of equality of resources and John Rawls's theory of justice. That theory is sufficiently rich to provide a question of connection at two different levels. First, how far do the arguments in favor of equality of resources, as described, follow the structure of argument Rawls deploys? How far do they depend, that is, on the hypothesis that people in the original position Rawls described would choose the principles of equality of resources behind the veil? Second—and independently—how far are the requirements of equality of resources different from the two principles of justice that Rawls suggests people in that position would in fact choose?

It is obviously better to start with the second of these questions. The comparison in point is that between equality of resources and Rawls's second principle of justice, whose main component is the "difference" principle which requires no variation from absolute equality in "primary goods" save as works to the benefit of the worst-off economic class. (Rawls's first principle, which establishes what he calls the priority of liberty, has more to do with the topics I have set aside as belonging to political equality.) The difference principle, like our conception of equality of resources, works only contingently in the direction of equality of welfare on any conception of welfare. If we distinguish broadly between theories of equality of welfare and of resources, the difference principle is an interpretation of equality of resources.

But it is nevertheless a rather different interpretation than our conception. From the standpoint of our conception, the difference principle is not sufficiently fine-tuned in a variety of ways. There is a conceded degree of arbitrariness in the choice of any description of the worst-off group, and this is, in any case, a group whose fortunes can be charted only through some mythical average or representative member of that group. In particular, the structure seems insufficiently sensitive to the position of those with natural handicaps, physical or mental, who do not themselves constitute a worst-off group, because this is defined economically, and would not count as the representative or average member of any such group. Rawls calls attention to what he calls the principle of redress, which argues that compensation should be made to people so handicapped, as indeed it is, in the way I described, under our conception of equality. But he notes that the difference principle does not include the principle of redress, though it would tend in the same direction insofar as special training for the handicapped, for example, would work to the benefit of the economically worst-off class. But there is no reason to think that it would, at least in normal circumstances.

It has often been pointed out, moreover, that the difference principle is insufficiently sensitive to variations in distribution above the worst-off economic class. This complaint is sometimes illustrated with bizarre hypothetical questions. Suppose an existing economic system is in fact just. It meets the conditions of the difference principle because no further transfers of wealth to the worst-off class would in fact improve its position. Then some impending catastrophe (for example) presents officials with a choice. They can act so that the position of the representative member of the small worst-off class is worsened by a just noticeable amount or so that the position of everyone else is dramatically worsened and they become almost as poor as the worst-off. Does justice really require the much greater loss to everyone but the poorest in order to prevent a very small loss by them?

It may be a sufficient reply to such questions that circumstances of that sort are very unlikely to arise, and that in fact the fates of the various economic orders are or can easily be "chained" together so that improvements in the worst-off class will in fact be accompanied by improvement in at least the other classes just above them. But this reply does not remove the theoretical question whether, in all circumstances, it is really and exclusively the situation of the worst-off group that determines what is just.

Equality of resources, as described here, does not single out any group whose status has that position. It aims to provide a description (or rather a set of devices for aiming at) equality of resources person by person, and the considerations of each person's history that affect what he should have, in the name of equality, do not include his membership in any economic or social class. I do not mean that our theory, even as so far detailed, claims any impressive degree of accuracy for those devices. On the contrary, even in the artificially simple case we treated, we several times had to concede speculation and compromise, and sometimes even indeterminacy, in the statement of what equality would require in particular circumstances. But the theory nevertheless proposes that equality is in principle a matter of individual right rather than group position. Not, of course, in the sense that each has a predetermined share at his disposal regardless of what he does or what happens to others. On the contrary, the theory ties the fates of people together in the way that the dominant devices of actual and hypothetical markets are meant to describe. But in the different sense that the theory supposes that equality defines a relation among citizens that is individualized for each, and therefore can be seen to set entitlements as much from the point of view of each person as that of anyone else in the community. Even when our theory helps itself to the idea of an average utility curve, as it does in the construction of hypothetical insurance markets, it does so as a matter of probability judgments about particular people's particular tastes and ambitions, in the interests of giving them what they are, as individuals, entitled to have, rather than as part of any premise that equality is a matter of equality between groups. Rawls, on the other hand, assumes that the difference principle ties justice to a class, not as a matter of second-best practical accommodation to some deeper version of equality which is in principle more individualized, but because the choice in the original position, which defines what justice even at bottom is, would for practical reasons be framed in class terms from the start.[10]

It is impossible to say, a priori, whether the difference principle or equality of resources will work to achieve greater absolute equality in what Rawls calls primary goods. That would depend upon circumstances. Suppose, for example, that the tax necessary to provide the right coverage for handicaps and the unemployed has the long-term effect of discouraging investment and in this way reducing the primary-goods prospects of the representative member of the worst-off class. Certain individual members of the worst-off group who are handicapped or who are and will remain unemployed would be better off under the tax scheme (as would, we should notice, certain members of other classes as well) but the average or representative member of the worst-off class would be worse off. The difference principle, which looks to the worst-off group as a whole, would condemn the tax, but equality of resources would recommend it nevertheless.

In the circumstances of the familiar bizarre questions just described, when a just noticeable loss to the representative member of the worst-off class, from a just base, could be prevented only by very substantial losses to those better off, the difference principle is committed to preventing that small loss even at that cost. Equality of resources, on the contrary, would be sensitive to quantitative differences of just the sort that those who take

10. J. Rawls, *A Theory of Justice* (Cambridge, MA: Harvard University Press, 1971), p. 98.

objection to Rawls's theory on that account believe should matter. If the base is an equal division of resources, this means, not that any transfer to the worst-off group would work to the long-run loss of that group, which it might or might not, but that any such transfer would be an invasion of equality because it would be unfair to others. The fact that those at the bottom do not have more would not indicate that it is impossible to give them more, but rather that they have all that they are entitled to have. If some economic catastrophe is now threatened, a government that allows a much greater loss to fall on one citizen, in order to avert a much smaller loss to a second, would not be treating the former as an equal, because, since equality in itself requires no further special attention to the second, that government must have more concern with his fate than it has for the fate of others. So if the loss threatened to the financially worst-off is indeed really inconsequential to him, as the bizarre question assumes, then that is an end of the matter.

But it does not follow that equality of resources turns into utilitarianism in the face of examples like these. It is, in fact, sensitive to more, or at least different, quantitative information than either the difference principle or utilitarianism is. For suppose the impending catastrophe threatens the worst-off group, not with a trivial loss as in the original question, but with a substantial loss, though not as great, in aggregate, as the loss threatened to those better-off. Equality of resources must ask whether the calculations of the hypothetical insurance market, and of the tax scheme in force, took adequate account of the risk of the threat now about to materialize. It might not have. The possibility of a substantial loss from the unexpected quarter, if it had been anticipated, might have led the average buyer in that market to purchase either catastrophe or unemployment insurance at a higher level of coverage, and this fact might affect an official's present decision about how to distribute the coming loss. He might be persuaded, for example, that allowing the loss to fall on those better-off, in spite of the overall welfare loss, would reach a situation closer to the situation all would have been in had the tax scheme better reflected what people would have done in the hypothetical market with that additional information.

Such contrasts in the practical advice that the difference principle and equality of resources offer in particular circumstances are in fact myriad, and these examples are meant only to be suggestive of others. These contrasts are organized around the theoretical distinction I have already noticed. The difference principle is tuned to only one of the dimensions of equality that equality of resources recognizes. The former supposes that flat equality in primary goods, without regard to differences in ambition, taste, and occupation, or to differences in consumption, let alone differences in physical condition or handicap, is basic or true equality. Since (once the priority of liberty is satisfied) justice consists in equality, and since true equality is just this flat equality, any compromise or deviation can be justified only on the grounds that it is in the interests of the only people who might properly complain of the deviation.

This uni-dimensional analysis of equality would plainly be unsatisfactory if applied person by person. It would fall before the argument that it is not an equal division of social resources when someone who consumes more of what others want nevertheless has as much left over as someone who consumes less. Nor that someone who chooses to work at a more productive occupation, measured by what others want, should have no more resources in consequence than someone who prefers leisure. (It would fall before such arguments, that is, unless it were converted into a form of equality of welfare through the doubtful proposition that equality in primary goods, in spite of different consumption or occupational histories, is the best guarantee of equality of welfare.)

So (as Rawls, as I said, makes plain) the difference principle does not tie itself to groups rather than individuals as a second-best accommodation to some deeper vision of equality that is individualistic. Any such deeper vision would condemn the difference principle as inadequate. It ties itself to groups in principle, because the idea of equality among social groups, defined in economic terms, is especially congenial to the flat interpretation of equality. Indeed, the idea of equality as equality among economic groups permits no other interpretation. Since the members of any economic group will be widely diverse in tastes, ambitions, and conceptions of the good life, these must drop away from any principle stating what true equality among groups requires, and we are left with only the requirement that they must be equal in the only dimension on which they can, as groups, possibly differ. The tie between the difference principle and the group taken as its unit of social measure is close to definitional.

We must be wary in rushing from this fact to conclusions about Rawls's theory of justice as a whole. The first of his principles of justice is plainly meant to be individualistic in a way that the difference principle is not, and any evaluation of the role of the individual in the theory as a whole would require a careful analysis of that principle and of the manner in which the two principles might work in harness. But insofar as the difference principle is meant to express a theory of equality of resources, it expresses a theory different in its basic vocabulary and design from the theory sketched here. It might well be worthwhile to pursue that difference further, perhaps by elaborating and working out in more detail the differences between the consequences of the two theories in practical circumstances. But I shall turn instead to the first of the two issues of comparison I distinguished.

I have tried to show the appeal of equality of resources, as interpreted here, only by making plainer its motivation and defending its coherence and practical force. I have not tried to defend it in what might be considered a more direct way, by deducing it from more general and abstract political principles. So the question arises whether that sort of defense could be provided and, in particular, whether it could be found in Rawls's general method. The fact that equality of resources differs in various ways, some of them fundamental, from Rawls's own difference principle is not decisive against this possibility. For perhaps we might show that the people who inhabit Rawls's original position would choose, behind the veil of their ignorance, not his difference principle, but either equality of resources or some intermediate constitutional principles such that, when the veil was lifted, it would be discovered that equality of resources satisfied these principles better than the difference principle could.

I hope it is clear that I have not presented any such argument here. It is true that I have argued that an equal distribution is a distribution that would result from people's choices under certain circumstances, some of which, as in the case of the hypothetical insurance markets, require the counterfactual assumption that people are ignorant of what in fact they are very likely to know. But this argument is different from an argument from the original position in two ways. First, my arguments have been designed to permit people as much knowledge as it is possible to allow them without defeating the point of the exercise entirely. In particular, they allow people enough self-knowledge, as individuals, to keep relatively intact their sense of their own personality, and especially their theory of what is valuable in life, whereas it is central to the original position that this is exactly the knowledge people lack. Second, and more important, my arguments are constructed against the background of assumptions about what equality requires in principle. It is not intended, as Rawls's argument is intended, to establish that background. My arguments enforce rather than construct a basic design of justice, and that design must find support, if at all, elsewhere than in those arguments.

I do not mean to suggest, however, that I am simply agnostic about the project of supporting equality of resources as a political ideal by showing that people in the original position would choose it. I think that any such project must fail. Or rather that it is misconceived, because some theory of equality, like equality of resources, is necessary to explain why the original position is a useful device—or one among a number of useful devices—for considering what justice is. The project, as just described, would therefore be too self-sustaining. The device of an original position (as I have argued at length elsewhere)[11] cannot plausibly be taken as the starting point for political philosophy. It requires a deeper theory beneath it, a theory that explains why the original position has the features that it does and why the fact that people would choose particular principles in that position, if they would, certifies those principles as principles of justice. The force of the original position as a device for arguments for justice, or of any particular design of the original position for that purpose, depends, in my view, on the adequacy of an interpretation of equality of resources that supports it, not vice versa.

11. R. Dworkin, *Taking Rights Seriously* (Cambridge, Mass.: Harvard University Press, 1977), chap. 6.

16

Michael Walzer, "Complex Equality," from *Spheres of Justice*

Michael Walzer is Professor of Social Science at the Institute for Advanced Study in Princeton, New Jersey. He is the author of Just and Unjust Wars *and* On Toleration, *as well as a frequent contributor over many years to* Dissent *magazine.* Spheres of Justice, *the book from which this selection is drawn, grew out of a course on "Capitalism and Socialism" Walzer co-taught with Robert Nozick at Harvard University in the early 1970s.*

Complex Equality

Pluralism

Distributive justice is a large idea. It draws the entire world of goods within the reach of philosophical reflection. Nothing can be omitted; no feature of our common life can escape scrutiny. Human society is a distributive community. That's not all it is, but it is importantly that: we come together to share, divide, and exchange. We also come together to make the things that are shared, divided, and exchanged; but that very making—work itself—is distributed among us in a division of labor. My place in the economy, my standing in the political order, my reputation among my fellows, my material holdings: all these come to me from other men and women. It can be said that I have what I have rightly or wrongly, justly or unjustly; but given the range of distributions and the number of participants, such judgments are never easy.

The idea of distributive justice has as much to do with being and doing as with having, as much to do with production as with consumption, as much to do with identity and status as with land, capital, or personal possessions. Different political arrangements enforce, and different ideologies justify, different distributions of membership, power, honor, ritual eminence, divine grace, kinship and love, knowledge, wealth, physical security, work and leisure, rewards and punishments, and a host of goods more narrowly and materially conceived—food, shelter, clothing, trans-portation, medical care, commodities of every sort, and all the odd things (paintings, rare books, postage stamps) that human beings collect. And this multiplicity of goods is matched by a multiplicity of distributive procedures, agents, and criteria. There are such things as simple distribu-tive systems—slave galleys, monasteries, insane asylums, kindergartens (though each of these, looked at closely, might show unexpected complex-ities); but no full-fledged human society has ever avoided the multiplicity. We must study it all, the goods and the distributions, in many different times and places.

There is, however, no single point of access to this world of distributive arrangements and ideologies. There has never been a universal medium of exchange. Since the decline of the barter economy, money has been the most common medium. But the old maxim according to which there are some things that money can't buy is not only normatively but also fac-tually true. What should and should not be up for sale is something men and women always have to decide and have decided in many different ways. Throughout history, the market has been one of the most important mechanisms for the distribution of social goods; but it has never been, it nowhere is today, a complete distributive system.

Similarly, there has never been either a single decision point from which all distributions are controlled or a single set of agents making decisions. No state power has ever been so pervasive as to regulate all the patterns of sharing, dividing, and exchanging out of which a society takes shape. Things slip away from the state's grasp; new patterns are worked out—familial networks, black markets, bureaucratic alliances, clandestine politi-cal and religious organizations. State officials can tax, conscript, allocate, regulate, appoint, reward, punish, but they cannot capture the full range of goods or substitute themselves for every other agent of distribution. Nor can anyone else do that: there are market coups and cornerings, but there has never been a fully successful distributive conspiracy.

And finally, there has never been a single criterion, or a single set of interconnected criteria, for all distributions. Desert, qualification, birth and blood, friendship, need, free exchange, political loyalty, democratic decision: each has had its place, along with many others, uneasily coexist-ing, invoked by competing groups, confused with one another.

In the matter of distributive justice, history displays a great variety of arrangements and ideologies. But the first impulse of the philosopher is to resist the displays of history, the world of appearances, and to search for some underlying unity: a short list of basic goods, quickly abstracted to a single good; a single distributive criterion or an interconnected set; and the philosopher himself standing, symbolically at least, at a single decision point. I shall argue that to search for unity is to misunderstand the subject matter of distributive justice. Nevertheless, in some sense the philosophical impulse is unavoidable. Even if we choose pluralism, as I shall do, that choice still requires a coherent defense. There must be principles that justify the choice and set limits to it, for pluralism does not require us to endorse every proposed distributive criteria or to accept every would-be agent. Conceivably, there is a single principle and a single legitimate kind of pluralism. But this would still be a pluralism that encompassed a wide range of distributions. By contrast, the deepest assumption of most of the philosophers who have written about justice, from Plato onward, is that there is one, and only one, distributive system that philosophy can rightly encompass.

Today this system is commonly described as the one that ideally rational men and women would choose if they were forced to choose impartially, knowing nothing of their own situation, barred from making particularist claims, confronting an abstract set of goods.[1] If these constraints on knowing and claiming are suitably shaped, and if the goods are suitably defined, it is probably true that a singular conclusion can be produced. Rational men and women, constrained this way or that, will choose one, and only one, distributive system. But the force of that singular conclusion is not easy to measure. It is surely doubtful that those same men and women, if they were transformed into ordinary people, with a firm sense of their own identity, with their own goods in their hands, caught up in everyday troubles, would reiterate their hypothetical choice or even recognize it as their own. The problem is not, most importantly, with the particularism of interest, which philosophers have always assumed they could safely—that is, uncontroversially—set aside. Ordinary people can do that too, for the sake, say, of the public interest. The greater problem is with the particularism of history, culture, and membership. Even if they are committed to impartiality, the question most likely to arise in the minds of the members of a political community is not, What would rational individuals choose under universalizing conditions of such-and-such a sort? But rather, What would individuals like us choose, who are situated as we are, who share a culture and are determined to go on sharing it? And this is a question that is readily transformed into, What choices have we already made in the course of our common life? What understandings do we (really) share?

Justice is a human construction, and it is doubtful that it can be made in

---

1. See John Rawls, *A Theory of Justice* (Cambridge, Mass., 1971); Jürgen Habermas, *Legitimation Crisis*, trans. by Thomas McCarthy (Boston, 1975), esp. p. 113; Bruce Ackerman, *Social Justice in the Liberal State* (New Haven, 1980).

only one way. At any rate, I shall begin by doubting, and more than doubting, this standard philosophical assumption. The questions posed by the theory of distributive justice admit of a range of answers, and there is room within the range for cultural diversity and political choice. It's not only a matter of implementing some singular principle or set of principles in different historical settings. No one would deny that there is a range of morally permissible implementations. I want to argue for more than this: that the principles of justice are themselves pluralistic in form; that different social goods ought to be distributed for different reasons, in accordance with different procedures, by different agents; and that all these differences derive from different understandings of the social goods themselves—the inevitable product of historical and cultural particularism.

A Theory of Goods

Theories of distributive justice focus on a social process commonly described as if it had this form:

People distribute goods to (other) people.

Here, "distribute" means give, allocate, exchange, and so on, and the focus is on the individuals who stand at either end of these actions: not on producers and consumers, but on distributive agents and recipients of goods. We are as always interested in ourselves, but, in this case, in a special and limited version of ourselves, as people who give and take. What is our nature? What are our rights? What do we need, want, deserve? What are we entitled to? What would we accept under ideal conditions? Answers to these questions are turned into distributive principles, which are supposed to control the movement of goods. The goods, defined by abstraction, are taken to be movable in any direction.

But this is too simple an understanding of what actually happens, and it forces us too quickly to make large assertions about human nature and moral agency—assertions unlikely, ever, to command general agreement. I want to propose a more precise and complex description of the central process:

People conceive and create goods, which they then distribute among themselves.

Here, the conception and creation precede and control the distribution. Goods don't just appear in the hands of distributive agents who do with them as they like or give them out in accordance with some general principle.[2] Rather, goods with their meanings—because of their meanings—are the crucial medium of social relations; they come into people's minds before they come into their hands; distributions are patterned in accordance with shared conceptions of what the goods are and what they are for. Distributive agents are constrained by the goods they hold; one might almost say that goods distribute themselves among people.

> Things are in the saddle
> And ride mankind.[3]

But these are always particular things and particular groups of men and women. And, of course, we make the things—even the saddle. I don't want to deny the importance of human agency, only to shift our attention from distribution itself to conception and creation: the naming of the goods, and the giving of meaning, and the collective making. What we need to explain and limit the pluralism of distributive possibilities is a theory of goods. For our immediate purposes, that theory can be summed up in six propositions.

1. All the goods with which distributive justice is concerned are social goods. They are not and they cannot be idiosyncratically valued. I am not sure that there are any other kinds of goods; I mean to leave the question open. Some domestic objects are cherished for private and sentimental reasons, but only in cultures where sentiment regularly attaches to such objects. A beautiful sunset, the smell of new-mown hay, the excitement of an urban vista: these perhaps are privately valued goods, though they are also, and more obviously, the objects of cultural assessment. Even new inventions are not valued in accordance with the ideas of their inventors; they are subject to a wider process of conception and creation. God's goods, to be sure, are exempt from this rule—as in the first chapter of Genesis: "and God saw every thing that He had made, and, behold, it was very good" (1:31). That evaluation doesn't require the agreement of mankind (who might be doubtful), or of a majority of men and women, or of any group of men and women meeting under ideal conditions (though Adam and Eve in Eden would probably endorse it). But I can't think of any other exemptions. Goods in the world have shared meanings because conception and creation are social processes. For the same reason, goods

---

2. Robert Nozick makes a similar argument in *Anarchy, State, and Utopia* (New York, 1974), pp. 149–50, but with radically individualistic conclusions that seem to me to miss the social character of production.

3. Ralph Waldo Emerson, "Ode," in *The Complete Essays and Other Writings*, ed. by Brooks Atkinson (New York, 1940), p. 770.

have different meanings in different societies. The same "thing" is valued for different reasons, or it is valued here and disvalued there. John Stuart Mill once complained that "people like in crowds," but I know of no other way to like or to dislike social goods.[4] A solitary person could hardly understand the meaning of the goods or figure out the reasons for taking them as likable or dislikable. Once people like in crowds, it becomes possible for individuals to break away, pointing to latent or subversive meanings, aiming at alternative values—including the values, for example, of notoriety and eccentricity. An easy eccentricity has sometimes been one of the privileges of the aristocracy: it is a social good like any other.

2. Men and women take on concrete identities because of the way they conceive and create, and then possess and employ social goods. "The line between what is me and mine," wrote William James, "is very hard to draw."[5] Distributions can not be understood as the acts of men and women who do not yet have particular goods in their minds or in their hands. In fact, people already stand in a relation to a set of goods; they have a history of transactions, not only with one another but also with the moral and material world in which they live. Without such a history, which begins at birth, they wouldn't be men and women in any recognizable sense, and they wouldn't have the first notion of how to go about the business of giving, allocating, and exchanging goods.

3. There is no single set of primary or basic goods conceivable across all moral and material worlds—or, any such set would have to be conceived in terms so abstract that they would be of little use in thinking about particular distributions. Even the range of necessities, if we take into account moral as well as physical necessities, is very wide, and the rank orderings are very different. A single necessary good, and one that is always necessary—food, for example—carries different meanings in different places. Bread is the staff of life, the body of Christ, the symbol of the Sabbath, the means of hospitality, and so on. Conceivably, there is a limited sense in which the first of these is primary, so that if there were twenty people in the world and just enough bread to feed the twenty, the primacy of bread-as-staff-of-life would yield a sufficient distributive principle. But that is the only circumstance in which it would do so; and even there, we can't be sure. If the religious uses of bread were to conflict with

4. John Stuart Mill, *On Liberty*, in *The Philosophy of John Stuart Mill*, ed. by Marshall Cohen (New York, 1961), p. 255. For an anthropological account of liking and not liking social goods, see Mary Douglas and Baron Isherwood, *The World of Goods* (New York, 1979).

5. William James, quoted in C. R. Snyder and Howard Fromkin, *Uniqueness: The Human Pursuit of Difference* (New York, 1980), p. 108.

its nutritional uses—if the gods demanded that bread be baked and burned rather than eaten—it is by no means clear which use would be primary. How, then, is bread to be incorporated into the universal list? The question is even harder to answer, the conventional answers less plausible, as we pass from necessities to opportunities, powers, reputations, and so on. These can be incorporated only if they are abstracted from every particular meaning—hence, for all practical purposes, rendered meaningless.

4. But it is the meaning of goods that determines their movement. Distributive criteria and arrangements are intrinsic not to the good-in-itself but to the social good. If we understand what it is, what it means to those for whom it is a good, we understand how, by whom, and for what reasons it ought to be distributed. All distributions are just or unjust relative to the social meanings of the goods at stake. This is in obvious ways a principle of legitimation, but it is also a critical principle.* When medieval Christians, for example, condemned the sin of simony, they were claiming that the meaning of a particular social good, ecclesiastical office, excluded its sale and purchase. Given the Christian understanding of office, it followed—I am inclined to say, it necessarily followed—that office holders should be chosen for their knowledge and piety and not for their wealth. There are presumably things that money can buy, but not this thing. Similarly, the words *prostitution* and *bribery*, like *simony*, describe the sale and purchase of goods that, given certain understandings of their meaning, ought never to be sold or purchased.

5. Social meanings are historical in character; and so distributions, and just and unjust distributions, change over time. To be sure, certain key goods have what we might think of as characteristic normative structures, reiterated across the lines (but not all the lines) of time and space. It is

---

*Aren't social meanings, as Marx said, nothing other than "the ideas of the ruling class," "the dominant material relationships grasped as ideas"?[6] I don't think that they are ever only that or simply that, though the members of the ruling class and the intellectuals they patronize may well be in a position to exploit and distort social meanings in their own interests. When they do that, however, they are likely to encounter resistance, rooted (intellectually) in those same meanings. A people's culture is always a joint, even if it isn't an entirely cooperative, production; and it is always a complex production. The common understanding of particular goods incorporates principles, procedures, conceptions of agency, that the rulers would not choose if they were choosing *right now*—and so provides the terms of social criticism. The appeal to what I shall call "internal" principles against the usurpations of powerful men and women is the ordinary form of critical discourse.

6. Karl Marx, *The German Ideology*, ed. by R. Pascal (New York, 1947), p. 89.

because of this reiteration that the British philosopher Bernard Williams is able to argue that goods should always be distributed for "relevant reasons"—where relevance seems to connect to essential rather than to social meanings.[7] The idea that offices, for example, should go to qualified candidates—though not the only idea that has been held about offices—is plainly visible in very different societies where simony and nepotism, under different names, have similarly been thought sinful or unjust. (But there has been a wide divergence of views about what sorts of position and place are properly called "offices.") Again, punishment has been widely understood as a negative good that ought to go to people who are judged to deserve it on the basis of a verdict, not of a political decision. (But what constitutes a verdict? Who is to deliver it? How, in short, is justice to be done to accused men and women? About these questions there has been significant disagreement.) These examples invite empirical investigation. There is no merely intuitive or speculative procedure for seizing upon relevant reasons.

6. When meanings are distinct, distributions must be autonomous. Every social good or set of goods constitutes, as it were, a distributive sphere within which only certain criteria and arrangements are appropriate. Money is inappropriate in the sphere of ecclesiastical office; it is an intrusion from another sphere. And piety should make for no advantage in the marketplace, as the marketplace has commonly been understood. Whatever can rightly be sold ought to be sold to pious men and women and also to profane, heretical, and sinful men and women (else no one would do much business). The market is open to all comers; the church is not. In no society, of course, are social meanings entirely distinct. What happens in one distributive sphere affects what happens in the others; we can look, at most, for relative autonomy. But relative autonomy, like social meaning, is a critical principle—indeed, as I shall be arguing throughout this book, a radical principle. It is radical even though it doesn't point to a single standard against which all distributions are to be measured. There is no single standard. But there are standards (roughly knowable even when they are also controversial) for every social good and every distributive sphere in every particular society; and these standards are often violated, the goods usurped, the spheres invaded, by powerful men and women.

7. Bernard Williams, *Problems of the Self: Philosophical Papers, 1956–1972* (Cambridge, 1973), pp. 230–49 ("The Idea of Equality"). This essay is one of the starting points of my own thinking about distributive justice. See also the critique of Williams's argument (and of an earlier essay of my own) in Amy Gutmann, *Liberal Equality* (Cambridge, 1980), chap. 4.

Dominance and Monopoly

In fact, the violations are systematic. Autonomy is a matter of social meaning and shared values, but it is more likely to make for occasional reformation and rebellion than for everyday enforcement. For all the complexity of their distributive arrangements, most societies are organized on what we might think of as a social version of the gold standard: one good or one set of goods is dominant and determinative of value in all the spheres of distribution. And that good or set of goods is commonly monopolized, its value upheld by the strength and cohesion of its owners. I call a good dominant if the individuals who have it, because they have it, can command a wide range of other goods. It is monopolized whenever a single man or woman, a monarch in the world of value—or a group of men and women, oligarchs—successfully hold it against all rivals. Dominance describes a way of using social goods that isn't limited by their intrinsic meanings or that shapes those meanings in its own image. Monopoly describes a way of owning or controlling social goods in order to exploit their dominance. When goods are scarce and widely needed, like water in the desert, monopoly itself will make them dominant. Mostly, however, dominance is a more elaborate social creation, the work of many hands, mixing reality and symbol. Physical strength, familial reputation, religious or political office, landed wealth, capital, technical knowledge: each of these, in different historical periods, has been dominant; and each of them has been monopolized by some group of men and women. And then all good things come to those who have the one best thing. Possess that one, and the others come in train. Or, to change the metaphor, a dominant good is converted into another good, into many others, in accordance with what often appears to be a natural process but is in fact magical, a kind of social alchemy.

No social good ever entirely dominates the range of goods; no monopoly is ever perfect. I mean to describe tendencies only, but crucial tendencies. For we can characterize whole societies in terms of the patterns of conversion that are established within them. Some characterizations are simple: in a capitalist society, capital is dominant and readily converted into prestige and power; in a technocracy, technical knowledge plays the same part. But it isn't difficult to imagine, or to find, more complex social arrangements. Indeed, capitalism and technocracy are more complex than their names imply, even if the names do convey real information about the most important forms of sharing, dividing, and exchanging. Monopolistic control of a dominant good makes a ruling class, whose members stand atop the distributive system—much as philosophers, claiming to have the wisdom they love, might like to do. But since dominance is always incomplete and monopoly imperfect, the rule of every ruling class is unstable. It is continually challenged by other groups in the name of alternative patterns of conversion.

Distribution is what social conflict is all about. Marx's heavy emphasis on productive processes should not conceal from us the simple truth that the struggle for control of the means of production is a distributive struggle. Land and capital are at stake, and these are goods that can be shared, divided, exchanged, and endlessly converted. But land and capital are not the only dominant goods; it is possible (it has historically been possible) to come to them by way of other goods—military or political power, religious office and charisma, and so on. History reveals no single dominant good and no naturally dominant good, but only different kinds of magic and competing bands of magicians.

The claim to monopolize a dominant good—when worked up for public purposes—constitutes an ideology. Its standard form is to connect legitimate possession with some set of personal qualities through the medium of a philosophical principle. So aristocracy, or the rule of the best, is the principle of those who lay claim to breeding and intelligence: they are commonly the monopolists of landed wealth and familial reputation. Divine supremacy is the principle of those who claim to know the word of God: they are the monopolists of grace and office. Meritocracy, or the career open to talents, is the principle of those who claim to be talented: they are most often the monopolists of education. Free exchange is the principle of those who are ready, or who tell us they are ready, to put their money at risk: they are the monopolists of movable wealth. These groups— and others, too, similarly marked off by their principles and possessions—compete with one another, struggling for supremacy. One group wins, and then a different one; or coalitions are worked out, and supremacy is uneasily shared. There is no final victory, nor should there be. But that is not to say that the claims of the different groups are necessarily wrong, or that the principles they invoke are of no value as distributive criteria; the principles are often exactly right within the limits of a particular sphere. Ideologies are readily corrupted, but their corruption is not the most interesting thing about them.

It is in the study of these struggles that I have sought the guiding thread of my own argument. The struggles have, I think, a paradigmatic form. Some group of men and women—class, caste, strata, estate, alliance, or social formation—comes to enjoy a monopoly or a near monopoly of some dominant good; or, a coalition of groups comes to enjoy, and so on. This dominant good is more or less systematically converted into all sorts of other things—opportunities, powers, and reputations. So wealth is seized by the strong, honor by the wellborn, office by the well educated. Perhaps the ideology that justifies the seizure is widely believed to be true. But resentment and resistance are (almost) as pervasive as belief. There are always some people, and after a time there are a great many, who think the seizure is not justice but usurpation. The ruling group does not possess, or does not uniquely possess, the qualities it claims; the conversion process violates the common understanding of the goods at stake. Social conflict is intermittent, or it is endemic; at some point, counterclaims are put forward. Though these are of many different sorts, three general sorts are especially important:

1. The claim that the dominant good, whatever it is, should be redistributed so that it can be equally or at least more widely shared: this amounts to saying that monopoly is unjust.
2. The claim that the way should be opened for the autonomous distribution of all social goods: this amounts to saying that dominance is unjust.
3. The claim that some new good, monopolized by some new group, should replace the currently dominant good: this amounts to saying that the existing pattern of dominance and monopoly is unjust.

The third claim is, in Marx's view, the model of every revolutionary ideology—except, perhaps, the proletarian or last ideology. Thus, the French Revolution in Marxist theory: the dominance of noble birth and blood and of feudal landholding is ended, and bourgeois wealth is established in its stead. The original situation is reproduced with different subjects and objects (this is never unimportant), and then the class war is immediately renewed. It is not my purpose here to endorse or to criticize Marx's view. I suspect, in fact, that there is something of all three claims in every revolutionary ideology, but that, too, is not a position that I shall try to defend here. Whatever its sociological significance, the third claim is not philosophically interesting—unless one believes that there is a naturally dominant good, such that its possessors could legitimately claim to rule the rest of us. In a sense, Marx believed exactly that. The means of production is the dominant good throughout history, and Marxism is a historicist doctrine insofar as it suggests that whoever controls the prevailing means legitimately rules.[8] After the communist revolution, we shall all control the means of production: at that point, the third claim collapses into the first. Meanwhile, Marx's model is a program for ongoing distributive struggle. It will matter, of course, who wins at this or that moment,

8. See Allen W. Wood, "The Marxian Critique of Justice," *Philosophy and Public Affairs* 1 (1972): 244–82.

but we won't know why or how it matters if we attend only to the successive assertions of dominance and monopoly.

Simple Equality

It is with the first two claims that I shall be concerned, and ultimately with the second alone, for that one seems to me to capture best the plurality of social meanings and the real complexity of distributive systems. But the first is the more common among philosophers; it matches their own search for unity and singularity; and I shall need to explain its difficulties at some length.

Men and women who make the first claim challenge the monopoly but not the dominance of a particular social good. This is also a challenge to monopoly in general; for if wealth, for example, is dominant and widely shared, no other good can possibly be monopolized. Imagine a society in which everything is up for sale and every citizen has as much money as every other. I shall call this the "regime of simple equality." Equality is multiplied through the conversion process, until it extends across the full range of social goods. The regime of simple equality won't last for long, because the further progress of conversion, free exchange in the market, is certain to bring inequalities in its train. If one wanted to sustain simple equality over time, one would require a "monetary law" like the agrarian laws of ancient times or the Hebrew sabbatical, providing for a periodic return to the original condition. Only a centralized and activist state would be strong enough to force such a return; and it isn't clear that state officials would actually be able or willing to do that, if money were the dominant good. In any case, the original condition is unstable in another way. It's not only that monopoly will reappear, but also that dominance will disappear.

In practice, breaking the monopoly of money neutralizes its dominance. Other goods come into play, and inequality takes on new forms. Consider again the regime of simple equality. Everything is up for sale, and everyone has the same amount of money. So everyone has, say, an equal ability to buy an education for his children. Some do that, and others don't. It turns out to be a good investment: other social goods are, increasingly, offered for sale only to people with educational certificates. Soon everyone invests in education; or, more likely, the purchase is universalized through the tax system. But then the school is turned into a competitive world within which money is no longer dominant. Natural talent or family upbringing or skill in writing examinations is dominant instead, and educational success and certification are monopolized by some new group. Let's call them (what they call themselves) the "group of the talented."

Eventually the members of this group claim that the good they control should be dominant outside the school: offices, titles, prerogatives, wealth too, should all be possessed by themselves. This is the career open to talents, equal opportunity, and so on. This is what fairness requires; talent will out; and in any case, talented men and women will enlarge the resources available to everyone else. So Michael Young's meritocracy is born, with all its attendent inequalities.[9]

What should we do now? It is possible to set limits to the new conversion patterns, to recognize but constrain the monopoly power of the talented. I take this to be the purpose of John Rawls's difference principle, according to which inequalities are justified only if they are designed to bring, and actually do bring, the greatest possible benefit to the least advantaged social class.[10] More specifically, the difference principle is a constraint imposed on talented men and women, once the monopoly of wealth has been broken. It works in this way: Imagine a surgeon who claims more than his equal share of wealth on the basis of the skills he has learned and the certificates he has won in the harsh competitive struggles of college and medical school. We will grant the claim if, and only if, granting it is beneficial in the stipulated ways. At the same time, we will act to limit and regulate the sale of surgery—that is, the direct conversion of surgical skill into wealth.

This regulation will necessarily be the work of the state, just as monetary laws and agrarian laws are the work of the state. Simple equality would require continual state intervention to break up or constrain incipient monopolies and to repress new forms of dominance. But then state power itself will become the central object of competitive struggles. Groups of men and women will seek to monopolize and then to use the state in order to consolidate their control of other social goods. Or, the state will be monopolized by its own agents in accordance with the iron law of oligarchy. Politics is always the most direct path to dominance, and political power (rather than the means of production) is probably the most important, and certainly the most dangerous, good in human history.*

---

9. Michael Young, *The Rise of the Meritocracy, 1870–2033* (Harmondsworth, England, 1961)—a brilliant piece of social science fiction.

10. Rawls, *Theory of Justice* pp. 75 ff.

*I should note here what will become more clear as I go along, that political power is a special sort of good. It has a twofold character. First, it is like the other things that men and women make, value, exchange, and share: sometimes dominant, sometimes not; sometimes widely held, sometimes the possession of a very few. And, second, it is unlike all the other things because, however it is had and whoever has it, political power is the regulative agency for social goods generally. It is used

Hence the need to constrain the agents of constraint, to establish constitutional checks and balances. These are limits imposed on political monopoly, and they are all the more important once the various social and economic monopolies have been broken.

One way of limiting political power is to distribute it widely. This may not work, given the well-canvassed dangers of majority tyranny; but these dangers are probably less acute than they are often made out to be. The greater danger of democratic government is that it will be weak to cope with re-emerging monopolies in society at large, with the social strength of plutocrats, bureaucrats, technocrats, meritocrats, and so on. In theory, political power is the dominant good in a democracy, and it is convertible in any way the citizens choose. But in practice, again, breaking the monopoly of power neutralizes its dominance. Political power cannot be widely shared without being subjected to the pull of all the other goods that the citizens already have or hope to have. Hence democracy is, as Marx recognized, essentially a reflective system, mirroring the prevailing and emerging distribution of social goods.[11] Democratic decision making will be shaped by the cultural conceptions that determine or underwrite the new monopolies. To prevail against these monopolies, power will have to be centralized, perhaps itself monopolized. Once again, the state must be very powerful if it is to fulfill the purposes assigned to it by the difference principle or by any similarly interventionist rule.

Still, the regime of simple equality might work. One can imagine a more or less stable tension between emerging monopolies and political constraints, between the claim to privilege put forward by the talented, say, and the enforcement of the difference principle, and then between the agents of enforcement and the democratic constitution. But I suspect that difficulties will recur, and that at many points in time the only remedy for private privilege will be statism, and the only escape from statism will be

---

to defend the boundaries of all the distributive spheres, including its own, and to enforce the common understandings of what goods are and what they are for. (But it can also be used, obviously, to invade the different spheres and to override those understandings.) In this second sense, we might say, indeed, that political power is always dominant—at the boundaries, but not within them. The central problem of political life is to maintain that crucial distinction between "at" and "in." But this is a problem that cannot be solved given the imperatives of simple equality.

11. See Marx's comment, in his "Critique of the Gotha Programme," that the democratic republic is the "form of state" within which the class struggle will be fought to a conclusion: the struggle is immediately and without distortion reflected in political life (Marx and Engels, *Selected Works* [Moscow, 1951], vol. II, p. 31) [this comment is omitted from the excerpt in this anthology].

private privilege. We will mobilize power to check monopoly, then look for some way of checking the power we have mobilized. But there is no way that doesn't open opportunities for strategically placed men and women to seize and exploit important social goods.

These problems derive from treating monopoly, and not dominance, as the central issue in distributive justice. It is not difficult, of course, to understand why philosophers (and political activists, too) have focused on monopoly. The distributive struggles of the modern age begin with a war against the aristocracy's singular hold on land, office, and honor. This seems an especially pernicious monopoly because it rests upon birth and blood, with which the individual has nothing to do, rather than upon wealth, or power, or education, all of which—at least in principle—can be earned. And when every man and woman becomes, as it were, a small-holder in the sphere of birth and blood, an important victory is indeed won. Birthright ceases to be a dominant good; henceforth, it purchases very little; wealth, power, and education come to the fore. With regard to these latter goods, however, simple equality cannot be sustained at all, or it can only be sustained subject to the vicissitudes I have just described. Within their own spheres, as they are currently understood, these three tend to generate natural monopolies that can be repressed only if state power is itself dominant and if it is monopolized by officials committed to the repression. But there is, I think, another path to another kind of equality.

Tyranny and Complex Equality

I want to argue that we should focus on the reduction of dominance—not, or not primarily, on the break-up or the constraint of monopoly. We should consider what it might mean to narrow the range within which particular goods are convertible and to vindicate the autonomy of distributive spheres. But this line of argument, though it is not uncommon historically, has never fully emerged in philosophical writing. Philosophers have tended to criticize (or to justify) existing or emerging monopolies of wealth, power, and education. Or, they have criticized (or justified) particular conversions—of wealth into education or of office into wealth. And all this, most often, in the name of some radically simplified distributive system. The critique of dominance will suggest instead a way of reshaping and then living with the actual complexity of distributions.

Imagine now a society in which different social goods are monopolistically held—as they are in fact and always will be, barring continual state intervention—but in which no particular good is generally convertible. As I go along, I shall try to define the precise limits on convertibility, but for now the general description will suffice. This is a complex egalitarian society. Though there will be many small inequalities, inequality will not be multiplied through the conversion process. Nor will it be summed across different goods, because the autonomy of distributions will tend to produce a variety of local monopolies, held by different groups of men and women. I don't want to claim that complex equality would necessarily be more stable than simple equality, but I am inclined to think that it would open the way for more diffused and particularized forms of social conflict. And the resistance to convertibility would be maintained, in large degree, by ordinary men and women within their own spheres of competence and control, without large-scale state action.

This is, I think, an attractive picture, but I have not yet explained just why it is attractive. The argument for complex equality begins from our understanding—I mean, our actual, concrete, positive, and particular understanding—of the various social goods. And then it moves on to an account of the way we relate to one another through those goods. Simple equality is a simple distributive condition, so that if I have fourteen hats and you have fourteen hats, we are equal. And it is all to the good if hats are dominant, for then our equality is extended through all the spheres of social life. On the view that I shall take here, however, we simply have the same number of hats, and it is unlikely that hats will be dominant for long. Equality is a complex relation of persons, mediated by the goods we make, share, and divide among ourselves; it is not an identity of possessions. It requires then, a diversity of distributive criteria that mirrors the diversity of social goods.

The argument for complex equality has been beautifully put by Pascal in one of his *Pensées*.

> The nature of tyranny is to desire power over the whole world and outside its own sphere.
>
> There are different companies—the strong, the handsome, the intelligent, the devout—and each man reigns in his own, not elsewhere. But sometimes they meet, and the strong and the handsome fight for mastery— foolishly, for their mastery is of different kinds. They misunderstand one another, and make the mistake of each aiming at universal dominion. Nothing can win this, not even strength, for it is powerless in the kingdom of the wise. . . .
>
> *Tyranny.* The following statements, therefore, are false and tyrannical: "Because I am handsome, so I should command respect." "I am strong, therefore men should love me. . . ." "I am . . . et cetera."
>
> Tyranny is the wish to obtain by one means what can only be had by

another. We owe different duties to different qualities: love is the proper response to charm, fear to strength, and belief to learning.[12]

Marx made a similar argument in his early manuscripts; perhaps he had this *pensée* in mind:

> Let us assume man to be man, and his relation to the world to be a human one. Then love can only be exchanged for love, trust for trust, etc. If you wish to enjoy art you must be an artistically cultivated person; if you wish to influence other people, you must be a person who really has a stimulating and encouraging effect upon others. . . . If you love without evoking love in return, i.e., if you are not able, by the manifestation of yourself as a loving person, to make yourself a beloved person—then your love is impotent and a misfortune.[13]

These are not easy arguments, and most of my book is simply an exposition of their meaning. But here I shall attempt something more simple and schematic: a translation of the arguments into the terms I have already been using.

The first claim of Pascal and Marx is that personal qualities and social goods have their own spheres of operation, where they work their effects freely, spontaneously, and legitimately. There are ready or natural conversions that follow from, and are intuitively plausible because of, the social meaning of particular goods. The appeal is to our ordinary understanding and, at the same time, against our common acquiescence in illegitimate conversion patterns. Or, it is an appeal from our acquiescence to our resentment. There is something wrong, Pascal suggests, with the conversion of strength into belief. In political terms, Pascal means that no ruler can rightly command my opinions merely because of the power he wields. Nor can he, Marx adds, rightly claim to influence my actions: if a ruler wants to do that, he must be persuasive, helpful, encouraging, and so on. These arguments depend for their force on some shared understanding of knowledge, influence, and power. Social goods have social meanings, and we find our way to distributive justice through an interpretation of those meanings. We search for principles internal to each distributive sphere.

12. Blaise Pascal, *The Pensées*, trans. by J. M. Cohen (Harmondsworth, England, 1961), p. 96 (no. 244).

13. Karl Marx, *Economic and Philosophical Manuscripts*, in *Early Writings*, ed. by T. B. Bottomore (London, 1963), pp. 193–94. It is interesting to note an earlier echo of Pascal's argument in Adam Smith's *Theory of Moral Sentiments* (Edinburgh, 1813), vol. 1, pp. 378–79; but Smith seems to have believed that distributions in his own society actually conformed to this view of appropriateness—a mistake neither Pascal nor Marx ever made.

The second claim is that the disregard of these principles is tyranny. To convert one good into another, when there is no intrinsic connection between the two, is to invade the sphere where another company of men and women properly rules. Monopoly is not inappropriate within the spheres. There is nothing wrong, for example, with the grip that persuasive and helpful men and women (politicians) establish on political power. But the use of political power to gain access to other goods is a tyrannical use. Thus, an old description of tyranny is generalized: princes become tyrants, according to medieval writers, when they seize the property or invade the family of their subjects.[14] In political life—but more widely, too—the dominance of goods makes for the domination of people.

The regime of complex equality is the opposite of tyranny. It establishes a set of relationships such that domination is impossible. In formal terms, complex equality means that no citizen's standing in one sphere or with regard to one social good can be undercut by his standing in some other sphere, with regard to some other good. Thus, citizen X may be chosen over citizen Y for political office, and then the two of them will be unequal in the sphere of politics. But they will not be unequal generally so long as X's office gives him no advantages over Y in any other sphere—superior medical care, access to better schools for his children, entrepreneurial opportunities, and so on. So long as office is not a dominant good, is not generally convertible, office holders will stand, or at least can stand, in a relation of equality to the men and women they govern.

But what if dominance were eliminated, the autonomy of the spheres established—and the same people were successful in one sphere after another, triumphant in every company, piling up goods without the need for illegitimate conversions? This would certainly make for an inegalitarian society, but it would also suggest in the strongest way that a society of equals was not a lively possibility. I doubt that any egalitarian argument could survive in the face of such evidence. Here is a person whom we have freely chosen (without reference to his family ties or personal wealth) as our political representative. He is also a bold and inventive entrepreneur. When he was younger, he studied science, scored amazingly high grades in every exam, and made important discoveries. In war, he is surpassingly brave and wins the highest honors. Himself compassionate and compelling, he is loved by all who know him. Are there such people? Maybe so, but I have my doubts. We tell stories like the one I have just told, but the stories are fictions, the conversion of power or money or academic talent into legendary fame. In any case, there aren't enough such people to constitute a

14. See the summary account in Jean Bodin, *Six Books of a Commonweale*, ed. by Kenneth Douglas McRae (Cambridge, Mass., 1962), pp. 210–18.

ruling class and dominate the rest of us. Nor can they be successful in every distributive sphere, for there are some spheres to which the idea of success doesn't pertain. Nor are their children likely, under conditions of complex equality, to inherit their success. By and large, the most accomplished politicians, entrepreneurs, scientists, soldiers, and lovers will be different people; and so long as the goods they possess don't bring other goods in train, we have no reason to fear their accomplishments.

The critique of dominance and domination points toward an open-ended distributive principle. *No social good x should be distributed to men and women who possess some other good y merely because they possess y and without regard to the meaning of x.* This is a principle that has probably been reiterated, at one time or another, for every *y* that has ever been dominant. But it has not often been stated in general terms. Pascal and Marx have suggested the application of the principle against all possible *y*'s, and I shall attempt to work out that application. I shall be looking, then, not at the members of Pascal's companies—the strong or the weak, the handsome or the plain—but at the goods they share and divide. The purpose of the principle is to focus our attention; it doesn't determine the shares or the division. The principle directs us to study the meaning of social goods, to examine the different distributive spheres from the inside.

Three Distributive Principles

The theory that results is unlikely to be elegant. No account of the meaning of a social good, or of the boundaries of the sphere within which it legitimately operates, will be uncontroversial. Nor is there any neat procedure for generating or testing different accounts. At best, the arguments will be rough, reflecting the diverse and conflict-ridden character of the social life that we seek simultaneously to understand and to regulate—but not to regulate until we understand. I shall set aside, then, all claims made on behalf of any single distributive criterion, for no such criterion can possibly match the diversity of social goods. Three criteria, however, appear to meet the requirements of the open-ended principle and have often been defended as the beginning and end of distributive justice, so I must say something about each of them. Free exchange, desert, and need: all three have real force, but none of them has force across the range of distributions. They are part of the story, not the whole of it.

FREE EXCHANGE

Free exchange is obviously open-ended; it guarantees no particular distributive outcome. At no point in any exchange process plausibly called "free" will it be possible to predict the particular division of social goods that will obtain at some later point.[15] (It may be possible, however, to predict the general structure of the division.) In theory at least, free exchange creates a market within which all goods are convertible into all other goods through the neutral medium of money. There are no dominant goods and no monopolies. Hence the successive divisions that obtain will directly reflect the social meanings of the goods that are divided. For each bargain, trade, sale, and purchase will have been agreed to voluntarily by men and women who know what that meaning is, who are indeed its makers. Every exchange is a revelation of social meaning. By definition, then, no x will ever fall into the hands of someone who possesses y, merely because he possesses y and without regard to what x actually means to some other member of society. The market is radically pluralistic in its operations and its outcomes, infinitely sensitive to the meanings that individuals attach to goods. What possible restraints can be imposed on free exchange, then, in the name of pluralism?

But everyday life in the market, the actual experience of free exchange, is very different from what the theory suggests. Money, supposedly the neutral medium, is in practice a dominant good, and it is monopolized by people who possess a special talent for bargaining and trading—the green thumb of bourgeois society. Then other people demand a redistribution of money and the establishment of the regime of simple equality, and the search begins for some way to sustain that regime. But even if we focus on the first untroubled moment of simple equality—free exchange on the basis of equal shares—we will still need to set limits on what can be exchanged for what. For free exchange leaves distributions entirely in the hands of individuals, and social meanings are not subject, or are not always subject, to the interpretative decisions of individual men and women.

Consider an easy example, the case of political power. We can conceive of political power as a set of goods of varying value, votes, influence, offices, and so on. Any of these can be traded on the market and accumulated by individuals willing to sacrifice other goods. Even if the sacrifices are real, however, the result is a form of tyranny—petty tyranny, given the conditions of simple equality. Because I am willing to do without my hat, I shall vote twice; and you who value the vote less than you value my hat, will not vote at all. I suspect that the result is tyrannical even with regard to the two of us, who have reached a voluntary agreement. It is certainly tyrannical with regard to all the other citizens who must now submit to my disproportionate power. It is not the case that votes can't be bargained for; on one

---

15. Cf. Nozick on "patterning," *Anarchy, State, and Utopia,* pp. 155 ff. [pp. 146ff. in this anthology].

interpretation, that's what democratic politics is all about. And democratic politicians have certainly been known to buy votes, or to try to buy them, by promising public expenditures that benefit particular groups of voters. But this is done in public, with public funds, and subject to public approval. Private trading is ruled out by virtue of what politics, or democratic politics, is—that is, by virtue of what we did when we constituted the political community and of what we still think about what we did.

Free exchange is not a general criterion, but we will be able to specify the boundaries within which it operates only through a careful analysis of particular social goods. And having worked through such an analysis, we will come up at best with a philosophically authoritative set of boundaries and not necessarily with the set that ought to be politically authoritative. For money seeps across all boundaries—this is the primary form of illegal immigration; and just where one ought to try to stop it is a question of expediency as well as of principle. Failure to stop it at some reasonable point has consequences throughout the range of distributions, but consideration of these belongs in a later chapter.

DESERT

Like free exchange, desert seems both open-ended and pluralistic. One might imagine a single neutral agency dispensing rewards and punishments, infinitely sensitive to all the forms of individual desert. Then the distributive process would indeed be centralized, but the results would still be unpredictable and various. There would be no dominant good. No x would ever be distributed without regard to its social meaning; for, without attention to what x is, it is conceptually impossible to say that x is deserved. All the different companies of men and women would receive their appropriate reward. How this would work in practice, however, is not easy to figure out. It might make sense to say of this charming man, for example, that he deserves to be loved. It makes no sense to say that he deserves to be loved by this (or any) particular woman. If he loves her while she remains impervious to his (real) charms, that is his misfortune. I doubt that we would want the situation corrected by some outside agency. The love of particular men and women, on our understanding of it, can only be distributed by themselves, and they are rarely guided in these matters by considerations of desert.

The case is exactly the same with influence. Here, let's say, is a woman widely thought to be stimulating and encouraging to others. Perhaps she deserves to be an influential member of our community. But she doesn't deserve that I be influenced by her or that I follow her lead. Nor would we want my followership, as it were, assigned to her by any agency capable of making such assignments. She may go to great lengths to stimulate and encourage me, and do all the things that are commonly called stimulating or encouraging. But if I (perversely) refuse to be stimulated or encouraged, I am not denying her anything that she deserves. The same argument holds by extension for politicians and ordinary citizens. Citizens can't trade their votes for hats; they can't individually decide to cross the boundary that separates the sphere of politics from the marketplace. But within the sphere of politics, they do make individual decisions; and they are rarely guided, again, by considerations of desert. It's not clear that offices can be deserved—another issue that I must postpone; but even if they can be, it would violate our understanding of democratic politics were they simply distributed to deserving men and women by some central agency.

Similarly, however we draw the boundaries of the sphere within which free exchange operates, desert will play no role within those boundaries. I am skillful at bargaining and trading, let's say, and so accumulate a large number of beautiful pictures. If we assume, as painters mostly do, that pictures are appropriately traded in the market, then there is nothing wrong with my having the pictures. My title is legitimate. But it would be odd to say that I deserve to have them simply because I am good at bargaining and trading. Desert seems to require an especially close connection between particular goods and particular persons, whereas justice only sometimes requires a connection of that sort. Still, we might insist that only artistically cultivated people, who deserve to have pictures, should actually have them. It's not difficult to imagine a distributive mechanism. The state could buy all the pictures that were offered for sale (but artists would have to be licensed, so that there wouldn't be an endless number of pictures), evaluate them, and then distribute them to artistically cultivated men and women, the better pictures to the more cultivated. The state does something like this, sometimes, with regard to things that people need—medical care, for example—but not with regard to things that people deserve. There are practical difficulties here, but I suspect a deeper reason for this difference. Desert does not have the urgency of need, and it does not involve having (owning and consuming) in the same way. Hence, we are willing to tolerate the separation of owners of paintings and artistically cultivated people, or we are unwilling to require the kinds of interference in the market that would be necessary to end the separation. Of course, public provision is always possible alongside the market, and so we might argue that artistically cultivated people deserve not pictures but museums. Perhaps they do, but they don't deserve that the rest of us contribute money or appropriate public funds for the purchase of pictures and the construction of buildings. They will have to persuade us that art is worth the money; they will have to stimulate and encourage our own artistic cultivation. And if they fail to do that, their own love of art may well turn out to be "impotent and a misfortune."

Even if we were to assign the distribution of love, influence, offices, works of art, and so on, to some omnipotent arbiters of desert, how would we select them? How could anyone deserve such a position? Only God, who knows what secrets lurk in the hearts of men, would be able to make the necessary distributions. If human beings had to do the work, the distributive mechanism would be seized early on by some band of aristocrats (so they would call themselves) with a fixed conception of what is best and most deserving, and insensitive to the diverse excellences of their fellow citizens. And then desert would cease to be a pluralist criterion; we would find ourselves face to face with a new set (of an old sort) of tyrants. We do, of course, choose people as arbiters of desert—to serve on juries, for example, or to award prizes; it will be worth considering later what the prerogatives of a juror are. But it is important to stress here that he operates within a narrow range. Desert is a strong claim, but it calls for difficult judgments; and only under very special conditions does it yield specific distributions.

NEED

Finally, the criterion of need. "To each according to his needs" is generally taken as the distributive half of Marx's famous maxim: we are to distribute the wealth of the community so as to meet the necessities of its members.[16] A plausible proposal, but a radically incomplete one. In fact, the first half of the maxim is also a distributive proposal, and it doesn't fit the rule of the second half. "From each according to his ability" suggests that jobs should be distributed (or that men and women should be conscripted to work) on the basis of individual qualifications. But individuals don't in any obvious sense need the jobs for which they are qualified. Perhaps such jobs are scarce, and there are a large number of qualified candidates: which candidates need them most? If their material needs are already taken care of, perhaps they don't need to work at all. Or if, in some non-material sense, they all need to work, then that need won't distinguish among them, at least not to the naked eye. It would in any case be odd to ask a search committee looking, say, for a hospital director to make its choice on the basis of the needs of the candidates rather than on those of the staff and the patients of the hospital. But the latter set of needs, even if it isn't the subject of political disagreement, won't yield a single distributive decision.

16. Marx, "Gotha Programme," p. 23 [p. 89 in this anthology].

Nor will need work for many other goods. Marx's maxim doesn't help at all with regard to the distribution of political power, honor and fame, sailboats, rare books, beautiful objects of every sort. These are not things that anyone, strictly speaking, needs. Even if we take a loose view and define the verb *to need* the way children do, as the strongest form of the verb *to want*, we still won't have an adequate distributive criterion. The sorts of things that I have listed cannot be distributed equally to those with equal wants because some of them are generally, and some of them are necessarily, scarce, and some of them can't be possessed at all unless other people, for reasons of their own, agree on who is to possess them.

Need generates a particular distributive sphere, within which it is itself the appropriate distributive principle. In a poor society, a high proportion of social wealth will be drawn into this sphere. But given the great variety of goods that arises out of any common life, even when it is lived at a very low material level, other distributive criteria will always be operating alongside of need, and it will always be necessary to worry about the boundaries that mark them off from one another. Within its sphere, certainly, need meets the general distributive rule about x and y. Needed goods distributed to needy people in proportion to their neediness are obviously not dominated by any other goods. It's not having y, but only lacking x that is relevant. But we can now see, I think, that every criterion that has any force at all meets the general rule within its own sphere, and not elsewhere. This is the effect of the rule: different goods to different companies of men and women for different reasons and in accordance with different procedures. And to get all this right, or to get it roughly right, is to map out the entire social world.

Hierarchies and Caste Societies

Or, rather, it is to map out a particular social world. For the analysis that I propose is imminent and phenomenological in character. It will yield not an ideal map or a master plan but, rather, a map and a plan appropriate to the people for whom it is drawn, whose common life it reflects. The goal, of course, is a reflection of a special kind, which picks up those deeper understandings of social goods which are not necessarily mirrored in the everyday practice of dominance and monopoly. But what if there are no such understandings? I have been assuming all along that social meanings call for the autonomy, or the relative autonomy, of distributive spheres; and so they do much of the time. But it's not impossible to imagine a society where dominance and monopoly are not violations but enactments of meaning, where social goods are conceived in hierarchical terms. In feudal Europe, for example, clothing was not a commodity (as it is today) but a badge of rank. Rank dominated dress. The meaning of clothing was shaped in the image of the feudal order. Dressing in finery to which one wasn't entitled was a kind of lie; it made a false statement about who one was. When a king or a prime minister dressed as a commoner in order to learn something about the opinions of his subjects, this was a kind of politic deceit. On the other hand, the difficulties of enforcing the clothing code (the sumptuary laws) suggests that there was all along an alternative sense of what clothing meant. At some point, at least, one can begin to recognize the boundaries of a distinct sphere within which people dress in accordance with what they can afford or what they are willing to spend or how they want to look. The sumptuary laws may still be enforced, but now one can make—and ordinary men and women do, in fact, make— egalitarian arguments against them.

Can we imagine a society in which all goods are hierarchically conceived? Perhaps the caste system of ancient India had this form (though that is a far-reaching claim, and it would be prudent to doubt its truth: for one thing, political power seems always to have escaped the laws of caste). We think of castes as rigidly segregated groups, of the caste system as a "plural society," a world of boundaries.[17] But the system is constituted by an extraordinary integration of meanings. Prestige, wealth, knowledge, office, occupation, food, clothing, even the social good of conversation: all are subject to the intellectual as well as to the physical discipline of hierarchy. And the hierarchy is itself determined by the single value of ritual purity. A certain kind of collective mobility is possible, for castes or subcastes can cultivate the outward marks of purity and (within severe limits) raise their position in the social scale. And the system as a whole rests upon a religious doctrine that promises equality of opportunity, not in this life but across the lives of the soul. The individual's status here and now "is the result of his conduct in his last incarnation . . . and if unsatisfactory can be remedied by acquiring merit in his present life which will raise his status in the next."[18] We should not assume that men and women are ever entirely content with radical inequality. Nevertheless, distributions here and now are part of a single system, largely unchallenged, in which purity is dominant over other goods—and birth and blood are dominant over purity. Social meanings overlap and cohere.

17. J. H. Hutton, *Caste in India: Its Nature, Function, and Origins* (4th ed., Bombay, 1963), pp. 127–28. I have also drawn on Célestin Bouglé, *Essays on the Caste System,* trans. by D. F. Pocock (Cambridge, England, 1971), esp. Part III, chaps. 3 and 4; and Louis Dumont, *Homo Hierarchus: The Caste System and Its Implications* (revised English ed., Chicago, 1980).
18. Hutton, *Caste in India,* p. 125.

The more perfect the coherence, the less possible it is even to think about complex equality. All goods are like crowns and thrones in a hereditary monarchy. There is no room, and there are no criteria, for autonomous distributions. In fact, however, even hereditary monarchies are rarely so simply constructed. The social understanding of royal power commonly involves some notion of divine grace, or magical gift, or human insight; and these criteria for office holding are potentially independent of birth and blood. So it is for most social goods: they are only imperfectly integrated into larger systems; they are understood, at least sometimes, in their own terms. The theory of goods explicates understandings of this sort (where they exist), and the theory of complex equality exploits them. We say, for example, that it is tyrannical for a man without grace or gift or insight to sit upon the throne. And this is only the first and most obvious kind of tyranny. We can search for many other kinds.

Tyranny is always specific in character: a particular boundary crossing, a particular violation of social meaning. Complex equality requires the defense of boundaries; it works by differentiating goods just as hierarchy works by differentiating people. But we can only talk of a *regime* of complex equality when there are many boundaries to defend; and what the right number is cannot be specified. There is no right number. Simple equality is easier: one dominant good widely distributed makes an egalitarian society. But complexity is hard: how many goods must be autonomously conceived before the relations they mediate can become the relations of equal men and women? There is no certain answer and hence no ideal regime. But as soon as we start to distinguish meanings and mark out distributive spheres, we are launched on an egalitarian enterprise.

17

Will Kymlicka,
"Justice and Minority Rights,"
from *Multicultural Citizenship*

Will Kymlicka is the author of Liberalism, Community, and Culture *and* Contemporary Political Philosophy: An Introduction. *In this selection from his book* Multicultural Citizenship, *Kymlicka discusses the bearing of equality upon claims by cultural and ethnic groups for group-specific rights.*

Justice and Minority Rights

I have argued that access to a societal culture is essential for individual freedom. I have also argued that most people have a deep bond to their own culture, and that they have a legitimate interest in maintaining this bond. But what particular claims are justified by this interest? Not all interests can be satisfied in a world of conflicting interests and scarce resources. Protecting one person's cultural membership has costs for other people and other interests, and we need to determine when these trade-offs are justified.

Many liberals believe that people's interest in cultural membership is adequately protected by the common rights of citizenship, and that any further measures to protect this interest are illegitimate. They argue that a system of universal individual rights already accommodates cultural differences, by allowing each person the freedom to associate with others in the pursuit of shared religious or ethnic practices. Freedom of association enables people from different backgrounds to pursue their distinctive ways of life without interference. Every individual is free to create or join various associations, and to seek new adherents for them, in the "cultural marketplace." Every way of life is free to attract adherents, and if some ways of life are unable to maintain or gain the voluntary adherence of people that may be unfortunate, but it is not unfair. On this view, giving political recognition or support to particular cultural practices or associations is unnecessary and unfair. It is unnecessary, because a valuable way of life will have no difficulty attracting adherents. And it is unfair, because it subsidizes some people's choices at the expense of others.

From *Multicultural Citizenship*, by Will Kymlicka (Oxford: Clarendon Press, 1995). Reprinted by permission of Oxford University Press.

Proponents of this "strict separation of state and ethnicity" view need not deny that people have a deep bond to their own culture (although some do). They may just argue that cultures do not need state assistance to survive. If a societal culture is worth saving, one could argue, the members of the culture will sustain it through their own choices. If the culture is decaying, it must be because some people no longer find it worthy of their allegiance. The state, on this view, should not interfere with the cultural market-place—it should neither promote nor inhibit the maintenance of any particular culture. Rather, it should respond with "benign neglect" to ethnic and national differences.

I think this common view is not only mistaken, but actually incoherent. The idea of responding to cultural differences with "benign neglect" makes no sense. Government decisions on languages, internal boundaries, public holidays, and state symbols unavoidably involve recognizing, accommodating, and supporting the needs and identities of particular ethnic and national groups. The state unavoidably promotes certain cultural identities, and thereby disadvantages others. Once we recognize this, we need to rethink the justice of minority rights claims. In this chapter, I will argue that some self-government rights and polyethnic rights are consistent with, and indeed required by, liberal justice. I will consider three sorts of arguments that attempt to defend these measures within a broadly liberal framework: equality, historical agreement, and diversity.[1] I will argue that each has some merit, although the latter two depend in part on the first. In each case, I will first consider how these arguments apply to the self-government rights of national minorities, and then examine their application to the polyethnic rights of ethnic groups.

1. The Equality Argument

Many defenders of group-specific rights for ethnic and national minorities insist that they are needed to ensure that all citizens are treated with genuine equality. On this view, "the accommodation of differences is the essence of true equality,"[2] and group-specific rights are needed to accommodate our differences. I think this argument is correct, within certain limits.

Proponents of "benign neglect" will respond that individual rights already allow for the accommodation of differences, and that true equality

1. [This excerpt is limited to Kymlicka's discussion of arguments that appeal to equality.—D.J.]

2. This phrase is from the judgement of the Canadian Supreme Court in explaining its interpretation of the equality guarantees under the Canadian Charter of Rights (*Andrews v. Law Society of British Columbia* 1 SCR 143; 56 DLR (4th) 1).

requires equal rights for each individual regardless of race or ethnicity. This assumption that liberal equality precludes group-specific rights is relatively recent, and arose in part as an (over-)generalization of the racial desegregation movement in the United States. It has some superficial plausibility. In many cases, claims for group-specific rights are simply an attempt by one group to dominate and oppress another.

But some minority rights eliminate, rather than create, inequalities. Some groups are unfairly disadvantaged in the cultural market-place, and political recognition and support rectify this disadvantage. I will start with the case of national minorities. The viability of their societal cultures may be undermined by economic and political decisions made by the majority. They could be outbid or outvoted on resources and policies that are crucial to the survival of their societal cultures. The members of majority cultures do not face this problem. Given the importance of cultural membership, this is a significant inequality which, if not addressed, becomes a serious injustice.

Group-differentiated rights—such as territorial autonomy, veto powers, guaranteed representation in central institutions, land claims, and language rights—can help rectify this disadvantage, by alleviating the vulnerability of minority cultures to majority decisions. These external protections ensure that members of the minority have the same opportunity to live and work in their own culture as members of the majority.

These rights may impose restrictions on the members of the larger society, by making it more costly for them to move into the territory of the minority (e.g., longer residency requirements, fewer government services in their language), or by giving minority members priority in the use of certain land and resources (e.g., indigenous hunting and fishing rights). But the sacrifice required of non-members by the existence of these rights is far less than the sacrifice members would face in the absence of such rights.

Where these rights are recognized, members of the majority who choose to enter the minority's homeland may have to forgo certain benefits they are accustomed to. This is a burden. But without such rights, the members of many minority cultures face the loss of their culture, a loss which we cannot reasonably ask people to accept.

Any plausible theory of justice should recognize the fairness of these external protections for national minorities. They are clearly justified, I believe, within a liberal egalitarian theory, such as Rawls's and Dworkin's, which emphasizes the importance of rectifying unchosen inequalities. Indeed inequalities in cultural membership are just the sort which Rawls says we should be concerned about, since their effects are "profound and pervasive and present from birth."

This equality-based argument will only endorse special rights for national minorities if there actually is a disadvantage with respect to cultural membership, and if the rights actually serve to rectify the disadvantage. Hence the legitimate scope of these rights will vary with the circumstances. In North America, indigenous groups are more vulnerable to majority decisions than the Québécois or Puerto Ricans, and so their external protections will be more extensive. For example, restrictions on the sale of land which are necessary in the context of indigenous peoples are not necessary, and hence not justified, in the case of Quebec or Puerto Rico.

At some point, demands for increased powers or resources will not be necessary to ensure the same opportunity to live and work in one's culture. Instead, they will simply be attempts to gain benefits denied to others, to have more resources to pursue one's way of life than others have. This was clearly the case with apartheid, where whites constituting under 20 per cent of the population controlled 87 per cent of the land mass of the country, and monopolized all the important levers of state power.

One could imagine a point where the amount of land reserved for indigenous peoples would not be necessary to provide reasonable external protections, but rather would simply provide unequal opportunities to them. Justice would then require that the holdings of indigenous peoples be subject to the same redistributive taxation as the wealth of other advantaged groups, so as to assist the less well off in society. In the real world, of course, most indigenous peoples are struggling to maintain the bare minimum of land needed to sustain the viability of their communities. But it is possible that their land holdings could exceed what justice allows.

The legitimacy of certain measures may also depend on their timing. For example, many people have suggested that a new South African constitution should grant a veto power over certain important decisions to some or all of the major national groups. This sort of veto power is a familiar feature of various "consociational democracies" in Europe, and under certain circumstances it can promote justice. But it would probably be unjust to give privileged groups a veto power before there has been a dramatic redistribution of wealth and opportunities. A veto power can promote justice if it helps protect a minority from unjust policies that favour the majority; but it is an obstacle to justice if it allows a privileged group the leverage to maintain its unjust advantages.

So the ideal of "benign neglect" is not in fact benign. It ignores the fact that the members of a national minority face a disadvantage which the members of the majority do not face. In any event, the idea that the government could be neutral with respect to ethnic and national groups is patently false. One of the most important determinants of whether a

culture survives is whether its language is the language of government—
i.e., the language of public schooling, courts, legislatures, welfare agencies,
health services, etc. When the government decides the language of public
schooling, it is providing what is probably the most important form of
support needed by societal cultures, since it guarantees the passing on of
the language and its associated traditions and conventions to the next
generation. Refusing to provide public schooling in a minority language,
by contrast, is almost inevitably condemning that language to ever-
increasing marginalization.

The government therefore cannot avoid deciding which societal cultures will be supported. And if it supports the majority culture, by using
the majority's language in schools and public agencies, it cannot refuse
official recognition to minority languages on the ground that this violates
"the separation of state and ethnicity." This shows that the analogy between religion and culture is mistaken. Many liberals say that just as the
state should not recognize, endorse, or support any particular church, so it
should not recognize, endorse, or support any particular cultural group or
identity. But the analogy does not work. It is quite possible for a state not
to have an established church. But the state cannot help but give at least
partial establishment to a culture when it decides which language is to be
used in public schooling, or in the provision of state services. The state can
(and should) replace religious oaths in courts with secular oaths, but it
cannot replace the use of English in courts with no language.

This is a significant embarrassment for the "benign neglect" view, and
it is remarkable how rarely language rights are discussed in contemporary
liberal theory. As Brian Weinstein put it, political theorists have had a lot
to say about "the language of politics"—that is, the symbols, metaphors,
and rhetorical devices of political discourse—but have had virtually nothing to say about "the politics of language"—that is, the decisions about
which languages to use in political, legal, and educational forums.[3] Yet
language rights are a fundamental cause of political conflict, even violence,
throughout the world, including Canada, Belgium, Spain, Sri Lanka, the
Baltics, Bulgaria, Turkey, and many other countries.

One could argue that decisions about the language of schooling and
public services should be determined, not by officially recognizing the
existence of various groups, but simply by allowing each political subunit
to make its own language policy on a democratic basis. If a national
minority forms a majority in the relevant unit, they can decide to have
their mother tongue adopted as an official language in that unit. But this is

3. Brian Weinstein, *The Civic Tongue: Political Consequences of Language Choices*
(New York: Longman, 1983), pp. 7–13.

because they are a local majority, not because the state has officially recognized them as a "nation."

This is sometimes said to be the American approach to language rights, since there is no constitutional definition of language rights in the United States. But in fact the American government has historically tried to make sure that such "local" decisions are always made by political units that have an anglophone majority. Decisions about state borders, or about when to admit territories as states, have been explicitly made with the aim of ensuring that there will be an anglophone majority. States in the American south-west and Hawaii were only offered statehood when the national minorities residing in those areas were outnumbered by settlers and immigrants. And some people oppose offering statehood to Puerto Rico precisely on the grounds that it will never have an anglophone majority.

This illustrates a more general point. Leaving decisions about language to political subunits just pushes back the problem. What are the relevant political units—what level of government should make these decisions? Should each neighbourhood be able to decide on the language of public schooling and public services in that neighbourhood? Or should this decision be left to larger units, such as cities or provinces? And how do we decide on the boundaries of these subunits? If we draw municipal or provincial boundaries in one way, then a national minority will not form even a local majority. But if we draw the boundaries another way, then the national minority will form a local majority. In a multination state, decisions on boundaries and the division of powers are inevitably decisions about which national group will have the ability to use which state powers to sustain its culture.

For example, the Inuit in Canada wish to divide the Northwest Territories into two, so that they will form the majority in the eastern half. This is seen as essential to the implementation of their right of self-government. Some liberals object that this proposal violates the separation of state and ethnicity by distributing public benefits and state powers so as to make it easier for a specific group to preserve its culture. But all decisions regarding boundaries and the distribution of powers in multination states have this effect. We can draw boundaries and distribute legislative powers so that a national minority has an increased ability within a particular region to protect its societal culture; or we can draw boundaries and distribute legislative powers so that the majority nation controls decisions regarding language, education, immigration, etc. on a country-wide basis.

The whole idea of "benign neglect" is incoherent, and reflects a shallow understanding of the relationship between states and nations. In the areas of official languages, political boundaries, and the division of powers, there is no way to avoid supporting this or that societal culture, or deciding which groups will form a majority in political units that control culture-affecting decisions regarding language, education, and immigration.

So the real question is, what is a fair way to recognize languages, draw boundaries, and distribute powers? And the answer, I think, is that we should aim at ensuring that all national groups have the opportunity to maintain themselves as a distinct culture, if they so choose. This ensures that the good of cultural membership is equally protected for the members of all national groups. In a democratic society, the majority nation will always have its language and societal culture supported, and will have the legislative power to protect its interests in culture-affecting decisions. The question is whether fairness requires that the same benefits and opportunities should be given to national minorities. The answer, I think, is clearly yes.

Hence group-differentiated self-government rights compensate for unequal circumstances which put the members of minority cultures at a systemic disadvantage in the cultural market-place, regardless of their personal choices in life. This is one of many areas in which true equality requires not identical treatment, but rather differential treatment in order to accommodate differential needs.

This does not mean that we should entirely reject the idea of the cultural market-place. Once the societal cultures of national groups are protected, through language rights and territorial autonomy, then the cultural market-place does have an important role to play in determining the character of the culture. Decisions about which particular aspects of one's culture are worth maintaining and developing should be left to the choices of individual members. For the state to intervene at this point to support particular options or customs within the culture, while penalizing or discouraging others, would run the risk of unfairly subsidizing some people's choices. But that is not the aim or effect of many rights for national minorities, which are instead concerned with external protections.

Let me now turn to polyethnic rights for ethnic groups. I believe there is an equality-based argument for these rights as well, which also invokes the impossibility of separating state from ethnicity, but in a different way. The context of choice for immigrants, unlike national minorities, primarily involves equal access to the mainstream culture(s). Having uprooted themselves from their old culture, they are expected to become members of the national societies which already exist in their new country. Hence promoting the good of cultural membership for immigrants is primarily a matter of enabling integration, by providing language training and fighting patterns of discrimination and prejudice. Generally speaking, this is more a matter of rigorously enforcing the common rights of citizenship than providing group-differentiated rights. In so far as common rights of citizenship in fact create equal access to mainstream culture, then equality with respect to cultural membership is achieved.

But even here equality does justify some group-specific rights. Consider the case of public holidays. Some people object to legislation that exempts Jews and Muslims from Sunday closing legislation, on the ground that this violates the separation of state and ethnicity. But almost any decision on public holidays will do so. In the major immigration countries, public holidays currently reflect the needs of Christians. Hence government offices are closed on Sunday, and on the major religious holidays (Easter, Christmas). This need not be seen as a deliberate decision to promote Christianity and discriminate against other faiths (although this was undoubtedly part of the original motivation). Decisions about government holidays were made when there was far less religious diversity, and people just took it for granted that the government work-week should accommodate Christian beliefs about days of rest and religious celebration.

But these decisions can be a significant disadvantage to the members of other religious faiths. And having established a work-week that favours Christians, one can hardly object to exemptions for Muslims or Jews on the ground that they violate the separation of state and ethnicity. These groups are simply asking that their religious needs be taken into consideration in the same way that the needs of Christians have always been taken into account. Public holidays are another significant embarrassment for the "benign neglect" view, and it is interesting to note how rarely they are discussed in contemporary liberal theory.

Similar issues arise regarding government uniforms. Some people object to the idea that Sikhs or Orthodox Jews should be exempted from requirements regarding headgear in the police or military. But here again it is important to recognize how the existing rules about government uniforms have been adopted to suit Christians. For example, existing dress-codes do not prohibit the wearing of wedding rings, which are an important religious symbol for many Christians (and Jews). And it is virtually inconceivable that designers of government dress-codes would have ever considered designing a uniform that prevented people from wearing wedding rings, unless this was strictly necessary for the job. Again, this should not be seen as a deliberate attempt to promote Christianity. It simply would have been taken for granted that uniforms should not unnecessarily conflict with Christian religious beliefs. Having adopted dress-codes that meet Christian needs, one can hardly object to exemptions for Sikhs and Orthodox Jews on the ground that they violate "benign neglect."

One can multiply the examples. For example, many state symbols such as flags, anthems, and mottoes reflect a particular ethnic or religious background ("In God We Trust"). The demand by ethnic groups for some symbolic affirmation of the value of polyethnicity (e.g., in government declarations and documents) is simply a demand that their identity be given the same recognition as the original Anglo-Saxon settlers.

It may be possible to avoid some of these issues by redesigning public holidays, uniforms, and state symbols. It is relatively easy to replace religious oaths with secular ones, and so we should. It would be more difficult, but perhaps not impossible, to replace existing public holidays and work-weeks with more "neutral" schedules for schools and government offices.

But there is no way to have a complete "separation of state and ethnicity." In various ways, the ideal of "benign neglect" is a myth. Government decisions on languages, internal boundaries, public holidays, and state symbols unavoidably involve recognizing, accommodating, and supporting the needs and identities of particular ethnic and national groups. Nor is there any reason to regret this fact. There is no reason to regret the existence of official languages and public holidays, and no one gains by creating unnecessary conflicts between government regulations and religious beliefs. The only question is how to ensure that these unavoidable forms of support for particular ethnic and national groups are provided fairly—that is, how to ensure that they do not privilege some groups and disadvantage others. In so far as existing policies support the language, culture, and identity of dominant nations and ethnic groups, there is an argument of equality for ensuring that some attempts are made to provide similar support for minority groups, through self-government and polyethnic rights.

18

Iris Marion Young, "Displacing the Distributive Paradigm," from *Justice and the Politics of Difference*

In this selection from her book, Justice and the Politics of Difference, *Young criticizes many theorists of justice—including several whose conceptions of equality are represented in this anthology—for focusing on the allocation of material goods and neglecting or distorting inequalities that stem from social relations.*

Displacing the Distributive Paradigm

It was in general a mistake to make a fuss about so-called distribution *and put the principal stress on it. Any distribution whatever of the means of consumption is only a consequence of the distribution of the conditions of production themselves. The latter distribution, however, is a feature of the mode of production itself.*
—Karl Marx

Thousands of buses converge on the city, and tens of thousands of people of diverse colors, ages, occupations, and life styles swarm onto the mall around the Washington Monument until the march begins. At midday people move into the streets, chanting, singing, waving wild papier-mâché missiles or effigies of government officials. Many carry signs or banners on which a simple slogan is inscribed: "Peace, Jobs, and Justice."

This scene has occurred many times in Washington, D.C., in the last decade, and many more times in other U.S. cities. What does "justice" mean in this slogan? In this context, as in many other political contexts today, I suggest that social justice means the elimination of institutionalized domination and oppression. Any aspect of social organization and practice relevant to domination and oppression is in principle subject to evaluation by ideals of justice.

Contemporary philosophical theories of justice, however, do not conceive justice so broadly. Instead, philosophical theories of justice tend to restrict the meaning of social justice to the morally proper distribution of benefits and burdens among society's members. In this chapter I define and assess this distributive paradigm. While distributive issues are crucial to a satisfactory conception of justice, it is a mistake to reduce social justice to distribution.

I find two problems with the distributive paradigm. First, it tends to focus thinking about social justice on the allocation of material goods such as things, resources, income, and wealth, or on the distribution of social positions, especially jobs. This focus tends to ignore the social structure and institutional context that often help determine distributive patterns. Of particular importance to the analyses that follow are issues of decision-making power and procedures, division of labor, and culture.

One might agree that defining justice in terms of distribution tends to bias thinking about justice toward issues concerning wealth, income, and other material goods, and that other issues such as decisionmaking power or the structure of the division of labor are as important, and yet argue that distribution need not be restricted to material goods and resources. Theorists frequently consider issues of the distribution of such nonmaterial goods as power, opportunity, or self-respect. But this widening of the concept of distribution exhibits the second problem with the distributive paradigm. When metaphorically extended to nonmaterial social goods, the concept of distribution represents them as though they were static things, instead of a function of social relations and processes.

In criticizing distributively oriented theories I wish neither to reject distribution as unimportant nor to offer a new positive theory to replace the distributive theories. I wish rather to displace talk of justice that regards persons as primarily possessors and consumers of goods to a wider context that also includes action, decisions about action, and provision of the means to develop and exercise capacities. The concept of social justice includes all aspects of institutional rules and relations insofar as they are subject to potential collective decision. The concepts of domination and oppression, rather than the concept of distribution, should be the starting point for a conception of social justice.

The Distributive Paradigm

A distributive paradigm runs through contemporary discourse about justice, spanning diverse ideological positions. By "paradigm" I mean a configuration of elements and practices which define an inquiry: metaphysical presuppositions, unquestioned terminology, characteristic questions, lines of reasoning, specific theories and their typical scope and mode of application. The distributive paradigm defines social justice as the morally proper distribution of social benefits and burdens among society's members. Paramount among these are wealth, income, and other material resources. The distributive definition of justice often includes, however, nonmaterial social goods such as rights, opportunity, power, and self-respect. What marks the distributive paradigm is a tendency to conceive social justice and distribution as coextensive concepts.

A review of how some major theorists define justice makes apparent the prevalence of this conceptual identification of justice with distribution. Rawls defines a "conception of justice as providing in the first instance a standard whereby the distributive aspects of the basic structure of society are to be assessed."[1]

. . .

Michael Walzer is interestingly ambiguous in relation to the distributive paradigm. Walzer asserts that philosophers' criticisms of the injustice of a social system usually amount to claims that a dominant good should be more widely distributed, that is, that monopoly is unjust. It is more appropriate, he says, to criticize the structure of dominance itself, rather than merely the distribution of the dominant good. Having one sort of social good—say, money—should not give one automatic access to other social goods. If the dominance of some goods over access to other goods is broken, then the monopoly of some group over a particular good may not be unjust.[2] Walzer's analysis here has resonances with my concern to focus primarily on the social structures and processes that produce distributions rather than on the distributions. At the same time, however, Walzer repeatedly and unambiguously uses the language of distribution to discuss social justice, in sometimes reifying and strange ways. In his chapter on the family, for example, he speaks of the just distribution of love and affection.

Most theorists take it as given, then, that justice is about distributions. The paradigm assumes a single model for all analyses of justice: all situations in which justice is at issue are analogous to the situation of persons dividing a stock of goods and comparing the size of the portions individuals have. Such a model implicitly assumes that individuals or other agents lie as nodes, points in the social field, among whom larger or smaller bundles of social goods are assigned. The individuals are externally related to the goods they possess, and their only relation to one another that matters from the point of view of the paradigm is a comparison of the amount of goods they possess. The distributive paradigm thus implicitly

1. John Rawls, *A Theory of Justice* (Cambridge, Mass.: Harvard University Press, 1971), p. 9.

2. Michael Walzer, *Spheres of Justice: A Defense of Pluralism and Equality* (New York: Basic Books, 1983), pp. 10–13 [pp. 216–219 in this anthology].

assumes a social atomism, inasmuch as there is no internal relation among persons in society relevant to considerations of justice.

The distributive paradigm is also pattern oriented. It evaluates justice according to the end-state pattern of persons and goods that appear on the social field. Evaluation of social justice involves comparing alternative patterns and determining which is the most just. Such a pattern–oriented conceptualization implicitly assumes a static conception of society.

I find two problems with this distributive paradigm, which I elaborate in the next two sections. First, it tends to ignore, at the same time that it often presupposes, the institutional context that determines material distributions. Second, when extended to nonmaterial goods and resources, the logic of distribution misrepresents them.

The Distributive Paradigm Presupposes and Obscures Institutional Context

Most theorizing about social justice focuses on the distribution of material resources, income, or positions of reward and prestige. Contemporary debates among theorists of justice, as Charles Taylor points out, are inspired largely by two practical issues.[3] First, is the distribution of wealth and income in advanced capitalist countries just, and if not, does justice permit or even require the provision of welfare services and other redistributive measures? Second, is the pattern of the distribution of positions of high income and prestige just, and if not, are affirmative action policies just means to rectify that injustice? Nearly all of the writers I cited earlier who define justice in distributive terms identify questions of the equality or inequality of wealth and income as the primary questions of social justice. . . . They usually subsume the second set of questions, about the justice of the distribution of social positions, under the question of economic distribution, since "more desirable" positions usually correspond to those that yield higher income or greater access to resources.

Applied discussions of justice too usually focus on the distribution of material goods and resources. Discussions of justice in medical care, for example, usually focus on the allocation of medical resources such as treatment, sophisticated equipment, expensive procedures, and so on. Similarly, issues of justice enter discussion in environmental ethics largely through consideration of the impact that alternative policies might have on the distribution of natural and social resources among individuals and groups.

3. Charles Taylor, "The Nature and Scope of Distributive Justice," in *Philosophy and the Human Sciences* (Cambridge: Cambridge University Press, 1985).

The social context of welfare capitalist society helps account for this tendency to focus on the distribution of income and other resources. Public political dispute in welfare corporate society is largely restricted to issues of taxation, and the allocation of public funds among competing social interests. Public discussions of social injustice tend to revolve around inequalities of wealth and income, and the extent to which the state can or should mitigate the suffering of the poor.

There are certainly pressing reasons for philosophers to attend to these issues of the distribution of wealth and resources. In a society and world with vast differences in the amount of material goods to which individuals have access, where millions starve while others can have anything they want, any conception of justice must address the distribution of material goods. The immediate provision of basic material goods for people now suffering severe deprivation must be a first priority for any program that seeks to make the world more just. Such a call obviously entails considerations of distribution and redistribution.

But in contemporary American society, many public appeals to justice do not concern primarily the distribution of material goods. Citizens in a rural Massachusetts town organize against a decision to site a huge hazardous waste treatment plant in their town. Their leaflets convince people that state law has treated the community unjustly by denying them the option of rejecting the plant. Citizens in an Ohio city are outraged at the announcement that a major employer is closing down its plant. They question the legitimacy of the power of private corporate decisionmakers to throw half the city out of work without warning, and without any negotiation and consultation with the community. Discussion of possible compensation makes them snicker; the point is not simply that we are out of jobs and thus lack money, they claim, but that no private party should have the right to decide to decimate the local economy. Justice may require that former workers and other members of the community have the option of taking over and operating the plant themselves. These two cases concern not so much the justice of material distributions as the justice of decisionmaking power and procedures.

Black critics claim that the television industry is guilty of gross injustice in its depictions of Blacks. More often than not, Blacks are represented as criminals, hookers, maids, scheming dealers, or jiving connivers. Blacks rarely appear in roles of authority, glamour, or virtue. Arab Americans are outraged at the degree to which television and film present recognizable Arabs only as sinister terrorists or gaudy princes, and conversely that terrorists are almost always Arab. Such outrage at media stereotyping issues in claims about the injustice not of material distribution, but of cultural imagery and symbols.

In an age of burgeoning computer technology, organizations of clerical workers argue that no person should have to spend the entirety of her working day in front of a computer terminal typing in a set of mindless numbers at monitored high speeds. This claim about injustice concerns not the distribution of goods, for the claim would still be made if VDT operators earned $30,000 annually. Here the primary issues of justice concern the structure of the division of labor and a right to meaningful work.

There are many such claims about justice and injustice in our society which are not primarily about the distribution of income, resources, or positions. A focus on the distribution of material goods and resources inappropriately restricts the scope of justice, because it fails to bring social structures and institutional contexts under evaluation. Several writers make this claim about distributive theories specifically with regard to their inability to bring capitalist institutions and class relations under evaluation. . . .

Other writers criticize distributive theories of justice, especially Rawls's, for presupposing at the same time that they obscure the context of class inequality that the theories are unable to evaluate. . . .

Many who make this Marxist criticism of the distributive focus of theories of justice conclude that justice is a concept of bourgeois ideology and thus not useful for a socialist normative analysis. Others disagree, and this dispute has occupied much of the Marxist literature on justice. . . . I wish to focus on the point on which both sides in this dispute agree, namely, that predominant approaches to justice tend to presuppose and uncritically accept the relations of production that define an economic system.

The Marxist analysis of the distributive paradigm provides a fruitful starting point, but it is both too narrow and too general. On the one hand, capitalist class relations are not the only phenomena of social structure or institutional context that the distributive paradigm fails to evaluate. Some feminists point out, for example, that contemporary theories of justice presuppose family structure, without asking how social relations involving sexuality, intimacy, childrearing, and household labor ought best to be organized. . . . Like their forebears, contemporary liberal theorists of justice tend to presume that the units among which basic distributions take place are families, and that it is as family members, often heads of families, that individuals enter the public realm where justice operates. Thus they neglect issues of justice within families—for example, the issue of whether the traditional sexual division of labor still presupposed by much law and employment policy is just.

While the Marxist criticism is too narrow, it is also too vague. The claim that the distributive paradigm fails to bring class relations under evaluation is too general to make clear what specific nondistributive issues are at stake. While property is something distributed, for example, in the form of goods, land, buildings, or shares of stock, the legal relations that define entitlement, possible forms of title, and so on are not goods to be distributed. The legal framework consists of rules defining practices and rights to make decisions about the disposition of goods. Class domination is certainly enacted by agents deciding where to invest their capital—a distributive decision; but the social rules, rights, procedures, and influences that structure capitalist decisionmaking are not distributed goods. In order to understand and evaluate the institutional framework within which distributive issues arise, the ideas of "class" and "mode of production" must be concretized in terms of specific social processes and relations. . . .

The general criticism I am making of the predominant focus on the distribution of wealth, income, and positions is that such a focus ignores and tends to obscure the institutional context within which those distributions take place, and which is often at least partly the cause of patterns of distribution of jobs or wealth. Institutional context should be understood in a broader sense than "mode of production." It includes any structures or practices, the rules and norms that guide them, and the language and symbols that mediate social interactions within them, in institutions of state, family, and civil society, as well as the workplace. These are relevant to judgments of justice and injustice insofar as they condition people's ability to participate in determining their actions and their ability to develop and exercise their capacities.

Many discussions of social justice not only ignore the institutional contexts within which distributions occur, but often presuppose specific institutional structures whose justice they fail to bring under evaluation. Some political theories, for example, tend to assume centralized legislative and executive institutions separated from the day-to-day lives of most people in the society, and state officials with the authority to make and enforce policy decisions. They take for granted such institutions of the modern state as bureaucracies and welfare agencies for implementing and enforcing tax schemes and administering services (see, e.g., Rawls, 1971, pp. 274–84). Issues of the just organization of government institutions, and just methods of political decisionmaking, rarely get raised.

To take a different kind of example, . . . when philosophers ask about the just principles for allocating jobs and offices among persons, they typically assume a stratification of such positions. They assume a hierarchical division of labor in which some jobs and offices carry significant autonomy, decisionmaking power, authority, income, and access to resources, while others lack most of these attributes. Rarely do theorists explicitly ask whether such a definition and organization of social positions is just.

Many other examples of ways in which theorizing about justice frequently presupposes specific structural and institutional background conditions could be cited. In every case a clear understanding of these background conditions can reveal how they affect distribution—what there is to distribute, how it gets distributed, who distributes, and what the distributive outcome is. With Michael Walzer, my intention here is "to shift our attention from distribution itself to conception and creation: the naming of the goods, the giving of meaning, and the collective making" (Walzer, 1983, p. 7 [p. 212 in this anthology]). I shall focus most of my discussion on three primary categories of nondistributive issues that distributive theories tend to ignore: decisionmaking structure and procedures, division of labor, and culture.

Decisionmaking issues include not only questions of who by virtue of their positions have the effective freedom or authority to make what sorts of decisions, but also the rules and procedures according to which decisions are made. Discussion of economic justice, for example, often deemphasizes the decisionmaking structures which are crucial determinants of economic relations. Economic domination in our society occurs not simply or primarily because some persons have more wealth and income than others, as important as this is. Economic domination derives at least as much from the corporate and legal structures and procedures that give some persons the power to make decisions about investment, production, marketing, employment, interest rates, and wages that affect millions of other people. Not all who make these decisions are wealthy or even privileged, but the decisionmaking structure operates to reproduce distributive inequality and unjust constraints on people's lives. . . .

Division of labor can be understood both distributively and nondistributively. As a distributive issue, division of labor refers to how pregiven occupations, jobs, or tasks are allocated among individuals or groups. As a nondistributive issue, on the other hand, division of labor concerns the definition of the occupations themselves. Division of labor as an institutional structure involves the range of tasks performed in a given position, the definition of the nature, meaning, and value of those tasks, and the relations of cooperation, conflict, and authority among positions. Feminist claims about the justice of a sexual division of labor, for example, have been posed both distributively and nondistributively. On the one hand, feminists have questioned the justice of a pattern of distribution of positions that finds a small proportion of women in the most prestigious jobs. On the other hand, they have also questioned the conscious or unconscious association of many occupations or jobs with masculine or feminine characteristics, such as instrumentality or affectivity, and this is not itself a distributive issue. . . .

Culture is the most general of the three categories of nondistributive issues I focus on. It includes the symbols, images, meanings, habitual comportments, stories, and so on through which people express their experience and communicate with one another. Culture is ubiquitous, but nevertheless deserves distinct consideration in discussions of social justice. The symbolic meanings that people attach to other kinds of people and to actions, gestures, or institut'ons often significantly affect the social standing of persons and their opportunities. . . .

Overextending the Concept of Distribution

The following objection might be made to my argument thus far. It may be true that philosophical discussions of justice tend to emphasize the distribution of goods and to ignore institutional issues of decisionmaking structure and culture. But this is not a necessary consequence of the distributive definition of justice. Theories of distributive justice can and should be applied to issues of social organization beyond the allocation of wealth, income, and resources. Indeed, this objection insists, many theorists explicitly extend the scope of distributive justice to such nonmaterial goods.

Rawls, for example, regards the subject of justice as "the way in which the major social institutions distribute fundamental rights and duties" (Rawls, 1971, p. 7 [p. 124 in this anthology]), and for him this clearly includes rights and duties related to decisionmaking, social positions, power, and so on, as well as wealth or income. . . .

The distributive paradigm of justice may have a bias toward focusing on easily identifiable distributions, such as distributions of things, income, and jobs. Its beauty and simplicity, however, consists in its ability to accommodate any issue of justice, including those concerning culture, decisionmaking structures, and the division of labor. To do so the paradigm simply formulates the issue in terms of the distribution of some material or nonmaterial good among various agents. Any social value can be treated as some thing or aggregate of things that some specific agents possess in certain amounts, and alternative end-state patterns of distribution of that good among those agents can be compared. For example, neoclassical economists have developed sophisticated schemes for reducing all intentional action to a matter of maximizing a utility function in which the utility of all conceivable goods can be quantified and compared.

But this, in my view, is the main problem with the distributive paradigm: it does not recognize the limits to the application of a logic of distribution. Distributive theorists of justice agree that justice is the primary normative concept for evaluating all aspects of social institutions, but at the same time they identify the scope of justice with distribution. This entails applying a logic of distribution to social goods which are not material things or measurable quantities. Applying a logic of distribution to such goods produces a misleading conception of the issues of justice involved. It reifies aspects of social life that are better understood as a function of rules and relations than as things. And it conceptualizes social justice primarily in terms of end-state patterns, rather than focusing on social processes. This distributive paradigm implies a misleading or incomplete social ontology.

But why should issues of social ontology matter for normative theorizing about justice? Any normative claims about society make assumptions about the nature of society, often only implicitly. Normative judgments of justice are about something, and without a social ontology we do not know what they are about. The distributive paradigm implicitly assumes that social judgments are about what individual persons have, how much they have, and how that amount compares with what other persons have. This focus on possession tends to preclude thinking about what people are doing, according to what institutionalized rules, how their doings and havings are structured by institutionalized relations that constitute their positions, and how the combined effect of their doings has recursive effects on their lives. Before developing this argument further, let us look at some examples of the application of the distributive paradigm to three nonmaterial goods frequently discussed by theorists of justice: rights, opportunity, and self-respect.

I quoted Rawls earlier to the effect that justice concerns the distribution of "rights and duties," and talk of distributing rights is by no means limited to him. But what does distributing a right mean? One may talk about having a right to a distributive share of material things, resources, or income. But in such cases it is the good that is distributed, not the right. What can it mean to distribute rights that do not refer to resources or things, like the right of free speech, or the right of trial by jury? We can conceive of a society in which some persons are granted these rights while others are not, but this does not mean that some people have a certain "amount" or "portion" of a good while others have less. Altering the situation so that everyone has these rights, moreover, would not entail that the formerly privileged group gives over some of its right of free speech or trial by jury to the rest of society's members, on analogy with a redistribution of income.

Rights are not fruitfully conceived as possessions. Rights are relationships, not things; they are institutionally defined rules specifying what people can do in relation to one another. Rights refer to doing more than having, to social relationships that enable or constrain action.

Talk of distributing opportunities involves a similar confusion. If by opportunity we mean "chance," we can meaningfully talk of distributing opportunities, of some people having more opportunities than others, while some have none at all. When I go to the carnival I can buy three chances to knock over the kewpie doll, and my friend can buy six, and she will have more chances than I. Matters are rather different, however, with other opportunities. James Nickel defines opportunities as "states of affairs that combine the absence of insuperable obstacles with the presences of means—internal or external—that give one a chance of overcoming the obstacles that remain."[4] Opportunity in this sense is a condition of enablement, which usually involves a configuration of social rules and social relations, as well as an individual's self-conception and skills.

We may mislead ourselves by the fact that in ordinary language we talk about some people having "fewer" opportunities than others. When we talk that way, the opportunities sound like separable goods that can be increased or decreased by being given out or withheld, even though we know that opportunities are not allocated. Opportunity is a concept of enablement rather than possession; it refers to doing more than having. A person has opportunities if he or she is not constrained from doing things, and lives under the enabling conditions for doing them. Having opportunities in this sense certainly does often entail having material possessions, such as food, clothing, tools, land, or machines. Being enabled or constrained refers more directly, however, to the rules and practices that govern one's action, the way other people treat one in the context of specific social relations, and the broader structural possibilities produced by the confluence of a multitude of actions and practices. It makes no sense to speak of opportunities as themselves things possessed. Evaluating social justice according to whether persons have opportunities, therefore, must involve evaluating not a distributive outcome but the social structures that enable or constrain the individuals in relevant situations.

Consider educational opportunity, for example. Providing educational opportunity certainly entails allocating specific material resources—money, buildings, books, computers, and so on—and there are reasons to think that the more resources, the wider the opportunities offered to

4. James Nickel, "Equal Opportunity in a Pluralistic Society," in *Equal Opportunity*, Ellen Frankel Paul, Fred D. Miller, Jeffrey Paul, and John Ahrens, eds. (Oxford: Blackwell, 1988), p. 110.

children in an educational system. But education is primarily a process taking place in a complex context of social relations. In the cultural context of the United States, male children and female children, working-class children and middle-class children, Black children and white children often do not have equally enabling educational opportunities even when an equivalent amount of resources has been devoted to their education. This does not show that distribution is irrelevant to educational opportunity, only that opportunity has a wider scope than distribution.

Many writers on justice, to take a final example, not only regard self-respect as a primary good that all persons in a society must have if the society is to be just, but also talk of distributing self-respect. But what can it mean to distribute self-respect? Self-respect is not an entity or measurable aggregate, it cannot be parceled out of some stash, and above all it cannot be detached from persons as a separable attribute adhering to an otherwise unchanged substance. Self-respect names not some possession or attribute a person has, but her or his attitude toward her or his entire situation and life prospects. While Rawls does not speak of self-respect as something itself distributed, he does suggest that distributive arrangements provide the background conditions for self-respect (Rawls, 1971, pp. 148–50). It is certainly true that in many circumstances the possession of certain distributable material goods may be a condition of self-respect. Self-respect, however, also involves many nonmaterial conditions that cannot be reduced to distributive arrangements.

People have or lack self-respect because of how they define themselves and how others regard them, because of how they spend their time, because of the amount of autonomy and decisionmaking power they have in their activities, and so on. Some of these factors can be conceptualized in distributive terms, but others cannot. Self-respect is at least as much a function of culture as it is of goods, for example. . . . The point here is that none of the forms and not all of the conditions of self-respect can meaningfully be conceived as goods that individuals possess; they are rather relations and processes in which the actions of individuals are embedded.

These, then, are the general problems with extending the concept of distribution beyond material goods or measurable quantities to non-material values. First, doing so reifies social relations and institutional rules. Something identifiable and assignable must be distributed. In accord with its implicit social ontology that gives primacy to substance over relations, moreover, the distributive paradigm tends to conceive of individuals as social atoms, logically prior to social relations and institutions. Conceiving justice as a distribution of goods among individuals involves analytically separating the individuals from those goods. Such an atomistic conception of the individual as a substance to which attributes adhere fails to appreciate that individual identities and capacities are in many respects themselves the products of social processes and relations. Societies do not simply distribute goods to persons who are what they are apart from society, but rather constitute individuals in their identities and capacities. In the distributive logic, however, there is little room for conceiving persons' enablement or constraint as a function of their relations to one another. Such an atomistic social ontology ignores or obscures the importance of social groups for understanding issues of justice.

Second, the distributive paradigm must conceptualize all issues of justice in terms of patterns. It implies a static social ontology that ignores processes. In the distributive paradigm individuals or other agents lie as points in the social field, among whom larger or smaller packets of goods are assigned. One evaluates the justice of the pattern by comparing the size of the packages individuals have and comparing the total pattern to other possible patterns of assignment.

Robert Nozick argues that such a static or end-state approach to justice is inappropriately ahistorical.[5] End-state approaches to justice, he argues, operate as though social goods magically appear and get distributed. They ignore the processes that create the goods and produce distributive patterns, which they find irrelevant for evaluating justice. For Nozick, only the process is relevant to evaluating distributions. If individuals begin with holdings they are justly entitled to, and undertake free exchanges, then the distributive outcomes are just, no matter what they are. This entitlement theory shares with other theories a possessively individualist social ontology. Society consists only of individuals with "holdings" of social goods which they augment or reduce through individual production and contractual exchange. The theory does not take into account structural effects of the actions of individuals that they cannot foresee or intend, and to which they might not agree if they could. Nevertheless, Nozick's criticism of end-state theories for ignoring social processes is apt.

Important and complex consequences ensue when a theory of justice adopts a narrowly static social ontology. . . . Action theorists have developed sophisticated accounts of social relations from the point of view of acting subjects with intentions, purposes, and reasons, but they have tended to abstract from the temporal flow of everyday life, and instead talk about isolated acts of isolated individuals. For a theory of justice, this means ignoring the relevance of institutions to justice. Structuralism and functionalist social theories, on the other hand, provide conceptual tools

5. Robert Nozick, *Anarchy, State, and Utopia* (New York: Basic Books, 1974), chap. 7 [pp. 146–154 in this anthology].

for identifying and explaining social regularities and large-scale institutional patterns. Because they also abstract from the temporal flow of everyday interaction, however, they tend to hypostatize these regularities and patterns and often fail to connect them with accounts of individual action. For a theory of justice, this means separating institutions from choice and normative judgment. . . . Individuals are not primarily receivers of goods or carriers of properties, but actors with meanings and purposes, who act with, against, or in relation to one another. We act with knowledge of existing institutions, rules, and the structural consequences of a multiplicity of actions, and those structures are enacted and reproduced through the confluence of our actions. Social theory should conceptualize action as a producer and reproducer of structures, which only exist in action; social action, on the other hand, has those structures and relationships as background, medium, or purpose.

This identification of a weakness in traditional social theory can be applied to the distributive paradigm of justice. I disagree with Nozick that end-state patterns are irrelevant to questions of justice. Because they inhibit the ability of some people to live and be healthy, or grant some people resources that allow them to coerce others, some distributions must come into question no matter how they came about. Evaluating patterns of distribution is often an important starting point for questioning about justice. For many issues of social justice, however, what is important is not the particular pattern of distribution at a particular moment, but rather the reproduction of a regular distributive pattern over time.

For example, unless one begins with the assumption that all positions of high status, income, and decisionmaking power ought to be distributed in comparable numbers to women and men, finding that very few top corporate managers are women might not involve any question of injustice. It is in the context of a social change involving more acceptance of women in corporate management, and a considerable increase in the number of women who obtain degrees in business, that a question of injustice becomes most apparent here. Even though more women earn degrees in business, and in-house policies of some companies aim to encourage women's careers, a pattern of distribution of managerial positions that clusters women at the bottom and men at the top persists. Assuming that justice ultimately means equality for women, this pattern is puzzling, disturbing. We are inclined to ask: what's going on here? why is this general pattern reproduced even in the face of conscious efforts to change it? Answering that question entails evaluation of a matrix of rules, attitudes, interactions, and policies as a social process that produces and reproduces that pattern. An adequate conception of justice must be able to understand and evaluate the processes as well as the patterns.

One might object that this account confuses the empirical issue of what causes a particular distribution with the normative issue of whether the distribution is just. As will be apparent in the chapters that follow, however, in the spirit of critical social theory I do not accept this division between empirical and normative social theory. While there is a distinction between empirical and normative statements and the kinds of reasons required for each, no normative theory meant to evaluate existing societies can avoid empirical inquiry, and no empirical investigation of social structures and relations can avoid normative judgments. Inquiry about social justice must consider the context and causes of actual distributions in order to make normative judgments about institutional rules and relations.

The pattern orientation of the distributive paradigm, then, tends to lead to abstraction from institutional rules and relations and a consequent failure to bring them into evaluation. For many aspects of social structure and institutional context cannot be brought into view without examining social processes and the unintended cumulative consequences of individual actions. Without a more temporal approach to social reality, for example, a theory of justice cannot conceptualize exploitation, as a social process by which the labor of some unreciprocally supports the privilege of others.

Problems with Talk of Distributing Power

I have argued that regarding such social values as rights, opportunities, and self-respect as distributable obscures the institutional and social bases of these values. Some theorists of justice might respond to my criticism of the distributive paradigm as follows: What is in question is indeed not goods, but social power; the distributive paradigm, however, can accommodate these issues by giving more attention to the distribution of power. Certainly I agree that many of the issues I have said are confused or obscured by the distributive paradigm concern social power. While talk of the distribution of power is common, however, I think this is a particularly clear case of the misleading and undesirable implications of extending the concept of distribution beyond material goods.

Distributional theorists of justice disagree on how to approach power. Some explicitly exclude power from the scope of their theories. . . . Ronald Dworkin explicitly brackets issues of power in his discussion of equality, and chooses to consider only issues of welfare, the distribution of goods, services, income, and so on.[6]

6. Ronald Dworkin, "What is Equality? Part 1: Equality of Welfare," *Philosophy and Public Affairs* 10 (1981): 185–246.

Other philosophers and political theorists, however, clearly include questions of power within the scope of the concept of justice. Many would agree that a theory of justice must be concerned not only with end-state patterns, but also with the institutional relations that produce distributions. Their approach to such questions takes the form of assessing the distribution of power in a society or a specific institutional context.

Talk about power in terms of distribution is so common that it does not warrant special notice. The following passage from William Connolly's *Terms of Political Discourse* is typical:

> When one speaks of a power structure one conveys, first, the idea that power in at least some domains is distributed unequally; second, that those with more power in one domain are likely to have it in several important domains as well; third, that such a distribution is relatively persistent; and fourth (but not necessarily), that there is more than a random connection between the distribution of power and the distribution of income, status, privilege, and wealth in the system under scrutiny.[7]

Common though it is, bringing power under the logic of distribution, I suggest, misconstrues the meaning of power. Conceptualizing power in distributive terms means implicitly or explicitly conceiving power as a kind of stuff possessed by individual agents in greater or lesser amounts. From this perspective a power structure or power relations will be described as a pattern of the distribution of this stuff. There are a number of problems with such a model of power.

First, regarding power as a possession or attribute of individuals tends to obscure the fact that power is a relation rather than a thing. While the exercise of power may sometimes depend on the possession of certain resources—money, military equipment, and so on—such resources should not be confused with power itself. The power consists in a relationship between the exerciser and others through which he or she communicates intentions and meets with their acquiescence.

Second, the atomistic bias of distributive paradigms of power leads to a focus on particular agents or roles that have power, and on agents over whom these powerful agents or roles have power. Even when they recognize its relational character, theorists often treat power as a dyadic relation, on the model of ruler and subject. This dyadic modeling of power misses the larger structure of agents and actions that mediates between two agents in a power relation. One agent can have institutionalized power over another only if the actions of many third agents support and execute the

7. William Connolly, *The Terms of Political Discourse,* 2nd ed. (Princeton: Princeton University Press, 1983), p. 117.

will of the powerful. A judge may be said to have power over a prisoner, but only in the context of a network of practices executed by prison wardens, guards, recordkeepers, administrators, parole officers, lawyers, and so on. Many people must do their jobs for the judge's power to be realized, and many of these people will never directly interact with either the judge or the prisoner. A distributive understanding of power as a possession of particular individuals or groups misses this supporting and mediating function of third parties.

A distributive understanding of power, which treats power as some kind of stuff that can be traded, exchanged, and distributed, misses the structural phenomena of domination. By domination, I mean structural or systemic phenomena which exclude people from participating in determining their actions or the conditions of their actions. Domination must be understood as structural precisely because the constraints that people experience are usually the intended or unintended product of the actions of many people, like the actions which enable the judge's power. In saying that power and domination have a structural basis, I do not deny that it is individuals who are powerful and who dominate. Within a system of domination some people can be identified as more powerful and others as relatively powerless. Nevertheless a distributive understanding misses the way in which the powerful enact and reproduce their power.

The structured operation of domination whose resources the powerful draw upon must be understood as a process. A distributive conceptualization of power, however, can construct power relations only as patterns. Conceptualizing power as relational rather than substantive, as produced and reproduced through many people outside the immediate power dyad, brings out the dynamic nature of power relations as an ongoing process. A distributive understanding of power obscures the fact that, as Foucault puts it, power exists only in action:

> What, by contrast, should always be kept in mind is that power, if we do not take too distant a view of it, is not that which makes the difference between those who exclusively possess and retain it, and those who do not have it and submit to it. Power must be analyzed as something that circulates, or rather something which only functions in the form of a chain. It is never localized here or there, never in anybody's hands, never appropriated as a commodity or piece of wealth. Power is employed and exercised through a net-like organization. And not only do individuals circulate between its threads; they are always in the position of simultaneously undergoing and exercising their power.[8]

8. Michel Foucault, *Power/Knowledge* (New York: Pantheon, 1980), p. 98.

The logic of distribution, in contrast, makes power a machine or instrument, held in ready and turned on at will, independently of social processes.

Finally, a distributive understanding of power tends to conceive a system of domination as one in which power, like wealth, is concentrated in the hands of a few. Assuming such a condition is unjust, a redistribution of power is called for, which will disperse and decentralize power so that a few individuals or groups no longer have all or most of the power. For some systems of domination such a model may be appropriate. As I will argue in the next two chapters, however, it is not appropriate for understanding the operation of domination and oppression in contemporary welfare corporate societies. For these societies witness the ironic situation in which power is widely dispersed and diffused, yet social relations are tightly defined by domination and oppression. When power is understood as "productive," as a function of dynamic processes of interaction within regulated cultural and decisionmaking situations, then it is possible to say that many widely dispersed persons are agents of power without "having" it, or even being privileged. Without a structural understanding of power and domination as processes rather than patterns of distribution, the existence and nature of domination and oppression in these societies cannot be identified.

Defining Injustice as Domination and Oppression

Because distributive models of power, rights, opportunity, and self-respect work so badly, justice should not be conceived primarily on the model of the distribution of wealth, income, and other material goods. Theorizing about justice should explicitly limit the concept of distribution to material goods, like things, natural resources, or money. The scope of justice is wider than distributive issues. Though there may be additional nondistributive issues of justice, my concerns in this book focus on issues of decisionmaking, division of labor, and culture.

Political thought of the modern period greatly narrowed the scope of justice as it had been conceived by ancient and medieval thought. Ancient thought regarded justice as the virtue of society as a whole, the well-orderedness of institutions that foster individual virtue and promote happiness and harmony among citizens. Modern political thought abandoned the notion that there is a natural order to society that corresponds to the proper ends of human nature. Seeking to liberate the individual to define "his" own ends, modern political theory also restricted the scope of justice to issues of distribution and the minimal regulation of action among such self-defining individuals.

While I hardly intend to revert to a full-bodied Platonic conception of justice, I nevertheless think it is important to broaden the understanding of justice beyond its usual limits in contemporary philosophical discourse. Agnes Heller proposes one such broader conception in what she calls an incomplete ethico-political concept of justice. According to her conception, justice names not principles of distribution, much less some particular distributive pattern. This represents too narrow and substantive a way of reflecting on justice. Instead, justice names the perspectives, principles, and procedures for evaluating institutional norms and rules. Developing Habermas's communicative ethics, Heller suggests that justice is primarily the virtue of citizenship, of persons deliberating about problems and issues that confront them collectively in their institutions and actions, under conditions without domination or oppression, with reciprocity and mutual tolerance of difference. She proposes the following test of the justice of social or political norms:

> Every valid social and political norm and rule (every law) must meet the condition that the foreseeable consequences and side effects the general observance of that law (norm) exacts on the satisfaction of the needs of each and every individual would be accepted by everyone concerned, and that the claim of the norm to actualize the universal values of freedom and/or life could be accepted by each and every individual, regardless of the values to which they are committed.[9]

. . . I endorse and follow this general conception of justice derived from a conception of communicative ethics. The idea of justice here shifts from a focus on distributive patterns to procedural issues of participation in deliberation and decisionmaking. For a norm to be just, everyone who follows it must in principle have an effective voice in its consideration and be able to agree to it without coercion. For a social condition to be just, it must enable all to meet their needs and exercise their freedom; thus justice requires that all be able to express their needs.

As I understand it, the concept of justice coincides with the concept of the political. Politics as I defined it in the Introduction includes all aspects of institutional organization, public action, social practices and habits, and cultural meanings insofar as they are potentially subject to collective evaluation and decisionmaking. Politics in this inclusive sense certainly concerns the policies and actions of government and the state, but in principle can also concern rules, practices, and actions in any other institutional context.

The scope of justice, I have suggested, is much wider than distribution,

9. Agnes Heller, *Beyond Justice* (New York: Basic Books, 1987), pp. 240–241.

and covers everything political in this sense. This coheres with the meaning of justice claims of the sort mentioned at the outset of this chapter. When people claim that a particular rule, practice, or cultural meaning is wrong and should be changed, they are often making a claim about social injustice. Some of these claims involve distributions, but many also refer to other ways in which social institutions inhibit or liberate persons.

Some writers concur that distribution is too narrow a focus for normative evaluation of social institutions, but claim that going beyond this distributive focus entails going beyond the norms of justice per se. Charles Taylor, for example, distinguishes questions of distributive justice from normative questions about the institutional framework of society.[10] Norms of justice help resolve disputes about entitlements and deserts within a particular institutional context. They cannot evaluate that institutional context itself, however, because it embodies a certain conception of human nature and the human good. According to Taylor, confusions arise in theoretical and political discussion when norms of distributive justice are applied across social structures and used to evaluate basic structures. For example, both right and left critics of our society charge it with perpetrating injustices, but according to Taylor the normative perspective from which each side speaks involves a project to construct different institutional forms corresponding to specific conceptions of the human good, a project beyond merely articulating principles of justice.

· · ·

I am sympathetic with [this critique, but . . .] I see no reason to conclude with Taylor . . . that this critique reveals the limits of the concept of justice which a normative social philosophy must transcend. I disagree to some extent, moreover, with Taylor's . . . suggestion that such a wider normative social philosophy merges questions of justice with questions of the good life.

Like many other writers . . . , Taylor assumes that justice and distribution are coextensive, and therefore that broader issues of institutional context require other normative concepts. Many Marxist theorists who argue that justice is a merely bourgeois concept take a similar position. Whether normative theorists who focus attention on issues of decision-making, division of labor, culture, and social organization beyond the distribution of goods call these issues of justice or not is clearly a matter of choice. I can give only pragmatic reasons for my own choice.

Since Plato "justice" has evoked the well-ordered society, and it con-

10. Charles Taylor, "The Nature and Scope of Distributive Justice," in *Philosophy and the Human Sciences* (Cambridge: Cambridge University Press, 1985).

tinues to carry those resonances in contemporary political discussion. Appeals to justice still have the power to awaken a moral imagination and motivate people to look at their society critically, and ask how it can be made more liberating and enabling. Philosophers interested in nurturing this emancipatory imagination and extending it beyond questions of distribution should, I suggest, lay claim to the term justice rather than abandon it.

To a certain extent Heller, Taylor, and Benhabib are right that a post-modern turn to an enlarged conception of justice, reminiscent of the scope of justice in Plato and Aristotle, entails more attention to the definition of ends than the liberal conception of justice allows. Nevertheless, questions of justice do not merge with questions of the good life. The liberal commitment to individual freedom, and the consequent plurality of definitions of the good, must be preserved in any reenlarged conception of justice. The modern restriction of the concept of justice to formal and instrumental principles was meant to promote the value of individual self-definition of ends, or "plans of life," as Rawls calls them. In displacing reflection about justice from a primary focus on distribution to include all institutional and social relations insofar as they are subject to collective decision, I do not mean to suggest that justice should include all moral norms in its scope. Social justice in the sense I intend continues to refer only to institutional conditions, and not to the preferences and ways of life of individuals or groups.

Any normative theorist in the postmodern world is faced with a dilemma. On the one hand, we express and justify norms by appealing to certain values derived from a conception of the good human life. In some sense, then, any normative theory implicitly or explicitly relies on a conception of human nature. On the other hand, it would seem that we should reject the very idea of a human nature as misleading or oppressive.

Any definition of a human nature is dangerous because it threatens to devalue or exclude some acceptable individual desires, cultural characteristics, or ways of life. Normative social theory, however, can rarely avoid making implicit or explicit assumptions about human beings in the formulation of its vision of just institutions. Even though the distributive paradigm carries an individualist conception of society, which considers individual desires and preferences private matters outside the sphere of rational discourse, it assumes a quite specific conception of human nature. It implicitly defines human beings as primarily consumers, desirers, and possessors of goods. . . .

The idea of human beings that guides normative social theorizing under the distributive paradigm is an image, rather than an explicit theory of human nature. It makes plausible to the imagination both the static picture of social relations entailed by this distributive paradigm and the notion of separate individuals already formed apart from social goods. Displacing the distributive paradigm in favor of a wider, process-oriented understanding of society, which focuses on power, decisionmaking structures, and so on, likewise shifts the imagination to different assumptions about human beings. Such an imaginative shift could be as oppressive as consumerist images if it is made too concrete. As long as the values we appeal to are abstract enough, however, they will not devalue or exclude any particular culture or way of life.

Persons certainly are possessors and consumers, and any conception of justice should presume the value of meeting material needs, living in a comfortable environment, and experiencing pleasures. Adding an image of people as doers and actors helps to displace the distributive paradigm. As doers and actors, we seek to promote many values of social justice in addition to fairness in the distribution of goods: learning and using satisfying and expansive skills in socially recognized settings; participating in forming and running institutions, and receiving recognition for such participation; playing and communicating with others, and expressing our experience, feelings, and perspective on social life in contexts where others can listen. Certainly many distributive theorists of justice would recognize and affirm these values. The framework of distribution, however, leads to a deemphasizing of these values and a failure to inquire about the institutional conditions that promote them.

This, then, is how I understand the connection between justice and the values that constitute the good life. Justice is not identical with the concrete realization of these values in individual lives; justice, that is, is not identical with the good life as such. Rather, social justice concerns the degree to which a society contains and supports the institutional conditions necessary for the realization of these values. The values comprised in the good life can be reduced to two very general ones: (1) developing and exercising one's capacities and expressing one's experience, and (2) participating in determining one's action and the conditions of one's action. These are universalist values, in the sense that they assume the equal moral worth of all persons, and thus justice requires their promotion for everyone. To these two general values correspond two social conditions that define injustice: oppression, the institutional constraint on self-development, and domination, the institutional constraint on self-determination.

Oppression consists in systematic institutional processes which prevent some people from learning and using satisfying and expansive skills in socially recognized settings, or institutionalized social processes which inhibit people's ability to play and communicate with others or to express their feelings and perspective on social life in contexts where others can listen. While the social conditions of oppression often include material deprivation or maldistribution, they also involve issues beyond distribution.

Domination consists in institutional conditions which inhibit or prevent people from participating in determining their actions or the conditions of their actions. Persons live within structures of domination if other persons or groups can determine without reciprocation the conditions of their action, either directly or by virtue of the structural consequences of their actions. Thorough social and political democracy is the opposite of domination.

I think the concepts of oppression and domination overlap, but there is nevertheless reason to distinguish them. Oppression usually includes or entails domination, that is, constraints upon oppressed people to follow rules set by others. But each face of oppression also involves inhibitions not directly produced by relations of domination. Not everyone subject to domination is also oppressed. Hierarchical decisionmaking structures subject most people in our society to domination in some important aspect of their lives. Many of those people nevertheless enjoy significant institutionalized support for the development and exercise of their capacities and their ability to express themselves and be heard.

Further Readings

In addition to the books from which some of the readings in this anthology are drawn (especially the works by Tawney, Rawls, Nozick, and Walzer), readers may be interested in the following works.

ANTHOLOGIES

Mason, Andrew, ed. *Ideals of Equality* (Oxford: Blackwell, 1988).

Pennock, J. Roland, and John W. Chapman, eds. *Nomos IX: Equality* (New York: Atherton, 1967).

Pojman, Louis P., and Robert Westmoreland, eds. *Equality: Selected Readings* (New York and Oxford: Oxford University Press, 1997).

ARTICLES

Arneson, Richard. "Equality and Equality of Opportunity for Welfare." *Philosophical Studies* 56 (1989): 77–93.

Frankfurt, Harry. "Equality as a Moral Ideal." *Ethics* 98 (1987): 21–43. Reprinted in Pojman and Westmoreland.

Parfit, Derek. "Equality or Priority?" Lindley Lecture, University of Kansas, 1995. Reprinted in abridged form in Mason.

Raz, Joseph. "Principles of Equality." *Mind* 87 (1978): 321–342.

Schaar, John. "Equality of Opportunity and Beyond." In Pennock and Chapman. Reprinted in Pojman and Westmoreland.

Vlastos, Gregory. "Justice and Equality." In *Social Justice*, ed. by Richard B. Brandt (Englewood Cliffs, N.J.: Prentice-Hall, 1962), pp. 31–72. Reprinted in Pojman and Westmoreland.

Westen, Peter, "The Empty Idea of Equality." *Harvard Law Review* 95 (1982): 537–596.

Williams, Bernard. "The Idea of Equality." In Peter Laslett and W. G. Runciman, eds. *Philosophy, Politics and Society*, Second Series (Oxford: Blackwell, 1962), pp. 110–131. Reprinted in Pojman and Westmoreland.

BOOKS

Gutmann, Amy. *Liberal Equality* (Cambridge: Cambridge University Press, 1980).

Hayek, Friedrich A. *Law, Legislation, and Liberty, vol. 2: The Mirage of Social Justice* (Chicago: University of Chicago Press, 1976).

Nagel, Thomas. *Equality and Partiality* (New York and Oxford: Oxford University Press, 1991).

Nielsen, Kai. *Equality and Liberty: A Defense of Radical Egalitarianism* (Totowa, N.J.: Rowman & Allanheld, 1985).

Rae, Douglas et al. *Equalities,* 2nd ed. (Cambridge, Mass.: Harvard University Press, 1989).

Roemer, John E. *Theories of Distributive Justice* (Cambridge, Mass.: Harvard University Press, 1996).

Sen, Amartya. *Inequality Re-Examined* (Cambridge, Mass., and New York: Harvard University Press and Russell Sage Foundation, 1992).

Van Parijs, Philippe. *Real Freedom for All: What If Anything Can Justify Capitalism?* (Oxford: Clarendon Press, 1995).

Westen, Peter. *Speaking of Equality: An Analysis of the Rhetorical Force of 'Equality' in Moral and Legal Discourse* (Princeton: Princeton University Press, 1990).